To

Gus Fletcher

with admiration and

from friend and author,

or, in other words

ข้าพเจ้าขึ้นข้าพ Fletcher ด้วยยินดีแด่

ขึ้นแยงดด, อาก เขียนดีแด่ ข้วยได้ด้ว

John Cross
Pokhara
15 November 2003

FIRST IN, LAST OUT

AN UNCONVENTIONAL BRITISH OFFICER IN INDO-CHINA (1945-46 AND 1972-76)

J P Cross

BRASSEY'S (UK)

LONDON • WASHINGTON • NEW YORK

First English edition 1992

UK editorial offices: Brassey's, 50 Fetter Land, London EC4A 1 AA
Orders: Brassey's, Purnell Distribution Centre, Paulton, Bristol BS18 5LQ

USA editorial offices: Brassey's, 8000 Westpark Drive, First Floor,
McLean, Virginia 22102
Orders: Macmillan Publishing Company, Front and Brown Streets,
Riverside, NJ 08072

Distributed in North America to booksellers and wholesalers by the
Macmillan Publishing Company, N.Y., N.Y.

Library of Congress Cataloging in Publication Date
Available

British Library Cataloguing Date
A catalogue record for this book is available from the British Library

ISBN 0-08-041787-6

[Literals amended and minor alterations added in 2003]

Printed in Great Britain in B.P.C.C. Wheatons Ltd., Exeter

BLURB

TO
The underdogs of Indo-China
Beneath the bane of bandits, bullies and bigots
For centuries past:
May it not be another hundred years?
Before release from there
MALICE and BLUNDERS

Contents

* Regrettably all place names in the text are not on the map but the their location is easily understood from the narrative.

List of Illustrations

Glossary

ARVN	Army of the Republic of Vietnam, South Vietnamese Army
CIA	Central Intelligence Agency
CPLA	Chinese People's Liberation Army
DA	Defence Attaché
FAN	Forces Armeé Neutralistes
FCO	Foreign and Commonwealth Office
GR	Gurkha Rifles
	1/1 GR: in full 1st King George V's Own Gurkha Rifles
	8 Gorkha Rifles, post-partition Indian Army
	4/10 GR
GRU	Soviet Military Intelligence Agency
ICSC	International Control and Supervision Commission
IMA	Indian Military Academy
KMT	Chinese Nationalist Army, Kuomintang
LPF	Lao Patriotic Front
LPLA	Lao People's Liberation Army
MOD	Ministry of Defence
MMF	Mission Militaire Française: French Military Mission
MR	Military Region
NVA	North Vietnamese Army
PGNU	Provisional Government of National Union
PL	Pathet Lao
PS	Pakse [in MR 4 helicopter landing] Site
RLA	Royal Lao Army
RLAF	Royal Lao Air Force
RLG	Royal Lao Government, Vientiane Regime
RTA	Royal Thai Army
RTAF	Royal Thai Air Force
USAF	United States Air Force

Dramatis Personae

[Laotians and those non-Lao people accredited to Laos have * against their names]

*Abundo, D. R. Jnr, Colonel, Filipino Defence Attaché
Attlee, C., British Prime Minister
*Bailey, B., Jnr, Colonel, US Army Attaché
*Bakhshi, S. P., Brigadier, Indian Army, ICSC
Balesor Rana, Subedar Major, 1/1 GR
*Boun Oum, Prince, Inspector General of the Realm
*Bounphone Maktapharaks, Lieutenant General, Commander-in-Chief, RLA
*Calder, A., Major, Assistant British Attaché and British Embassy pilot
Callaghan, L. J., British labour politician
*Cape, D.B., British Ambassador
*Chao Savang, Brigadier General, RLA. Commander Military Region 1
*Chapman, C., US Chargé d'Affairs
*Chen Shu-lin., Chinese Defence Attaché
*Chesney, E. R., WOI, British Embassy
*Chi, Nguyen Huu, Colonel, South Vietnamese Defence Attaché
*Chok Di, DA's houseboy
Clark, R. W., Major, 1/1 GR
*Curry, H. C., Colonel, US Air Attaché
*Davidson, A. E., British Ambassador
*Dean, J., American diplomat
*Denny, B. L., First Secretary British Embassy
*Derpol, A. B., Colonel, Filipino Defence Attaché
Dewey, P., Lieutenant Colonel, US Army, son of
Dewey, T. E., USA Presidential candidate
*Douang Pi, Colonel, RLA
Edwardes, J. S. M., Major, Training Wing Commander ARVN troops, Jungle Warfare School
*Etam Singvongsa, Brigadier General, RLA. Director Psychological Operations
Everard, T., British Consul General, North Vietnam
*Fairweather, P., Head of Chancery, British Embassy
*Fearn, R., Head of Chancery, British Embassy
Foot, M, British politician
Frolik J, Czech spy, friend of J H Wilson, British Prime Minister
Fujiwara Yositoke, famous Japanese sword maker
*Gharekan, C. R., Indian Chairman ICSC
Giap, Vo Nguyen, General, NVA
*Godley, G. McM., US Ambassador
*Golden Fairy, Princess – *see under* Inkham Rangsi, Princess
*Gretchanine, V. P., Colonel, USSR Defence Attaché
Gracy, D. D., Major General, Indian Army
Hart, J., Ms, British Minister
Heath, E. R. G., British Prime Minister
*Hinphed Phouybanhdyt, Colonel, RLA

*Sisouk Na Champassak, Prince, Minister, RLG
*Soloviev, V., Colonel, (Assistant) Soviet Defence Attaché
*Somneuk, Siharaj, Colonel, RLA
*Sorokin, Y. G., Lieutenant, GRU
*Soth Phetrasi, PL official
*Souk Vongsak, PL offical
*Soupraseut, General, LPF
*Souridh Don Sasorith, Major General, Commander RLAF
*Soutchai, Brigadier General, RLA. Commander Military Region 4
*Souvannouvong, a.k.a. Red Prince, President, Democratic Republic of Laos
*Souvanna Phouma, Prince, Prime Minister, RLG
Stalin, J., *de facto* leader, USSR
Stewart, J. A. B., British representative to the Mayor of Hanoi then Ambassador, North Vietnam
Takahashi, Major, Imperial Japanese Army battalion commander
*Tao Ly Lidiluja, Brigadier General, RLA. Commander Scorpion Division later
Director of Intelligence
*Thao Ma, Brigadier General, RLAF
Thatcher, M. H., Mrs, British Prime Minister
*Thong Damdouane, LPF official
*Thonglit, Brigadier General, RLA. Commander Military Region 5
*Thursby-Pelham, D., Colonel, British Defence Attaché
*Tsarkov, N., Colonel, Soviet Defence Attaché
Turk, Colonel, French Army attached to 1/1 GR
*Vang Pao, Major General, RLA. Commander Military Region 2
*Varamit, M., Colonel, Thai attaché
Vassall, J., British Admiralty clerk, USSR spy from 1955
Vaygaskus, R., Lithuanian spy
*West, C. P., Colonel, Australian Defence Attaché
Whitehead, J., Brigadier, British Army
Whitlam, E. G., Australian Prime Minister
Wilson, J. H., British Prime Minister
*Wood, J. L., Colonel, USAF, Defence Attaché
Yamagishi, Captain, Imperial Japanese Army battalion commander

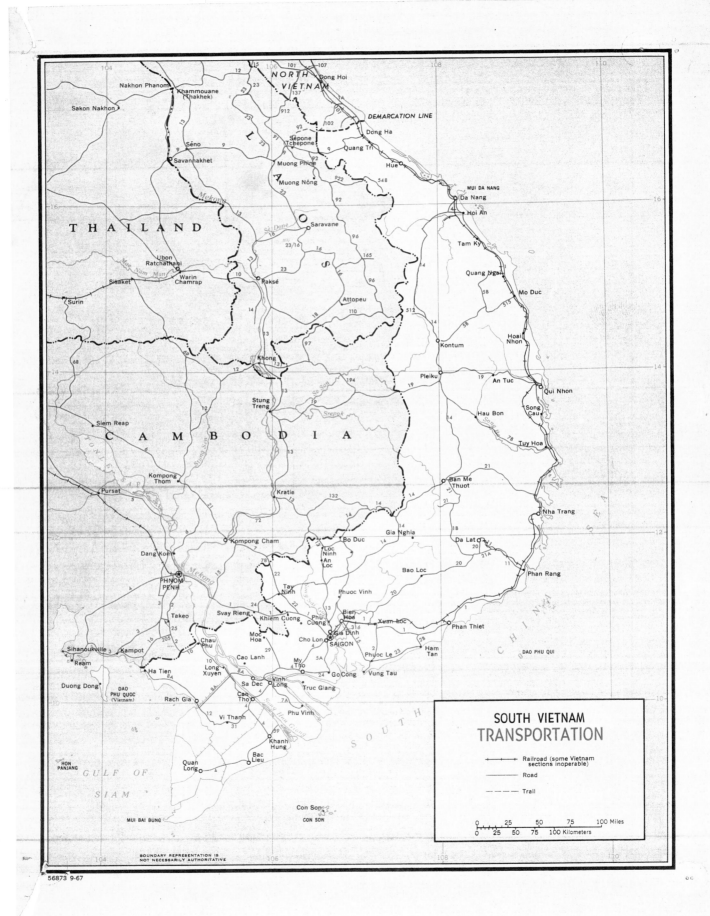

SOUTH VIETNAM TRANSPORTATION

Railroad (some Vietnam sections inoperable)

Road

Trail

0   25   50   75   100 Miles

0   25   50   75   100 Kilometers

56873 9-67

Antescsript

The Gurkha was so angry with the Vietnamese officer that he had to be dragged away and then restrained by three of us sitting on him – he was one of those thin, wiry types with a flash-point temper and strength to match. Subdued yet seething, he still wanted to chop the Viet's head off with his kukri. He sat beside his pack waiting to move off, honing the blade with quiet relish and determination. The early morning jungle mist had not yet fully cleared, the smell of the coloured smoke and thunderflashes used to simulate battle effects made the air acrid, mixing with the smell of sweat, dirty clothes and decaying undergrowth. It was the culmination of the final exercise ever to be run by the British Army's Jungle Warfare School: Vietnamese attacking a 'guerilla' camp in the jungle with the Gurkha 'enemy' dressed as Vietminh guerillas, in black pyjamas.

October 1971: we were the only part of the British Army left in Malaysia prior to pull-out from east of Suez at the end of the year. We had been instructing officers of the Army of the Republic of Vietnam (ARVN), armed forces of a third-world, non-Commonwealth country, in jungle warfare, using the Gurkha Independent Parachute Company as demonstration-cum-enemy troops. All of us would be involved in a most unpleasant international row if any blood were shed – or any more, as the Gurkha had a bleeding mouth. He had been lying doggo, feigning death, and one of the Viets, who had become so immersed in the realism of noise, smoke, shouting, attacking and men in peasant dress, that he had run up to him and kicked him sharply, and painfully, in the face. I sympathized with the one, understood the other and could hush up what had happened so far, but serious injury or death would have to be brought out into the open, with all the attendant horrors of enquiries, unwanted publicity and bad international relations we could well do without. It was a situation fraught with unpleasantness.

Even were I not the school's commandant, I dared not let this incident get out of control. This was the culminating episode on that last morning of the last-ever course to be run after twenty-three years of instructing, not only major and minor units, as well as individuals, of the British Army, but individuals of twenty other countries from six continents also. I cancelled the exercise there and then and told the Vietnamese students to reform and wait my pleasure in an open glade nearby. I went over to the brooding, proud, angry Gurkha, whom I will call Rifleman Ramshor Pun, and sat down beside him.

I asked him why he was sharpening his kukri. The exercise was over so there was now no need to use it. "Put it away and get ready to move." He reluctantly sheathed his lethal knife before turning to me. I saw that his eyes were losing the redness they had in them when he was overpowered. "You saw him kick me in the mouth," he said. "Either he lies down so that I can kick him in the mouth or I will cut him with my kukri. One or the other, not both." He spoke with dignity and conviction. He had made up his mind and, like any good tactician, knew solid ground when he saw it. "No, that won't do," I countered. "You can't kill him. I won't let you. I'll get him to apologise and you will shake hands." Came the same reply. The Gurkha saw no alternative as, for him, there was none. Subtleties of international relations, of my having no Manual of Military Law to throw at the hapless Viet, or of the limits of my jurisdiction over a member of a foreign army in a third country, with none of us being citizens of the host country, were of no concern at all to Ramshor. "You can't stop me," he said. "No one can."

We talked it out in that dismal spot in the jungle. Gurkha stubbornness was nothing new. With drink taken a Gurkha can be very dangerous. An angry Gurkha is equally intractable. I had to diffuse the nastiness. I stood up. "On with your packs, lads. Time to go."

We soon reached the Vietnamese who were sitting in three ranks. The leading Gurkhas walked past them then turned round to face them. Ramshor refused to go any farther than the near edge of the clearing. This was tactically unsound as we were outnumbered by three to one, so I curtly told him to join the others.

Once at the other end Ramshor turned round, peering at the faces of the Vietnamese. He soon saw the man he was searching for. "He's the one," he said, almost to himself, taking off his pack and reaching for his kukri.

The senior Gurkha stopped him before he could withdraw it from the scabbard. I turned and, in the now-bright sunlight, noticed that the face of the Vietnamese who had been pointed out had turned a greenish tinge. All eyes were on me. "*Chao, Dai Ta*," chorused the students, wearing their not-our-fault smiles. I returned their welcome, but not their smiles. Pointing to the man with the green gills, I beckoned him forward. As he made his unwilling way towards me I told them that the Gurkha was very angry, so angry that only a personal apology, with a handshake, would solve the crisis. The kicker and the kicked had to meet, both standing up, and shaking hands.

The situation, tense in any case, became more so. I was only too well aware that numbers placed the Gurkhas – thirty Vietnamese, ten Gurkhas – and me, at a grave disadvantage. I, a thin piece of supposedly authoritative British meat in an Asian sandwich, could be brushed aside with no difficulty whatsoever. "Come nearer," I ordered the Vietnamese. "Reach forward and shake hands." I turned to Ramshor and gave the same orders in Nepali. The two men were too far apart from each other to be able to make contact so I stretched out with my left hand, grasped the Vietnamese's sweaty hand in mine and, lurching to the other flank, grasped the Gurkha's then pulled both men into the middle. Some six inches apart they both jerked their hand away and stared angrily at each other, then at me. "I said give me your hand." In Vietnamese and Nepali I tried to sound as stern as I could but the former language is tonal and the stress of severity is not an inflection in the voice – had my tone changed, goodness only knows what I would have said. However, my feelings were obvious enough to both men. Slowly and begrudgingly the men held out their arms and I got hold of their hands. A second time I pulled them towards each other and, just as they were about to touch hands, both men yanked them away. All eyes were on me.

I was desperate, though tried not to show it. If I were unable to get them to shake hands the third time, not only would I have failed in my attempt to remedy matters but I had no other idea how to resolve the crisis. My fear turned to anger. I mouthed an oath at Ramsor and, in as swift a movement as I could, took hold of the men's hands. Using all my strength, I got them together, feeling for all the world as though I were at some grotesque tug-of-war line-up. Shake hands they did, for just long enough for it to matter…

As the students left next day they warmly thanked me for having averted what they saw as a grave situation. I was thoroughly embarrassed by one of the more emotional coming up to me as the others were getting into their transport and giving me a resounding kiss. So totally unprepared was I for such an unasked for and surprising gesture that I was momentarily transfixed with dismay. Major Jon Edwardes, in charge of Vietnamese training and who had gone with me to South Vietnam in 1969, cackled with glee as he watched me push my assailant away. "That's not something we saw when we were over there, was it?" he remarked.

It most certainly was not, nor would I be the last person to be embarrassed by lingering and maladroit French influence over her erstwhile Indo-Chinese subjects.

The end of the Second World War brought peace and stability to few parts of Asia. The turmoil of war and the inability of the colonial powers to defend what they had looked on as theirs had stirred up a new political atmosphere in the whole region. The Japanese had shown that Asians could more than master Europeans: Asian nationalists took full advantage of the new situation.

Despite victory, Britain grew tired of sustaining her colonial empire. There were many reasons for this: emergence of new political and social forces, both in Britain and elsewhere, that were inimical to empires (unless they were thinly disguised in communist red rather than openly-painted imperial red of the British kind); the rise of those who felt uncomfortable in positions of authority in the mould of previous establishments; the unwelcome phenomenon of 'debunking' much of what people had cherished in the past (patriotism, thrift, good reputation, for instance); financial crises; and a growing awareness that monumental changes were in the air all combined to make Britain start looking less far afield than in previous decades. The French, on the other hand, were markedly more tenacious regarding their overseas colonial territories.

Disengagement in Asia started with the cataclysmic events in the Indian subcontinent that resulted in the jewel in the crown of the British Empire being fragmented and handed over to two lots of home-grown masters: the greatest act of statesmanship this century, so Prime Minister Attlee is reputed to have said. "*Apartheid* in the name of religion," said I – and haven't more deaths, more suffering and more hatred been caused by gods that are held to be true by one, false by another, than any other reason? Even with India's open and implied abnegation of most matters British, without which India would never have been a political entity let alone a regional power, it kept on six regiments of Gurkhas and the British Army absorbed the other four, sending them, in the nick of time, to save Malaya from a completely new phenomenon: Communist Revolutionary Warfare.

Despite the worldwide sands of time running out for 'imperialists' and 'colonialists', with communism (disguised as or aided by nationalism) trying to fill the vacuum, only the British in Malaya were successful in inflicting a military and political defeat on these same communists in terrain and on terms of the latter's choosing. It sounds easy when put like that but there were times when it seemed as if some of those on our side had a death wish of incompetence fostered by 'the slow defeat of seldom doing anything properly'. There, disengagement came ten later than in India. In Borneo disengagement was over and done with by 1967, leaving only a residual interest in Brunei and a completely different situation in Hong Kong.

In stark contrast to the British performance, patchy and marred though it was, in Indo-China neither the French, nor later the Americans, were successful in having their chosen people take over the reins of power. In the East Indies, the Dutch were eased out (blaming the British for starting the rot by quitting India prematurely) to make Indonesia and the Portuguese had 'withered on the vine' in Timor by 1975.

Whatever else the British do or don't, they seem to be able to 'hit it off' to a remarkable degree with various ethnic groups not of or in the motherland, often better than any others – empathy between the British and the Gurkhas epitomise this. The Americans are naïve and the French arrogant and cruel, to take two examples of other foreigners' approach. In my experience Asians can be worse than either, and then to their own sort. Western-type democracy, as Britain, certainly, and France, maybe in name only, had falteringly tried to implant in their former colonial subjects, was an alien graft, certainly in Asia. However, it had been around longer than any American influence had been on the Asian mainland and the pathological dislike of Americans to colonialism undermined the colonial powers residual influence even more. Added to all that, the double standards of the bullying communists made an explosive cocktail with insurgent nationalism that became old and stale even before the honeymoon had ended, often before it had been consummated.

Nowhere was this more starkly obvious than in Indo-China.

I had joined the army during the war when the sheltered lives and stereotyped existence of the children of middle-class gentry of prewar Britain and the confines of a classical education at a public school were, for most of us, still taken for granted as utterly normal and our non-plebian birthright. God still wore spats and had a fob watch in His waistcoat pocket. The squire in the manor still had his shoots, his keeper living in a tied cottage on the estate and the gentry still spoke as though a potato was in their mouth. Overseas service was, for many, still the mark of the black sheep. Feudal breeding may have been taboo as a conversational subject but it was still, for the officer class, regarded as a positive asset. When I was 'called up' as a private soldier it was regarded as decidedly strange but an indecent wartime aberration. But what I learnt about the raw material of soldiery paid me tremendous dividends and I could now understand how those other than my social peers 'ticked'. After six months my ageing company commander in the depôt told me I was useless as a lance corporal and to try my luck as a second lieutenant.

Till then I had always been in the shadow of a brilliant and dearly-loved elder brother and I suppose it was natural when, in the April of 1944, there was the chance of volunteering for officer training in India instead of the Isle of Man, Lance Corporal Cross jumped at it. I was not particularly keen to go to war or to India for any reason other than to see what I could do entirely on my own in a completely new circumstances and surroundings. 'Make or break,' I told myself, as I faced the selection board of senior Indian Army officers. Within a year I found myself an Emergency Commissioned officer serving with Gurkhas. During that time my elder brother needlessly died in Holland in 1944, shortly before his 21st birthday, because his English superior officer's orders to him, an Englishman, in English, were not clear enough to be properly understood. If I, with Gurkhas, operating in a foreign language, needlessly wasted lives because of a communication problem, I would have failed as an officer. I thereby saw language acquisition as being of vital importance and, over the years, mastered nine Asian languages, all of them to the extent of their being of tactical importance. They, plus French, made ten.

After the war, having nothing to go back to, I applied for and was granted a regular commission. At that time, 1946, many prewar British officers seemed to want to 'purge' their ranks of those who had joined them during the war, not having gone to a peacetime Sandhurst. The prewar barrier that had been between officer and man had broken down in the jungles of Burma and those officers who did not make the change were either killed or sent on the staff in far-away India. It was these latter who wanted to re-erect the old barriers, being suspicious of, even hostile to, those like me who found wartime camaraderie more congenial.

By then I had a firm and growing empathy with Gurkhas and I thought the world of them. I found I had absorbed sufficient of their skills and tenacity to be branded as an eccentric by my British Lords and Masters, who never quite knew how to treat me, unlike Asians who did, regarding eccentricity as an inner strength.

The British Army, like the Royal Academy, requires docility in her children and even originality has to be stereotyped. Nor does the British Army have much time or place for eccentrics, especially linguists and bachelors – I am both. The regimental dedication of the old Indian Army was not nearly such a strong feature of the British Army and those guilty of such heresy were distrusted as being 'narrow-minded and dogmatic'. This, in turn, led to personality clashes and even jealousies when those not imbued with such a strong personal bond with the rank and file found that they were unsuccessful in penetrating the barrier between leader and led. To many such, all joys of regimental service and activity had to be subsumed by 'career planning': a military confidence trick that even 'run of the mill' officers felt they had a good chance that a field marshal's baton was hiding somewhere in their knapsack and so suffering many inglorious postings the while – a recipe for regimental rancour, if not remorse.

By the time the British Army left mainland Asia (less Hong Kong) at the end of 1971 I had been in Asia, without a home posting, since 1944. By then I had spent a total of ten years in the jungle, to start with as a company commander of Gurkha infantry during the Malayan Emergency. In the Borneo Confrontation campaign I was first Commandant of the Border Scouts, disguised as a colonial policeman, and later commanded the Gurkha parachutists who operated in the reconnaissance rôle in small patrols. I had no European service to my credit. I had only ever done one low-grade job on the staff. However, during these long and exacting years I had learnt a lot about low-intensity operations in tropical rainforest terrain and the military counter to Communist Revolutionary Warfare. This put me beyond the pale for promotion above major as I was deemed completely unsuitable for conventional employment. It was only by the remotest chance that I was eventually promoted to lieutenant colonel and posted to the Jungle Warfare School, first as Chief Instructor and then as Commandant.

Dame Fortune, that most fickle of ladies, plays strange tricks. Most unusually I had found myself in Indo-China as a young man in 1945-46. Even more unexpectedly I found myself back there as the last-ever Defence Attaché, this time in Laos, for over three years, from late 1972 to early 1976. Here I tell the story of these two periods in Indo-China, where I was one of the first English military in and, thirty years later, the very last one out.

PART I

COCHIN-CHINA: 1945-46

'When the water level falls, the ants eat the fish . . .*

* Lao proverb

1

Black Flags of Surrender Flew . . .

"May we stop and buy a horizontal bomb?"

I turned to my Gurkha driver and asked him to repeat his request as I was sure I had not heard correctly.

"May we stop and buy a horizontal bomb? There's a mobile canteen on our way back and I can get one there."

It was shortly after the atom bombs had been dropped at the very end of the war. We were on our return from Headquarters 20 Division where I had been sent to collect a rarity in those days, an issue of beer. I had been serving with Gurkhas for all of eight months and had managed a fair degree of fluency, but this beat me.

We could spare the time and I was intrigued. We soon reached the canteen, one of a small fleet of converted trucks that visited units. Run by a gallant band of women called the Woman's Auxiliary Service (Burma), it provided a basic and much appreciated service of necessities and, until they ran out, 'char and wads'. I told the driver and his mate to go and see what was in the canteen and get a cup of tea. I sat back and waited.

I was twenty years old. Recently commissioned, I had been posted to the first battalion of the First Gurkha Rifles (1/1 GR) in Burma a few weeks before, having been trained for jungle warfare and service with Gurkhas for the past year in India. On my arrival, having steeled myself to fight the Japanese and reluctant to postpone my first 'moment of truth', I found the situation quiet. I fretted over the inevitable anticlimax caused by unexpected inactivity but I dared not be bored. A soft breeze stirred some metal strips that hung at the top of a pagoda opposite the parked vehicle, producing little ringing jingles, tinklingly mellifluous. There was a fragrance in the air, whether from joss or wild flowers I cannot remember.

As I mused about being so near the war though not yet a part of it, the two Gurkhas came back, looking slightly forlorn. They said that the canteen was no good, did not have what they wanted. I sympathised.

"'Didn't you get any tea?"
"Oh yes, we got our tea all right but we could not find any horizontal bombs."

So I had heard correctly, over the noise of the engine.

"Do you really want a horizontal bomb?"

Yes, they did.

"The memsahib inside the canteen said that there weren't any but we think we saw some."

Rather facetiously I suggested it was an 'etam bomb' they were looking for but soon realised my joke was in poor taste.

"No. It's not like that. It is small and cool."

In the end I went myself and asked one of the ladies if she had a horizontal bomb – one of the small, cool ones? The hapless woman was taken aback and, asking to be excused, went to consult her superior. I now wished I had never stopped at the canteen, thus avoiding this embarrassing situation. What exactly did I want? I made my strange request yet again only to be told that they had never heard of such a thing. I asked if I could call one of my men in – "just this once, please" – as they were sure some were in stock.

Reluctantly this was allowed ("we're really too busy to answer such queries") and my driver was allowed in. He looked around and, stiffening like a terrier scenting a rat, suddenly pounced on a small cardboard box on a shelf. He put his hand inside and, with the air of one who has known he was right all along, produced a small bottle.

"*Lo, saheb*, a 'horizontal bomb'," he said with quiet satisfaction. I read the label which clearly showed its contents – Oriental Balm.

He paid for it and we left in silence. Neither of us would ever know how many similarly stupid mistakes of misunderstanding were to be made between Asians and non-Asians over the next thirty years.

The war in Europe had been over for three months when, on 6 August 1945, the atomic bomb was dropped on Hiroshima. That, and the bomb dropped on Nagasaki a few days later, changed the face of the world. One of the many effects was to produce a completely new situation in southeast Asia.

At the Potsdam Conference, in July 1945, it had been decided temporarily to divide what was then known as French Indo-China into two prior to its future being settled, the northern sphere to the Chinese (a political decision insisted upon by the Americans), the southern to the British.

Of course, it was not as simple as that; the Americans, with strong anti-colonial feelings, treated the French as enemies and the British, as regards Malaya, Singapore, Hong Kong, Burma and India, not much better. The French were smarting, not least from loss of national prestige caused by wartime defeat, and were very desirous to regain their colony and rescue their prisoners-of-war. The British, not seeing Indo-China as their 'sphere of influence', wanted to sort their own problems out elsewhere, while the Vietnamese communists wanted to run their own country without the help of any outsider, communist or not. The wellsprings of hatred of the French that flowed from the Vietnamese and of contempt of the Vietnamese that flowed from the French provided the fatal doses of poison that could not have had more explosive ingredients to a recipe already ripe for chaos. Despite much dedicated, if often misguided, effort, there had been too many lost chances and too many mistakes made through expediency, ignorance or inefficiency for men's passions to be quieted and peace given a chance. The seeds of bitterness had already been sown; they were to flower foully for the next fifty years.

So much for the future: all we knew then was that momentous events were happening. The evening I brought back the beer, sitting in an upstairs room of a large Burmese house on stilts we used as a mess, the field telephone clanked its authority as we started to eat our super. Slightly vexed, the adjutant went to answer it and then followed one of those infuriatingly elusive, one-sided conversations that had us hanging on his words even after the last 'good night'.

The adjutant returned and put us out of our suspense by telling us that the Japanese had surrendered. Impromptu celebrations lasted well into the night so it was with a distinct jolt we learnt next morning that the message of the previous evening was wrong and the Japanese had not surrendered. Quite the reverse, so went the new message, a large party was infiltrating to our north and we were to go and deal with it immediately...

Peace was declared a week later and we were very relieved that the battalion had suffered no casualties during those last seven days, but that in no way countered an understandable tendency to lethargy.

Interest was revived and pressure re-applied by orders to move to French Indo-China, to disarm the Japanese and hand the country back to the French. Up to then our mental horizons had never been farther afield than Singapore and few of us had any but hazy notions of where French Indo-China was. I was detailed to pay a visit to the local Burmese head teacher and find out. He produced an atlas and I learnt where it was and that there were no less than five states with names that conjured up shades of schoolboy stamp albums; Cambodia, Laos, Tonkin, Annam and Cochin China. We were destined to go somewhere named Saigon that few of us had heard about and none of us could otherwise have placed without that atlas.

The battalion packed up, painting all the stores with a code name, MASTERON. The day before we were due to move we were ordered to repaint them all as MASTERDOM. I marvelled, in my innocence, how the army could take such matters so seriously. Official farewells to the villagers were paid and the battalion made its way by train to Rangoon – I drove the engine part of the way – ready for the next stage of its journey to an unknown country.

In early September we sailed in SS *Rajula*, touched at Singapore and, within five days or so, reached the coast of Cochin China. From Cap St Jacques upriver to Saigon we took in details of this new land, so depressingly like parts of the one we had just left. As all seemed so calm the men did not look upon it with any more tactical interest than is inbred in soldiers who have survived a hard war. But the calm was illusory.

'All Japanese forces in French Indo-China have been ordered to fly a black flag, denoting surrender.' That edict made a great impression on me, as indeed did the rules of conduct laid down for our relations with the surrendered Japanese forces:

> ...*There will be no fraternising whatever between Japanese and Allied forces. In dealing with Japanese your behaviour will be guarded and coldly polite. You will, in the case of senior Japanese officers, use their correct titles. You will not shake hands with them... In no case will British and Japanese officers feed in the same room, nor will tea be offered at any meeting. Any Japanese who come to receive orders or report should be kept at arm's length, e.g. with a table between you and them, and they should not be allowed to sit at the same table...*

All Japanese officers had to salute allied soldiers of all ranks.

To me there was something fitting and ultimate about having a black flag. For too long the Rising Sun of the Japanese flag had dominated too many places and now their sun was set. The Japanese, who had swept all before them at the start of the war, had been ordered to stop fighting. In Burma, where they had lost the war, that made sense to them. In Indo-China, where they had had no fighting, it was very difficult for them to understand how they had lost the war. Luckily for the allies the emperor's edict was final and the Japanese conformed. The rules of conduct, the restrictions and petty embarrassments were not harsh but designed to humble by loss of face.

The Vietnamese we came into contact with, condescendingly called Annamites by the French, were small, lithe people with faces not unlike Chinese but, in the main, darker skinned. Their language was beyond any of us; a high-pitched twittering as of many sparrows. The only way we could talk to them directly was by using French but even that had its problems as not all of them spoke it and those who did had an accent unfamiliar to our ears. If that was not enough, so little rapport was there between the locals and their colonial masters that we British had to speak French well enough to be understood but badly enough to be taken for someone who was not French. We were, initially, accepted in a friendly way.

The French, pro-Vichy colonials – and who was it who so aptly said that only French colonials like French colonials? – should have been in charge of Saigon but they were so ineffectual they soon had to hand their duties over, but to whom? We had been detailed to collect and back-load Japanese military stores from various installations so were unable to take on those French responsibilities. The only people who could were the Japanese but French national pride, or what was left of it, baulked at their soldiers handing over duties to the Japanese even if the Japanese could have been persuaded to take them over from the French. A compromise was reached: the British would take over from the French in the morning and hand over to the Japanese in the evening. In the event all went smoothly but there was one moment of tension when one Gurkha guard commander, a *naik* (corporal), found that his opposite number, a second lieutenant, had to draw his sword to salute with. Discipline on both sides prevailed but the Gurkha looked uncomfortable till the sword was sheathed.

Although none of us knew it at the time, we were to become embroiled in what is now known as Communist Revolutionary Warfare. Mao Tse-tung's doctrine, also practised by his formidable lieutenants-by-proxy, Ho Chi Minh, personality spokesman for North Vietnam, and General Vo Nguyen Giap, had insidiously started to spread in Asia. It set a pattern for the next two decades and more of unrest and violence, in one guise or another. Gone, for the most part, were the pitched battles of conventional armies as we knew them, changed were the priorities of the principles of war. The tactic of terror needed no front line nor the gospel of grief any slit trench. Slogans and ideas did not fill the belly, nor rice the mind, yet hungry men spurned food and thoughtful men disdained normal logic. What was this strange new happening and what moved men so violently? Surely not entirely the hatred of the European, nor solely the love of revolution? These two facets were, maybe, the catalyst that gave the impetus to swing the pendulum that moved the ratchet-wheel that slipped the cog that started to change the face of the world that John Roast-Beet and his Gallic neighbours had built. This was to be further changed by the two superpowers to the detriment of millions: 'three cheers for America'? or 'three Tsars for Russia'?

It is easy to forget that it is only when the pendulum has swung its full course does the ratchet-wheel move at all. Movement is life, no movement is death: yet in action the very reverse was often nearer the truth, and we were there to fight, not to philosophise. When I first tried to put my thoughts together, Indo-China/Vietnam had not soured men's souls nor had the post-war rash of history books yet analysed cause and effect. I put down my thoughts as they were then.

Not very long after we arrived it was evident that there was going to be trouble between the French civilians and the local population. The man in overall charge of the forces in the south was Major General Douglas Gracey. His orders were to control the area surrounding the two Japanese headquarters, one in Saigon itself and the other, at a hill station not far away, called Dalat. Gracey found himself in an unenviable position, squeezed from many sides: by the French and the Vietminh (the shortened form of 'Vietnam League of Independence'); by Lord Louis Mountbatten, the Supreme Commander, who was not only ambitious and politically motivated but was also at 'personality odds' with him; by a Labour government in Great Britain that was not sympathetic to matters colonial and heavily in debt; by the Viceroy and Commander-in-Chief in India wanting his army back without getting involved in someone else's war; by Indian politicians to whom the presence of Indian troops helping restore French colonialism (and Dutch in Java) was anathema; and by the Japanese army which was 'undefeated'.

The situation quickly deteriorated as the Vietminh came to realise that the French were to be given back control of the country, and incidents of shooting were a nightly occurrence. Both Saigon and its Chinatown, Cholon, were dangerous places. The arrogance of the French towards their colonies has been well documented; the cruel exploitation and brutal maltreatment and contempt of the Tonkinese, Annamites and others in Indo-China shown during that phase manured seeds of bitterness and frustration already sowed and a burning desire to be rid of their masters. General Giap (a student of Napoleon) the military commander of the Vietnamese main force and guerilla armies, who was to prove more than a match for both the French and the Americans, and Ho Chi Minh, the political boss who outwitted all adversaries, were both rampantly anti-French. Such bitterness does not accrue overnight. I know these feelings not to be the product of some left-wing historian's imagination. It was bitter irony for so many Vietnamese that, when the northern communists did eventually prevail, communism was as much a failure as it has been everywhere, with its mismanagement, corruption, privilege, repression, intransigence and cruelty on a par with the previous French colonial practice, however much Frenchmen would argue to the contrary.

Proof of further nastinesses was forthcoming when leaflets were smuggled into the Gia Dinh girls' school where the battalion was billeted. Headed '*Warning*', the message continued:

There is about to happen an armed struggle between ourselves, the Viet Minh and our enemies the French. We want to be friends with the British, so be prudent and never ramble about with the French.

So prudent we were, nor did we ramble about with them except occasionally when we went to swim at *Le Cercle Sportif*, irreverently re-christened 'The Sporting Gooly', where the women besported themselves with more faith than elastic.

One afternoon there was a film show in town that was supposed to be anti-Vichy in sentiment, and therefore unpopular with the local French inhabitants. In order to control any possible disturbances, I was ordered to take a platoon of Gurkhas to guard the cinema, inside and outside. At this unexpected display of force the audience could only give vent to their feelings with some fearsome-sounding Gallic oaths. Two hours later the crowd streamed out into the road. A car, slowly driven by a Japanese, came past and a woman cyclist, swerving to miss an obstruction, hit it. She fell off and immediately the French formed a circle around the car and started belabouring the hapless driver. Reactions pent up by frustrating inactivity in the cinema found an outlet. The Japanese sat steady, with an embarrassed smile, as blows smote him from all sides. The woman had, by this time, picked herself up and was rapidly disappearing. I was unhappy to see the luckless driver as a target of pent-up French emotions but I did not see how to redress the situation. More exploratorily than with conviction, I shouted 'Oy!' at the top of my voice and the effect was instant. The Frenchmen stepped back, glaring at me as I waved the Japanese on. The engine was still ticking over and he needed no second bidding. I found myself filling the vacuum and wished I had not been so impetuous.

To stop any Gallic onslaught I put my hand out and, subconsciously remembering being punished at school for getting a supposedly simple phrase wrong, brought it out unhesitatingly, loudly and with great authority. *"Ou sont les bagues de la reine?* which does not mean where are the queen's knickers," I added in English so a casual observer would not be muddled as I had been in those early days.

The effect was gratifyingly startling and, before the French crowd could realise that my message was inappropriate, albeit very well timed, I had reached the safety of my platoon, now reformed nearby. 'What did you say?' the driver asked me as we drove off. For a moment I toyed with the idea of giving a Nepali rendering of my few words but regretfully decided I was not up to it. I took a side step away from the truth and said I was invoking royalty.

Japanese units in the surrounding countryside also had to be disarmed and, at the same time, it was feared the unrest in Saigon was spreading. Troops were therefore deployed to the south and north and it was our 100 Brigade that went upcountry. 1/1 GR was to go to Thu Dau Mot, a peaceful little riverine town an hour's normal drive from the capital, 4/10 GR to Thu Duc, a small town nearer to Saigon and 3/14 Punjab Regiment to Bien Hoa, a sleepy village to the east, on the River Dong Nai. We moved off expecting trouble, I travelling with the Commanding Officer, Lieutenant Colonel C. E. Jarvis. We drove through open countryside along roads badly in need of repair, with peasants working normally in the fields.

The French Army camp at Thu Dau Mot consisted mainly of two three-storied buildings, two rows of cells – capable of being heavily guarded – a pleasantly sited officers' mess and some outbuildings. The perimeter was soon strengthened with *panjis*, sharp bamboo stakes, which were stuck into the ground to impale the inquisitive and the evil-minded. A football ground lay outside the perimeter. The barracks were a couple of miles from the town and built on a knoll overlooking paddy on one side, mixed jungle and scrub on two other sides and the River Saigon, half a mile wide, on the fourth. We were supported by machine-gunners of the 1st Royal Battalion of the 9th Jats and a section of Indian Artillery.

Convoys, known as 'Atlantics', reached us every other day from Saigon. I had been made Intelligence Officer and much of my work entailed visiting various Japanese installations and making inventories of items for back-loading. With elements of the navy, the air force – complete with an arsenal of 60 and 120 kilogram bombs – to say nothing of part of a Railway Company as well as more conventional army units, my work was unusual and interesting. Apart from my own Gurkha staff, I was also in charge of a small intelligence cell comprising an Annamite woman and two half-caste men. A French Army liaison officer, Colonel Turk, who had come from Madagascar, lived with us, practising his English. He was a narrow-minded, obstinate man who seemed to despise anyone not a European, so found himself at odds living in a Gurkha battalion. He was inclined to obesity, was of medium build and had a bad complexion. However, he was gratified at the respect paid to him and was useful on occasions.

100 Brigade's mission was to disarm the Japanese. However, the local Vietminh guerilla units were becoming more and more active as they tried to prevent this from happening. Roadblocks, ambushes and skirmishes dragged us into fighting when we should have been busy with our prime task. There were not enough troops to keep the guerillas at bay and to disarm the

Japanese. The official solution for the task of containing the guerillas was to use Japanese troops, but only those who had no adverse war record against the British.

It may not be generally known that two Japanese battalions operated under Indian Army command during this brief campaign, both under 1/1 GR. In the Japanese army a battalion, *butai*, took its name from its commander, normally a major. One was the *Takahashi Butai* under a major; the second was the *Yamagishi Butai*, under a captain. Both men were very experienced and shrewd operators who had spent many years fighting the Chinese. We came to know them well and found the restrictions imposed on us in our dealing with them irksome. Even so, relations were cordial. Both Japanese commanders sensed our unease and never, in any way, took advantage of our feelings. They had to come and report to us every evening. Their staff work, especially regarding reports, maps and diagrams, was faultless. As Intelligence Officer, I helped with these reports.

One day Major Takahashi and his interpreter marched in, stood to attention one side of the table behind which we were seated and saluted, bending forward from the waist as their hands came up to their hats, halfway between our army and navy salutes.

"Good evening, Gentlemen."
"Good evening."
"We have a report."
"Please give us your report."
"We have captured a Russian. Shall we kill him or bring him to you?"
"Bring him to us. How do you know he is a Russian?"
"Because of his uniform and because he is carrying a jar of coffee."

The information was given with the quiet authority of one who talks from a position of strength because what he says is true. We did not follow the logic of the coffee but had the manners not to seem puzzled. Later on we speculated among ourselves about this curious affair. Russian was one of the 'big four' and an ally. We could not believe it was capable of organising clandestine operations against wartime comrades in arms, but how wrong we were.

When the Russian appeared on the morrow he was clasping a large glass jar full of roasted coffee beans. Red-haired and stocky, he was wearing khaki drill, had a yellow hammer and sickle emblem on a red background on each lapel, with a similar badge stuck into his khaki forage cap. He was put in the cells and kept there until Higher Authority told us to send him to Saigon. We had his clothes laundered for him but drank his coffee, which was delicious.

We sent him south to Saigon three days later, he protesting volubly that he would talk to no one except the Soviet ambassador. He would not believe us when we told him that there was no Soviet representation in Saigon. We never heard of him again.

Guerilla activity increased in tempo. In November orders came to send a column, code-named 'Clarkol' – under Major Clark, hence its name – north to a village called Ben Cat. Its task was to locate and destroy a Vietminh force that had ambushed and caused casualties to a company of *Yamagishi Butai*. The infantry element was to be our own B Company and three rifle companies of the *Yamashi*. I was detailed as the column second-in-command. We moved north with a strong escort of armoured cars of the 16th Cavalry, commanded by Major Sawney, a versatile Indian officer who spoke impeccable English and quickly rose to great heights after Indian independence. The only all-British unit in the division, 114 Field Regiment, Royal Artillery, sent its contingent as did the Jat machine-gunners already in Thu Dau Mot.

We reached Ben Cat that evening, after a tiring day during which many Vietminh roadblocks of felled trees had to be cleared. Major Clark went to meet the Japanese commander at his house – the largest in the village – and was kept waiting for a quarter of an hour before he came downstairs with a Japanese woman. He was dealt with curtly. Some of the Gurkhas spat their disgust as the Japanese major and his 'keep' passed them. Troops were settled for the night and orders for the next day were to be given only when a Japanese patrol returned.

At 8 o'clock that evening elements of all interested groups assembled in the house where Major Clark had set up his headquarters. It appeared that there was a group of about fifty guerillas to our south in a triangle of country, the apex of which pointed to Saigon. The gunners were to remain on the northern 'base' road while the Jat machine-gunners and the armoured cars were to patrol the other two roads. The infantry was to sweep southwards, spread out widely at first but concentrating as the country tapered to a point. It was hoped to finish the operation in one day. Major Clark, being committed to overall command, I wondered how B Company, 1/1 GR, and the *Yamagishi Butai* would manage when my thoughts were rudely interrupted by hearing that 'Captain Cross is the commander of all the infantry.' We were to drive to as near where the Vietminh were suspected then patrol south of foot, searching for them.

The edict from the highest laid down that no Japanese would give orders to an ally. Military common sense, however, argued against me, with only ten months' commissioned service, commanding the equivalent of a battalion, three parts of it already with a commander who was battle-proven and with no common language.

I spent a restless night, going to bed with my head in a whirl. So nervous was I that I knocked over the only lamp there was in the house and we had to go to bed in the dark. I was severely cursed. In a vivid dream my elder brother, Timothy, who had been killed in Europe a year before and with whom I was very close, gave me advice on what to do on the morrow. "Be yourself, keep calm, you'll manage," he told me. I slept on comforted and was awoken at 3 o'clock, refreshed. I dressed and went outside to find the convoy assembling and the men falling in, an untidy jigsaw puzzle so cleverly putting itself together.

The convoy moved off at dawn. I was in the leading vehicle with three Gurkhas as bodyguards. Driving slowly along a winding road with cover on either side, shots rang out as guerillas opened fire on us. So much on tenterhooks was I that I was out of the truck with my three men, over a bank and towards the scene of firing before I realised it was pointless my barking with so many dogs under my command. Even so, my stupidity raised my morale and luckily had a depressing effect on the opposition because they were seen, in the half-light of dawn, running away. Japanese soldiers caught me up and joined in the firefight. We did not give chase as we were on a tight movement schedule. On we drove.

We moved off on foot dead on time. With me were Yamagishi and his staff, my three shadows and, on my right, the company of Gurkhas. One of Yamagishi's companies was on its right and the other two away on the left. We advanced steadily through elephant grass, scrub and patches of rubber trees for about two hours with no incident.

When firing broke out I was nonplussed. It came from a rubber plantation in front of us, about two hundred yards away. Between us and the guerillas the country was not very thick and sloped down to a small river that flowed across our front. I looked around and tried to pinpoint the fire. As I did a voice sounded in my ear and I turned to see the Japanese interpreter bending forward, hissing his respects, his solar pith helmet under his left arm, with a water bottle in his right hand and a Japanese-English dictionary in his left. He was newly appointed and very, very nervous. Probably we were both equally green.

"Respected sir, Captain Yamagishi sends his respects and respectfully requests you to adopt the lying position."

Looking around I saw that we two were the only ones not lying down and, in all probability, presenting good, though small, targets. We continued our conversation in the prone position.

"Respected sir," the interpreter hissed, looking happier now he was closer to nature than originally designed. "Captain Yamagishi respectfully asks your respected permission to fire his mortars."

The interpreter squirmed away to give my respected permission and the Japanese fired their mortars for about ten minutes, after which Captain Yamagishi and I, aided by the interpreter, held a short confabulation. I suggested, in my grandiose ignorance, a company attack. I was respectfully asked if I would mind if Yamagishi could have my permission to send a section. I gave it – having not much option – and was intrigued to see ten men, commanded by a second lieutenant armed only with a sword, disappear down the slope a few minutes later. After a short while they appeared some way up on the far side, near a rubber plantation. They cast about, turned and waved us forward.

The main body moved off downhill in extended line. My mind was already at the top of the hill when I reached the river so I was frightened out of my wits by seeing a Japanese head come up from between my knees and my crotch and felt myself being heaved into the air. Frightful visions of *harakiri* raced through my mind and I tried to kick out but my legs were firmly pinioned. I really did think I had 'had' it – miles in the middle of nowhere, yet another young and unsung embryonic hero serving King and Country – and it took a few moments to realise that I, like the Japanese officers and my three gunmen, were being given a pick-a-back across the river to save our feet from getting wet.

At the top of the hill were two casualties, both badly wounded by mortar fragments. In both cases a large lump of metal had penetrated near the top of the thigh and made a nasty hole in the neck. One was a young man, armed with a rifle; the other, a lad of about twelve, held a catapult in his hand.

About twenty yards away a section of Japanese soldiers distracted me by going through some sort of dumb pantomime. They were excitedly pointing down to something I could not see. I told the interpreter to calm them down. I was distressed on account of the wounded. We were miles from anywhere and, even to my untrained eye, there was little hope for their survival and carrying them out would badly delay us. In Yamagishi's headquarter group was a doctor with a medical satchel. He examined the casualties and spoke to the interpreter. I was approached and asked if I would authorise the doctor to despatch (I still can't use the word 'kill') the man and the boy by injecting sufficient morphia into their bloodstream for their end to be painless, as his limited medical supplies could help in no other way. I was appalled by being turned to for a decision and stalled. But apparently everything was in my hands and I made the fatal decision that I have had to live with ever since.

Feeling distraught, the antics of the Japanese soldiers, standing on the bank, grated on me.

"Stop them fooling about," I said, angrily, to the interpreter.

"Respected sir, they are afraid."

"Why?"

"They have seen a hand," was the enigmatic reply.

So I went to see what it was all about. The bank, maybe three feet high, had a ditch on the other side. Rubber trees were planted on the bank and the ditch was to hold water to help their growth. But now it was full of dry leaves and a skinny brown arm was waving about, palm upwards, not unlike an oriental Excalibur without his sword. So the soldiers had seen a hand!

"Pull it," I ordered callously.

"They are afraid to," answered the interpreter.

My temper snapped and, sensing that valour was the better part of discretion, the soldiers were quickly ordered to pull the hand. One man, braver than the rest, bent down ready to grasp it. A man caught him round the waist and a third the second likewise. In one movement the leading soldier grasped the hand and all three pulled. I watched, fascinated, as a small, stark naked man, with the star of Tonkin tattooed on his left shoulder, was jerked upwards, carrying a brand new machine-gun of curious shape. Almost in one movement he wriggled free of his captors, looked up at the near-cloudless sky, crouched low and, just as I noticed that the gun was loaded with a tray-like magazine, he bent both ends down and so jammed the weapon. He jumped up and down, shrieking. The Japanese were on him in a flash even as I turned to my nearest gunman and told him to give me his kukri. I took it and made as to decapitate the naked man. He ceased his shouting and looked sullen. I asked the interpreter for an explanation.

"Respected sir, the soldiers were in micturition [some quick overtime with his dictionary there] on the leaves when the hand appeared."

Then I understood why the man had looked at the sky on being so unexpectedly pulled out. When he felt the sudden surges of liquid wetting him he had put his hand up to see how heavily it was raining! He was part of the Vietminh stay-behind party who had left the two dying casualties as bait and presumably his mission was to shoot us up as we moved off burdened with the wounded. On seeing that there was scarcely a cloud in the sky, he was furious at having disclosed his position. The gun was of Czechoslovakian origin and, had the man not made the mistake he did, would undoubtedly have been used against us. I never knew what made him jam his weapon rather than try and kill us. (In future years, when I gave South Vietnamese army students lectures at the Jungle Warfare School, I used this incident as an example both of the need for constant vigilance when engaged on this type of operation and of the fact that secret weapons need not always be modern to be effective.)

During the next two hours we took about twenty more prisoners. We were about a hundred yards from the apex of the triangle in thick country when machine-guns of 16 Cavalry armoured cars opened fire dangerously close. There was no need for me to be reminded about lying down as we hit the ground as one man. Another burst smacked overhead. Apparently the remainder of the guerilla groups had slipped across the road and had been seen but not stopped so the subaltern in the nearest armoured car had fired into the thick undergrowth taking a gamble of hitting more men he believed might be following behind.

Once on the road I soon met up with Major Clark and Colonel Turk. The latter, with true Gallic courtesy, said, "You were very brave, I will recommend you for a decoration," in a heavy and guttural accent. We quarrelled badly a month later when I strongly objected to the manner in which the then-not-so-gallant colonel spoke to the Gurkhas. His Parthian shot then was to the effect that if I so insisted that when he had said to those f***ing Gurkhas was insulting, then he would cancel my decoration. But that was later and now he exuded bonhomie.

The drive back to Ben Cat had only one incident worth recording. The armoured escorts for the returning column had only reached the road junction at the apex of the search area a short while before my group did. The guerillas had dug so many holes in the road and felled so many trees athwart it that it had taken the whole day to make the road passable to vehicles as well as search the verges for ambush positions to ensure no hostiles were in the area. The Vietminh, as far as we knew, had all moved south so a quiet journey back was expected.

From the opposite direction came a French armoured jeep. It slammed on its brakes as it drew level with us and out stepped an officer, thin and foxy, limping on his right leg. He found Major Clark and asked him in good English if the road south to Saigon was clear. Clark told him that the Gurkhas had cleared down to the next road junction, some six miles away but he thought it unsafe to go farther south. He said that we were going to Ben Cat for the night and it would be dark soon. "We have a radio there if you want to use it. Come back with us." No. He had a personal despatch for le Général Le Clerc and had to get it to Saigon that night.

So saying, he hobbled back into the jeep and drove off. The country to left and right was clear of trees. We turned and watched him go and, fifty yards away, there was a muffled report and a spurt of dust from a punctured back tyre. I saw it happen. The vehicle slewed to a halt, reversed and drove back fast. The French officer's face was dark. He sought out Major Clark and angrily demanded why the road was so dangerously exposed to enemy fire when we claimed that we had cleared it. He was in no way pacified and flushed with pique when we pointed out that there was no place for a sniper for a considerable distance, that we were still standing there, safe and sound, and had not he better return with us? He drove the few miles back to Bet Cat on his punctured tyre, not bothering to change the wheel.

On arrival at Ben Cat we dismissed the troops. I waited until they were settled in their billets and, as I turned to go to mine, the French officer came out of a house a few yards away and strode off, neither leg in distress. He suddenly noticed me and, stopping only momentarily, limped away with his left leg obviously causing him distress.

That night, as I drowsed off to sleep, I reviewed the events of the day, so unusual I felt I could never forget them. I had, in a mild way, been tested, if not under exacting conditions, by much that was unexpected and unusual. While I would never say that I had been anything other than pedestrian in my military actions, I had not disgraced myself – frightened, angry and remorseful though I had been.

I had faced my 'moment of truth', not as I had expected in Burma but in an outlandish place far from British interests and farther still from anything ever remotely imagined, and I was still in one piece, mentally and physically. How strange it was that militarily I had come of age fighting Asians of no concern to Britain while commanding Britain's staunchest Asian friends and her most feared Asian enemies.

We drove back the next day with no incident. Brigade headquarters acknowledged what we had done by making a signal. The Indian signaller only made one mistake when he took it down: *From 100 Bde to Clarkol (.) immediate (.) unclassified (.) your 0058 of 10 Nov (.) well done CLARKOL keep it up and knock their BLACKS off.*

On the road between Thu Dau Mot and Saigon was a village favourable to the Vietminh, named Bung. A company was sent there to patrol the area and prevent road convoys from being ambushed. One day I had to visit the troops there and, as no trouble was anticipated, I only took a small escort. Approaching Bung we met scattered firing as we drove into an area of paddy, but we only saw two people, a man ploughing and a young woman. She was standing stock still, legs slightly apart, one in front of the other, her arms upraised. She was silhouetted against the sky and remained immobile the fifteen seconds for us to drive out of sight. But what was curious was that she was completely naked.

On the way back a grenade was thrown from the roadside into the truck in front of me. I saw it hit a soldier on the head and roll onto the floor. He picked it up and threw it away, superbly unruffled. It was a Japanese-type, lighter than the British 36 grenade, but even so the soldier was bareheaded and I presumed it would have hurt him. He did not even put his hand up to his head to feel if there was any damage while the grenade harmlessly exploded out of range.

Shortly afterwards I was made battalion quartermaster and had to devote my energies to the rapidly increasing amount of Japanese stores that were piling up. Their range was immense but now only a few of the more unusual items come to mind: Mauser pistols, aerial bombs, swords – at one time I had over a thousand of them in my stores – artillery pieces and unrecognisable bits of railway equipment.

By mid-December 1945 the two Japanese battalions that had supported us had to be disarmed, that is to say they had to surrender officially. By then *Takahashi Butai* had returned to Saigon but Yamagishi's unit was with us. A day was fixed for the disarming ceremony.

A week before the surrender parade, Yamagishi and his interpreter came to me one morning when I was working in the stores. I had no shirt on and was hot. I was counting 60-kilogram bombs and he asked me to spare a minute. He was immaculate in clean uniform and shining leather, belt and boots. There were some Gurkha soldiers counting stores and Yamagishi signified that he wanted to see me alone. By now there was a bond between us and, although we had never gone beyond the bounds of decorum laid down by the edict, I felt that, were other situations to prevail, we could become firm friends. Even so, the end of the war was only four months past and a tiny and uncharitable thought struck me – was this interview going to be violent? I need not have worried.

When we were out of sight of the others and by ourselves, the interpreter told me the history of Yamagishi's sword; the 250-odd years it had been in his family, the five personal fights he had had with it against the Chinese and now, before the surrender parade, he was going to give it to me. I felt too small for the occasion as, reaching out to take it from Yamagishi's hands, the interpreter said, "Respected sir, Captain Yamagishi says he wants to give you his sword because you are a true gentleman and cavalier."

I stammered my thanks, feeling that anything I said was superfluous. The sword indeed had five notches in the blade. I was also given a piece of paper on which was written:

To: Capt Cross

Q.M.A.L.F. Thu Dau Mot*

Brief History of a Sowrd

This sword was made by a famouth swardsmith called Fujiware yositoke who lived about

300 years ago in our country
We call these sword – Nippon-to, and this Nippon-to was a treasure of my house
I used this sword as my most favourite one on this great war's battlefield
Especially this sword is being kept in ancient shape, and is very sharp on its edge

Owner
Yamagishi Keisuke

18th Jan 1946   *2nd Battalion Commander*

[*Quarter master Allied Land Forces]

On the eve of the parade proper, preparations were made. Towards one end of the large parade square, equidistant from both sides, a flagpole was erected. Early on the morrow the Union Jack was flown. In front of it were tables and, in the rear, a row of chairs.

For the parade, the British officers stood either side of the flagpole and the Gurkha officers sat on chairs in front, the senior Gurkha officer, the Subedar Major, in the centre. The surrender was to be Asian to Asian. At 8 o'clock the *butai*, let by Yamagishi, marched up the road leading into the camp and onto the square. It formed up facing the flag and the men to whom they were to surrender, the commanding officer in front, all other officers six paces behind him, all warrant officers six more paces behind them, then the rank and file, at open-order, with sergeants behind as supernumeraries.

Yamagishi marched up to Subedar Major Balesor Rana, saluted, unbuckled his sword – his second best – laid it on the table between him and the Gurkha officers and saluted again. His face was wet with tears. He turned about and, one by one, the officers followed suit. The Gurkha officers' faces were granite-hewn in their immobility. Their expressions were a stern mask of unrelenting unforgivingness.

At a single command the warrant officers divested themselves of their swords and laid them on the ground. The supernumeraries, rank and file, bent down and, performing the drill movement of 'ground arms', laid their rifles alongside their right feet, pointing towards the front. Erect once more, they undid their leather belts and laid them down, complete with side arms. Ranks were close-ordered, a turn to the right was made and away they marched, inscrutable no longer, as an ineffably weary slouch to their shoulders and shuffling gait poignantly expressed their inexpressible comments.

A fatigue party bundled the surrendered stuff into the store where I had to make an inventory of it. It was ironic that, within ten days of the ceremony, all the swords had to be re-issued to the same Japanese to cut the grass along the verges of the route used by the convoys to prevent Vietminh ambushes.

2
. . . And a Blacker Hatred Grew

Hostile pressure was increasing: a local woman came to the jungle edge near our camp perimeter one day and enticed one of our Indian non-combatants, a water carrier, to meet her outside. She offered herself to him and was accepted. Vietminh stabbed him to death as he straddled her. They had waited until the intensity of his emotions prevented any reaction before striking. The woman pushed his corpse off her and made good her escape with the guerillas. His body was found two days later.

Three Indian machine gunners went to buy eggs at a small house not far from the camp entrance, almost in sight of the sentry. They were invited in by the woman of the house. Men, in hiding, tried to overpower them. They succeeded in subduing two of them and bind them. They were stabbed to death piercing their eyes with long skewers. The third broke soldier loose and ran away but, in his panic, turned down the road leading away from the camp. He was chased, captured and killed, then buried in the cemetery of the Paupers' Hospital.

Relations were getting strained. We, the British, had lost the popularity we had initially when it was thought we were going to hand the country over to the Vietnamese. Now that they could see we intended to hand their country back to the French, we were no longer welcome.

I went down into the market one morning with two Dodge 30-cwt trucks and a fatigue party to get some firewood. A man ran out from behind a wall and threw a grenade under the leading truck. It exploded. The driver jumped out, brandishing his kukri and gave chase. He caught our assailant up and tried to lop his head off. The terrified man lunged despairingly forward and the kukri streaked down, slicing off his left buttock. The mess was frightening. I had him bundled into the serviceable vehicle and sent up to the camp. I waited until a third vehicle came to tow us away. Colonel Turk upbraided me – we had not quarrelled then – for making myself so obviously a target "when you have a price on your head."

"How much?"
"Not as much as I have," he said, either with a touch of legitimate pride or merely pulling rank.

One of the suspects captured during the column up to Ben Cat was a woman. She stayed in the camp and made up numbers to two pairs for the intelligence cell looked after by Colonel Turk. One Saturday afternoon she came into my room. She seemed excited. She had some intelligence she wanted to impart. She alleged that she know where the body of an American officer was buried – in the cemetery of the Paupers' Hospital. This man, Lieutenant Colonel Peter Dewey, was the senior American in the Control Commission and had been killed in an ambush some months previously near Saigon. His body was never recovered.

A report about it was sent to the Control Commission in Saigon and, on an appointed day, two youthful American officers arrived in the convoy. It was planned to go to the cemetery on the morrow and exhume the body. I was detailed to be in charge.

There were some Vietminh prisoners in the camp cells and early next morning I went and chose the strongest-looking bunch. I also collected an escort from the duty rifle company and we drove down to the cemetery. The party consisted of myself, Colonel Turk, the two American officers, the grave-digging Viets armed with picks and shovels, and the soldiers. The cemetery was much larger than when viewed from the outside. The woman had given us a vague idea where to look, so many yards from the western end, and we tried to recognise the grave.

All the graves looked the same; I chose one and ordered the earth to be shovelled away. The coffin appeared and seemed new. The lid was prized open and revealed a very dead man with rotting flesh. A sickly-sweet smell pervaded the area and one of the soldiers vomited. We put the lid on and shovelled the earth back. We tried again. No luck, either, but my gaze fell on what had been a woman and before I looked away the picture of one of her breasts, which had burst open with a growth like a blood-red cauliflower and with the skin peeled back like a grotesque banana, imprinted itself on my brain. A large, lazy, black fly settled on the maggots and the lid was banged shut. Another man spewed.

The idea that our search would be narrowed if we only opened the larger coffins then struck me. Earth was cleared from a third box and a prisoner told to lie on top the better to judge the relative sizes of body. A glassy look came to his eyes and he was momentarily seized with fear. He struggled vigorously but was overcome by the others and stretched out on top. Poor brute! He really did think he was going to be buried alive. He was only kept there long enough for us to confirm that it could not be the one we were looking for as the coffin could not have contained Dewey's corpse.

I had high hopes when I looked in the next one we opened. The body had been squeezed into the coffin. The corpse's face, growing dark, suggested European features. The dress was normal issue khaki fatigue. The head was slewed round to one side and the body bent as though it had been an effort to fit it into the coffin. I directed a man to turn the head because it was rumoured that it was there that the bullet had struck the Colonel and there was the suspicion of such a mark. A hesitant hand reached down, grasped the skull and turned it. The underside was a sordid mess, flattened by its own weight, but I thought I saw a definite bullet wound. The Americans, watching closely, were not fully convinced. The man, sickened by where his hand was, jerked it away. The skull came off from above the temples, revealing decomposing mush. The Americans then wanted to see the shirt, so I got another man (the first had retired, eyes swimming and retching vilely) to lift the arm. He pulled too hard and the arm was jerked from its socket. By now I was weary of it all, the heat, the stench, the sight, the flies, so I asked the Americans to stop prevaricating and state whether it was the Colonel or not. And the only thing they had against it being Dewey's corpse was that a small piece of sacking had been tacked into the inside of the breast pocket. "That's not according to regulations so the body is not Dewey's." I was too emotionally drained to argue. We all felt deflated for some time after we left the cemetery. None of us touched meat for several days. Two days later a convoy was badly ambushed as it drove past where we had exhumed the three corpses and I couldn't help wondering if the woman was a spy.

Nor did this macabre episode end there. When in the United States in 1960 I tried to contact Dewey's father, then a presidential candidate, about it but was fobbed off when it was known why I wanted to see him. Later that year I talked with General Gracey and told him how I had been fobbed off telling Dewey senior about what I thought had happened to his son. The General told me he had expected Lord Louis Mountbatten to get rid of him because of Dewey's death – "he was looking for an excuse to give me the sack" – but all that was said about the incident was to ask why the flag on Dewey's vehicle was bigger than regulation size? "I never understood Mountbatten's unexpected attitude to me." When I said that in America the rumour was the Colonel was a 'natural' son whose existence might have embarrassed a presidential candidate, the General said he understood Mountbatten's reticence.

Very soon after that I had to go and investigate reports of an ammunition factory. It was almost light relief to find a humble carpenter's shop full of spears, poisoned darts and bows and arrows. It struck me as risible, if not paradoxical, to find ourselves engaged in such skulduggery so soon after we had read reports about the mushroom clouds.

The tempo was increasing and tempers were becoming frayed. An air strike had to be called for at short notice to extract the battalion from a tricky situation. The barracks were sniped at several nights in succession and the small 10-man French garrison in Thu Dau Mot became jittery and cruel. Prior to the war there had been considerable missionary work in French Indo-China. Devoted nuns had gone forth and some had spent the war unscathed. Now disturbing rumours filtered through about some of these nuns in our area disappearing and being abducted by the guerillas. I went out three times looking for them and always drew a blank. Once we only just escaped being ambushed and so were reluctant to go nun hunting on speculation. The French decided to do something about it, but they found nothing either.

One example of French cruelty was when the 10-man garrison reported that they had captured a young woman who was alleged to be a spy. They had bastinadoed her and she had been ravished by all except the cook. When she recovered consciousness she was dragged to the market place and publicly shot. We heard the shooting, so at least that part of their report could be substantiated.

Another example was when I was out in a French vehicle with a small French patrol. The driver was told to stop at the first man he saw. So he did and out jumped the French, overpowered him (that was not difficult for the man was frail) and, trussed like a fowl, threw him into the back. They drove on and started beating the man up. After one blow in the face with a rifle butt I stopped them. A furious argument ensued, the French saying the man was obviously a spy and had to be made to talk and I was trying to restrain them. When I got back to camp I found that a French officer had been tampering with the Japanese stores I was responsible for. He was still there, 'looking for' a pistol and I sent him away with a verbal lashing as I was in a very angry mood. Not only had I previously warned him against taking any weapon but also because I strongly suspected the same man of stealing rations.

It was incidents such as these that made me the target of French anger. Colonel Turk had, unbeknownst to any of us, reported on me adversely to General Le Clerc who, naturally enough, had reported me to General Gracey, my most senior officer. The first thing I knew about it was when I was sent for by the adjutant and shown his draft reply to the three charges proffered against me, namely interfering with the rescue of French citizens, refusing to co-operate and refusing to supply food and arms. The answers must have satisfied Authority because we heard no more. Colonel Turk was called to Saigon a few days later and never returned.

Meanwhile the surrendered stores continued to be meticulously listed and back-loaded. The work involved was considerable and time-consuming. I was working hard, often eighteen hours a day. Apart from the petty and needless frustrations of the job, I was nagged by the few low-type Frenchmen with access to the camp and abrasive to the point of a total breakdown in good relationships. It was just as well that I did not know that my carefully prepared lists were never read and the stores were never counted. Put on a boat, they were dumped at sea.

In mid-January 1946 the battalion was ordered back to India, having previously been alerted for the Celibes, for which maps had been issued, Bangkok and Singapore. We packed up and, without me, the battalion returned to Saigon, preparatory to embarkation. As quartermaster, brimming with confidence and now in my second year's commissioned service, I had to remain in Thu Dau Mot to hand over the barracks to their rightful owners. Our garrison had been over a thousand strong. Fifty Frenchmen took our place. They came with a flamboyant arrogance that boded ill. I remember hoping to effect the transfer without delay but the French seemed uninterested in any administrative details outside their immediate needs. They occupied part of the barrack block farthest from my small band of men; three Gurkhas (batman, signaller and driver) and an Indian soldier who manned the brigade communications set. The Indian came to report to me when I was talking to one of the French officers wanting to air his English. He immediately asked what language I was speaking.

"Urdu."
"What is that?"
"Hindustani," I answered inaccurately.
"Why bother to learn? Why not make them speak English"?
I explained the system in the Indian Army and he shrugged his shoulders. "In the French Army we make black men speak French."
"And if they can't?" I queried.
"They go 'ungry," was his laconic reply.

He asked what we did in the evenings after the day's parades were over. I told him that we played basketball or football when we had the chance. He was dumbfounded when he learnt that teams were mixed, British officers playing in company football teams with their men and, at times, officers against sergeants at basketball.

"But you must always win," he asserted.
"But we usually don't," I countered.
"If you don't win, 'ow do you keep discipline the next day?"

That night I found what few rations I had in store had been stolen along with my razor and washing kit. I went over to the French to make a complaint. I was taken into a room with some officers and had *vin rouge* given me. Yes, they were sympathetic. Yes, they would find the culprit. Yes, would I join them in their meal, now about to be served?

The meal over and nothing apparently having been set in motion, I again raised the query. Rations were not so much a problem but shaving kit was. I sensed that I was being regarded as a nuisance and an interloper. Their equivalent of a company sergeant major made an opportune entry, was briefed and left. Half an hour later the place was in an uproar. Sounds of shouting and laughing men running about filtered from the next floor up. The door burst open and in came a messenger. All the officers were called away and I was told to stay where I was. The shrill screaming of a treble voice was intermingled with manly bass-voiced baying. So intrigued was I that I went out and climbed the flight of stairs to the next floor. And in the dimly lit corridor I saw a small, stark naked Annamite boy being chased by a group of nude French soldiers, members erect, from one room to another. I was joined by an officer whose one remark was *'Vive le sport'*.

I found my washing kit neatly laid out when I returned to my room. Next morning I was delighted to leave the camp and return to Saigon, two days later than planned.

Back in Saigon morale was not high. Some callous, indiscriminate and heavy-handed French attacks had been made on the civil population with many fatalities. The sentries around General Le Clerc's residence fired their weapons every hour to let the guard commander that they were awake. Unfortunately their rifles were not always upright when fired and this caused gloom among those who found themselves in the path of bullets fired on such a low trajectory.

Some Gurkhas from 3/1 GR, in another brigade, were heavily outnumbered, captured and disappeared. They were never found. It was rumoured that they were forced to dig their own communal grave and were then lined up, bound hand and foot, and shot, their bodies falling into the grave, the lucky ones being killed outright.

The French ordered a sweep in part of Cholon. They were held up by 'three determined Annamites who have grenades'. A detachment of 16 Cavalry was asked to blow the house down. Major Sawney refused the request.

Angrily the French threatened action from the destroyer *Triomphe* lying alongside Saigon harbour. Her guns would act where Sawney wouldn't.

The tone of their answer was, so Sawney told me later, slanted and caused some of the embarrassment intended.

Sawney suggested a compromise. He would arrange for a section of Gurkhas to invest the house and the French could keep the 6-inch guns of the destroyer *Triomphe* in reserve.

So, as ever it should be, polite firmness, common sense and the ability not to lose one's head saved what could have been a nasty situation from developing. We English felt it so sad that the French never learnt that lesson.

The Gurkhas, who had known no other European than the paternalistic British, were dismayed by French behaviour and unimpressed by their military showing. The French did not look different from the British so why did they comport themselves with such arrogance and contempt for others? I asked one of my Gurkhas what he thought of the French and he summed them up in one word – careless – or should I write it care-less?

Our time in French Indo-China came to an end. Our own casualties were mercifully light but the French suffered as the tempo of events increased with tragic rapidity, taking as many casualties in a week as the whole of 20 Division had during our entire stay. As we sailed down river to the open sea there were no more black flags of surrender to be seen, but in that corner of Asia a black miasma of uncertainty seemed to be slowly and surely spreading, with a blacker hatred eating into men's hearts.

PART II

LAOS: 1972-76

. . . when the water level rises, the fish eat the ants.'

3

The Hyphen Between Indo And China

In late 1971, as I was closing down the British Army's Jungle Warfare School in Peninsular Malaysia, Major General James Lunt, the Vice Adjutant General, paid us a visit. He quizzed me on future possibilities for my employment. These seemed to be: the adviser on jungle warfare to the Royal Thai Army (the Thais said they would give me the rank of major general in their army); a Foreign and Commonwealth Office (FCO) adviser on jungle warfare to Thailand and South Vietnam, each for six months of every year; to raise, train and command a battalion of Singaporean Commandos and – what did I think of this one? – an attaché to an unspecified Indo-Chinese country. I said that I would do whatever I was told to, as each choice had its own advantages and disadvantages. The General advised me to stick in my own army if possible – always safer in the long run. This I agreed to. I was told I'd hear about my future in due course.

A few days later I received a telephone call from headquarters in Singapore. I recognised the voice as that of a Guardsman on the staff, who took his tame otter to his office and, strangely, when the climate was considered, was writing a pamphlet on warfare in snow-covered mountains. Had I a good knowledge of Indo-China? he queried. I told him that, apart from a visit to South Vietnam in 1969, I had been over there in 1945 when it was Cochin China.

"We disarmed the Japs, fought off the Vietminh and I hunted for nuns."
A pause: "You hunted for what?"
"Nuns. I never did find any but whether that was because there were none or I didn't know where to look for them is a moot point."

There was another pause as the staff officer considered, so I presumed, whether it was bad luck or carelessness that had prevented that part of my military career from showing any positive results. His next question did not reveal which he had plumped for as all he asked was would I would mind going back to Indo-China? I told him I was happy to be sent there if that was what was wanted. In February 1946 I learnt that I was to be the attaché in Laos from the following November – a job very different from any other I had ever tackled.

Britain's interest in what was traditionally a sphere of French, and, since the mid-1950s, American, influence, stemmed from July 1954 when it became, with the Soviet Union, one of the two Co-Chairmen of the Geneva Accords for Indo-China. From that date, which marked the end of French colonial domination, the United States became more and more enmeshed with the Vietnamese 'tar baby'. A few salient facts bear this out: even by June 1952 it was bearing one-third of the cost of the war and, by the time of the French collapse, 78 per cent of it; it took over training commitments from ARVN in February 1955; by December 1961 there were 3,200 US servicemen there; by April 1962, 4,500 as well as more in Thailand; by the end of 1962, 11,300, and by the end of July 1964, 21,000.

After the Gulf of Tonkin Resolution on 7 August 1964, US forces rapidly increased. By December 1965 bombing of Laos was intensified and, in April 1966, B-52 bombing started. There were then 245,000 US service personnel on land and 50,000 more offshore. By August 1967 there were 525,000 service personnel and the strength peaked in March 1969, at 541,000.

North Vietnam invaded Laos in early 1953, capturing the royal capital, Luang Prabang, on 30 April. That same month the NVA surrounded the Plain of Jars in the centre of the country. In 1962 the situation in Laos deteriorated once more so severely that another set of Geneva Accords was patched up, with the same Co-Chairmen.

In 'neutral' Cambodia Prince Sihanouk allowed the NVA to establish seven sanctuaries (the nearest only thirty miles from Saigon) and, between 1966 and 1969, the equivalent of eight years' supplies was provided to the communist Khmer Rouges, (21,000 metric tons of military equipment and 600 tons of Soviet rockets). Lieutenant General Lon Nol ousted Sihanouk in March 1970 and, for a few years, the country was known as the Khmer Republic, then as Kampuchea before eventually once again as Cambodia.

So much for bare facts and figures that give some inkling as to the scale of it all. During that time the Pathet Lao ('the country of Laos') and the Vietminh in South Vietnam were being directed to fight an unorthodox war for social and political aims, for people, rather than territory as such. Both groups had persuaded western liberal opinion that they were patriotic nationalists rather than communist guerillas. In 1972 the NVA, acting conventionally, made great use of Soviet-made tanks, missiles and armoured troop carriers. American bombing was suspended on 22 October, shortly before I got to Laos, and peace talks (for Vietnam and Laos) started.

By now Cochin China had become South Vietnam, a new country, with new money, a new flag, a new official language and some new place names, certainly in the provinces. French was only spoken as a second language by the over-40s: American English had taken its place for those of younger years. Also now the situation was completely different, not only because of the American presence, but also because of greatly enhanced American air power and sophisticated weaponry, ranging from bombs that sucked oxygen out of the air so suffocating people up to quite a distance to people sniffers. The French had heard their colonial death knell sounded over the octave of Easter, 1954, at Dien Bien Phu. Both French and Americans had made many fundamental mistakes.

A primitive warrior has always had advantages over better-trained and more sophisticated troops in tree-girt areas. In Europe, Germanic tribes, lurking in deep forests, gave the Roman legions, (which, by then, contained many non-Roman troops) much trouble, retaining the initiative and, with fewer men, tying down significant numbers of troops. The tribes were unable to make use of this advantage so the invaders won.

In Asia, centuries later, the Vietnamese did exactly the same against the French (whose forces in Indo-China also contained a minority of Frenchmen) and the Americans. This time the 'invaders' lost. In neither case were the wooded areas the scenes of final victory, however important they had been during the campaign. A colonial mentality had ever postulated that the superior initiative and intelligence, both individual and group, of the more civilised army resulted in a decisive result for them when conditions of firepower and terrain were equal. Whose national pride was hurt the most – the French or the Americans in having presumed that they could beat the Vietnamese; or the Vietnamese for being taken as inferior when they beat both the others?

The French had fought a war based on the mobility of armies, whereas the Vietnamese based their fighting on the mobility of the individual. The French tried to hold a fortress barrier but failed because they did not control the surrounding jungle and the North Vietnamese had the inestimable advantage of being able to use China as a sanctuary and having time on its side. The French then tried to match the Vietnamese mobility on foot with mechanical mobility but the Vietnamese used the jungle to nullify such action. In the final analysis, the French lost because they did not have the full backing of the government at home for a campaign of higher intensity, did not have troops on the ground in sufficient strength to defeat the Vietnamese (although they did have enough not to lose) and, supremely, they did not have the support of the Vietnamese people. Their political base was simply not strong enough. They were not wanted, they never had been; they never would be.

Although guilty of being wise after the event, it is worth mentioning, at this point, the political interests of the United Kingdom and other countries. I think it would be fair to say that the United Kingdom's main interest was to see hostilities cease as expeditiously as possible so that the British Government need no longer be involved in the prestigious-sounding (but, on closer acquaintance, boring and non-productive if not very expensive) Co-Chairmanship of those two Geneva Accords. A certain amount of solidarity with other non-communist nations was also needed to be shown; with Commonwealth countries, with America, for traditional reasons, and with European countries in an effort to make the European Community mean more than it did.

Apart from the USA, with its policy of trying to contain communism on mainland Asia in ruins and its wound-licking urge for 'Peace with Honor', the only other non-communist country with more than a passing interest in affairs Indo-Chinese, was France. Generations of French pride had been sunk almost without trace and, as it struck me later, there was an innate craving to be looked upon once more as a model of diplomacy, culture and trade.

On the communist front, the USSR and China saw the Indo-Chinese struggle as a wonderful chance to widen their influence, spread their ideology and humble the USA. This was too big an opportunity for overt factional quarrelling, so all cracks were papered over until victory could be consolidated.

Three women walked into my life after I got back to England on 9 May 1972, after a 107-day trek in Nepal, and, by the time I had finished my briefings and preparations to become the 'Defence, Military and Air Attaché (with navel representation) to Laos', they had all walked out. Two were language teachers, one for French and the other for Lao. ['Lao' is used for the language and the people.] The third, to whom I had recently become engaged, threw a wobbler shortly before we were due to be married prior to going to Laos and went into hiding when she learnt what an attaché's wife was meant to do. However warm the heart might have been, the feet were too cold. Better before than after, I felt, and put it down to experience. The Europeans only ever reappear as flickery shadows in the memory; the Asian – whom I met twice more – with unalloyed tenderness.

My attaché training was essentially in two parts, both equally important. The longer part was language instruction, initially only French – one hundred and sixty hours of individual teaching in two months, which represented a 5-year syllabus in government-run schools. My French teacher was a French lady. She was pert, chic and cosily responsive, had no pretensions to beauty. Initially I thought she had a new hairstyle when I saw the parting in her flaxen hair to be of a plain mouse colour. Although she was a very good teacher and had more than her fair share of patience, I became bored stiff with the inanities of the work script and the tedious question-and-answer periods. To keep myself awake I tried counting her teeth but I never did satisfy myself whether there were thirty-one or thirty-two as my eyes, dilated with concentration, put the poor dear off her stride and made me realise how rude I was being. It was only later that I discovered that she, unhappy with her husband, took my concentration as feelings of another sort.

My insistent asking Authority for permission to learn Lao, because I saw mastery of it being of greater importance than competence in French, eventuated in sixty hours' instruction being allowed. As no overall time could be allocated, this resulted in learning both languages simultaneously, averaging twelve hours' daily study for the second month.

My Lao teacher, Princess Inkham Rangsi, or Golden Fairy as her name translated, was a niece of the King of Laos. In her late twenties, she had exquisitely moulded features, smooth golden skin, raven-black hair and almond eyes. She held herself regally yet had a demure manner. Standing a little over five-and-a-half feet tall she had an eye-catching figure. Golden Fairy spoke fluent English, French and Thai. Her native tongue, which she taught me, was the not-so-common royal, Luang Prabang, dialect of northern Laos. Her silvery voice, rippling laughter and impish grin gave me a pang of regret that I was not twenty years younger, when not even diplomatic immunity would have prevented royal wrath at courtship by a commoner. It was only by intense concentration on my part that I made what linguistic progress I did.

The other phase of my briefings was technical. Apart from being taught how to use a camera, it concerned my status and what I was expected to do when 'in post'. There were four aspects to the job. First and foremost, I was to be an accredited representative of Her Britannic Majesty's Government, with full diplomatic immunity. Accreditation was to the Kingdom of Laos, not to one or other side of the quarrelling factions who were at war with one another. There were neither enemy nor own troops in the conventional way as it was not Britain's war.

Second, I was to be the adviser on all defence matters to the ambassador, hence back to the FCO, as well as keeping the relevant part of the MOD up to date with the very complicated military situation. I was not expected to make any impact for the first six months, nor were politics *per se* my concern.

The third aspect was that I might find pressure and temptations unusual to one who was used to living in a comparatively closeted atmosphere of an officers' mess as I would have a house in town. As a bachelor and a linguist I was of much interest to the communists, representing a challenge to them on both counts.

Lastly, being on the fringe of the intelligence world but not of it, I would be working on a 'need to know' basis. I was to operate entirely overtly, never covertly – dire consequences were threatened were I to disregard that strict rule. An attaché is the accredited military representative for the collection of open military information, collected by observation, extrapolation and common-sense methods. Never to betray a confidence or a source is of paramount importance and information is never to be obtained by financial or other untoward means. Being an attaché was not, I was told, all cocktail parties and gossip. Unlike the communist world, attachés of the old Commonwealth countries are not 'official spies'.

The situation in Indo-China was, at one, global, ideological and regional. It was global in that two superpowers, the USA and the USSR, were involved, the former more directly than the latter. Ideologically, the United States was fighting communism on the mainland of Asia, which the communists bitterly opposed. The tensions between the two could have spilled over into something far bigger had, for instance, US troops invaded North Vietnam. The regional aspect came from the North Vietnamese (by whatever name was in vogue) long-felt desire to control the whole area, most recently prevented by French aspirations of colonial grandeur.

As I saw it, Laos was only of any importance in relation to the countries surrounding it. It was regarded as a window on Thailand to its south. In the west, Burma was not seen as a military threat to Laos; there was considerable traffic in opium in the so-called 'Golden Triangle', centred on a small village, Ban Nam Kheun, near where the frontiers of Burma, Thailand and

Laos meet on the banks of the Mekong and where there were still some Chinese Nationalist soldiers, there since 1949, who acted more as brigands than as military men.

To the north China loomed as a giant, with the northwest province of Laos, Phong Saly, virtually Chinese, as all the Laotian provinces to the northeast were Vietnamese in all but name. To the southeast South Vietnam and the Khmer Republic were sucked into the vortex of combat.

Inside Laos I was to find the situation as complicated and difficult to understand as any I had ever come across. I simplified it with the analogy of a boxing ring: in the blue corner was the fighting arm of the Royal Lao Government (RLG), the Royal Lao Army (RLA) infuriatingly further complicated by partial use of its French nomenclature, seconded by the Americans. In the red corner was the fighting arm of the Lao Patriotic Front (LPF), the Pathet Lao (PL), seconded by the North Vietnamese. In fact it was not as simple and clear-cut as that because the Blue's seconds had some secret Thais and tame Lao Irregulars up their sleeves, while the Reds had some representatives of both communist empires and the satellites in the background. And both Blues and Reds boasted their own neutrals – weird, wonderful and insubstantial. The referees were a panel of three, the International Control and Supervision Commission (ICSC), comprising a neutral India, a pro-left-wing Poland and a pro-right-wing Canada. The sponsors were the Co-Chairmen of two lots of Geneva Accords who also looked left and right, the Soviet Union and the United Kingdom. The boxing ring was Laos and belonged to the King. The Blues wanted to keep it that way and the Reds did not.

Having had all that to absorb I was overwhelmed by the feeling of utter insignificance of my being part of the scene. The vastness of the vista, the plethora of players on the stage, the outpouring of such immeasurable quantities of blood and treasure, seemingly unstoppable, put me into invisible insignificance. Yet, if the policy of the powers-that-be wanted me there and thought I could be of some use, so be it. I had no false pretensions before I left England and even fewer when I arrived in Laos.

Shortly before I left England Major General Kouprasith Abhay, the Deputy Commander-in-Chief of the Royal Lao Army, visited as guest of the government. He was accompanied by an aide, Colonel Hinphed (many Laotian family names are, I was to find out, so tongue twisting that usually only the first names are mentioned here) and they were due to go from the Royal Lao embassy in London to the School of Infantry, in Warminster, Wiltshire. I was asked to go with them and, although at that juncture all the Lao I could speak were simple sentences like 'Auntie catches crabs in the swamp' and 'Grandfather scratches his buffalo on its back' (the only books I could get hold of being Lao readers for small children), the car journey with these two men both ways and the few hours spent at the school were to redound in my favour in later days.

I left England on Remembrance Sunday, 1972, as a bogus red-tabbed colonel. I say 'bogus' as the rank was local, for diplomatic door-opening only but it made me a VIP for the journey. The faintly-heard and monotonous whine of the Rolls Royce Pegasus engines that kept up their threnody was conducive to thought. I had always mentally rhymed 'Laos' with 'chaos' until I learnt it rhymed with 'mouse'. The old name, *Lane Xang*, '[The Land of a] Million Elephants', had been changed by the first European missionaries. One way or another the Lao had been fighting a war – or other people had been fighting for them or each other – since 1946 when, instead of finding themselves independent as the Japanese had decreed in 1945, the French came back and claimed Laos as a protectorate. How would I find the country, divided into a royalist zone and a communist 'liberated zone', with all the ingredients of revolutionary warfare and its counter (my staple for over two decades) which would make me want to take part and from which I was strictly forbidden to be anything else but a neutral spectator?

For the first time in my army life I was to be a watcher, not a doer, and that was, in its own way, a challenge. But even if I had been a doer, whoever heard of an Englishman making any difference to a situation where American pressures, French idiom and the communist Big Brothers were all jostling one another so blatantly, and the word 'English', if it meant anything at all, referred to a language some educated people spoke when they did not know French? What had the Desk Officer said during one of my briefings? Laos: the only under-populated country in southeast Asia, not far off the size of Great Britain, with a population of less than three million, a 20 per cent literacy rate, a life expectancy of between thirty to thirty-five years, fifty-eight different languages, to say nothing of a myriad dialects.

I flew by way of Hong Kong and was there long enough to touch my hat to the commander and to have some of the new British Army stone-coloured uniforms made up. The last leg of my journey was in a quarter-full Electra of Royal Air Lao – with its logo of a three-headed elephant surmounted by a nine-tiered parasol. I arrived at Wattay airport, Vientiane (Vieng Chan, 'the walled town in the shape of a [half] moon'), as dusk fell on 18 November. There was enough light to see the Mekong (Mé Khong, 'Mother River'), the world's thirteenth longest (then the longest unbridged) river before we touched down. I was met by the military side of the embassy staff, the outgoing attaché, Colonel Donald Thursby-Pelham, the assistant and embassy Beaver pilot, Major Alan Calder, and the chief clerk, Mr George Mottram, who whipped my passport off me and I was cleared in a jiffy. Also there were the Australian Colonel Cam West and Colonel Hinphed, this last being a rare Laotian gesture of welcome.

Before I had time to catch my breath I was whisked away in a flagged, chauffeur-driven car to meet the ambassador, Mr John Lloyd, before being dumped at a hotel. It was the start of as frenetically kaleidoscopic a week and depressingly difficult a 6-month period as I had ever experienced. I was lucky not to 'know the half of it'.

The week allowed for DAs to hand over responsibilities coincided with the second of two annual visits by the King, Vientiane being the commercial, not the royal capital. Days were therefore packed when official representation was mandatory at certain functions, leaving little time for being introduced to the senior members of the RLA and the rest of the attaché corps, less time still for office work and no time for domestic problems.

Next morning, dressed in smart uniform, I was picked up early and driven to the embassy. The 'Ten-Minute Town', as it was once known because it only took that time to drive through, was a mixture of old Buddhist and colonial French culture with a veneer of Americana. The main town roads were tarred and tree-lined but most of the others were bumpy dirt tracks that led to paddy fields in which old and new houses were to be found. Unexpected vegetable plots and domestic animals were also in built-up areas, where poverty jostled with prosperity.

The shops were almost all Chinese or Vietnamese, with the only cold storage, the Frizzy Bull, run by the French. In the middle of one of the main roads is a large concrete monument, topped by coloured and glinting designs, similar to those in Buddhist *wats*, as temples are called. Named the Monument of Independence (but referred to as the Cenotaph so as not to offend French susceptibilities), it was built with concrete donated by the Americans to make the airstrip at Wattay an all-weather one. It was a good indication of how seriously some elements in control took the prosecution of the war.

I was to find the embassy very different from the crisply efficient military life I had known till then. Here was a longer haired, less incisive, more verbose and Christian-named oriented set-up. Punctuality was to be a thing of the past and the morning repetition of the previous night's cocktail party trivia as irritatingly banal as it was spuriously inaccurate. As Donald and I were walking down the passage to the office we met the ambassador who greeted me with an unsmiling "Why are in that fancy dress, Colonel?" I tried not to register any surprise at the terseness of the question (I had been warned he was unpredictable) and answered that I was to be representational that morning with visits of introduction at the MOD.

It was here that I found my first big difficulty, the personality of the man to whom I had to be scrupulously loyal. The British tradition of reticence which in the 1970s still hung so heavily over all organisations, especially in Whitehall, made taboo even the most veiled understatements about other people, especially those in senior grades. It was so enshrined that, coupled with benevolently uncritical annual confidential reports, it perpetuated the odd miscarriage of common sense to the extent that some ducklings were always ugly, even when fully grown, without ever having had any swan-like pretensions.

John Lloyd was, in fact, never anything but kind to me and, once he saw that my personality was less abrasive than some of my peers and predecessors, he accepted me. He had been witness to Japanese horrors on the mainland of China at the outset of his career and that had given him a hatred of violence. He was an ardent pacifist with strong left-wing tendencies, anti-military and outspokenly critical of American policy. The stresses and strains as head of mission in a country at war, coupled with the frustrations of a family problem (second late marriage to an old flame to whom he told all secrets and admitted she was 'so emotional') and an impending retirement, had made him peevishly intolerant of normal procedures, and openly sympathetic to those who portrayed themselves as underdog fighters for social justice – in short a perfect and unconscious subject for communist ploys. Also, being anti-American, he was not trusted by the Americans – who as paymasters of the RLA as well as for much of the government, virtually ran the war – nor by the right-wing Laotian faction whom the British were there to represent under the terms of those two Geneva Accords. His indiscretions at various social functions were an embarrassing commonplace. It took me some time to realise that, although I should have been fully trusted by both the Americans and the Lao, they would spurn me, and that I would be shunned by the non-communist embassies as it were much better that nothing of substance be told me so that I would not be torn by divided loyalties.

I was given another inkling of future frustrations that first morning when we had a longer talk in the ambassador's office. He supposed that I liked killing people and that is why I had joined the army, "just like those Americans and their beastly bombers". At my first solo weekly briefing on the military situation I was abjured never to mention casualties. And, for good measure, I was instructed to let him know "if you find out anything sensitive that I can embarrass the Americans with. I want to punish them for all this bombing madness," I continued with my now anodyne briefing.

Only later was I told that Donald himself had betrayed American and Australian confidences, to say nothing of having insulted the Soviets, Chinese, Indians and French, so I was under a burden of double mistrust.

Mid-morning that first day we drove the short distance to the MOD at Phone Kheng to meet the Commander-in-Chief and his Deputy. The Chief was Lieutenant General Bounphone, called Jubilation by the Americans after some character in a strip cartoon. Paid the equivalent of £80 a month, he and all the other generals were powerful, political animals – robber barons – with many lucrative side jobs.

Housed in a modern, imposing-looking, white, three-storied building set in spacious grounds and surrounded by a high wall, we were allowed to drive straight in at the gates and, after a short delay, were escorted into the Commander-in-Chief's office. Bounphone was short and plump, had a vacuous grin and did not seem to have much intelligence although he had a reputation for a shrewd amount of low cunning. Dotted around the office were various military trophies of the sort that American influence seems to produce: banners, flags, regimental streamers, plaques, citations and photographs. On the wall were pictures of the King of Laos, King Savang Vatthana, dressed as a 7-star general, and the Prime Minister, Prince Souvanna Phouma. As we sipped our lukewarm, sugarless and milkless tea and nibbled at stale biscuits the conversation was desultory, shallow and difficult to follow as Donald spoke fast French – persisting, not at all successfully, in trying to get some concrete news of the current peace talks. The Chief declined to answer in more than grunts. He clearly disliked speaking French – his accent was heavy – and knew less English. He was delighted when I spoke some Lao to him and, in one, I saw that fluent Lao would be the passport to acceptability. I realised that I needed to improve my military vocabulary.

We next met the Deputy Chief, Major General Kouprasith Abhay, who greeted me warmly and asked me if I had yet had a copy of the photograph of him and me taken at Stonehenge on our way to Warminster. Donald then monopolised the conversation, pontificating on how he thought the conduct of the war in the future should be and where he thought that the planners had gone wrong in the past. I was fascinated and depressed by the fellow's gall. I admired the General's self-control and unruffled answers but his eyes were hooded and angry. No one likes being talked at condescendingly and critically by a non-combatant during a war, especially when the one is junior, a foreigner and not very experienced in fighting the communists. Donald was a Signaller.

As we drove away I tried to dispel the feeling of unreality that swamped me: here in a country that had known war for nearly thirty years there seemed to be no urgency and the outward calibre of the chief and his deputy gave no cause for optimism that much would, or even could, change.

It was then time for another side of my new job, an attaché luncheon, thrown by the out-going Thai. We drove to a restaurant run by a Taiwanese and here I met all the other attachés and the members of the ICSC. Only the Chinese DA, who took no part in such frivolities, was absent. I was an object of curiosity. Conversation alternated between English and French and was anodynely bland until the Thai ordered champagne. As the corks popped Donald looked at his Soviet counterpart, Vladimir Gretchanine, accusingly and said that it was like the NVA using Soviet ammunition. As the NVA's presence was still being sedulously denied, despite it being known to be in Laos in force and to be supplied by the Soviets and Chinese, the remark was considered to be offensive and in bad taste. The American, Colonel Broadus Bailey, Jnr, allowed himself a grin and the Russian glowered because, unknown to me then, relations between the two were more strained than usual: the Russian's secretary had recently defected to the Americans and been granted political asylum. (He was Yevgeniy Georgiyevich Sorokin, a GRU lieutenant. A year later he returned to the USSR and was jailed for twelve years. He had said that Donald could not have been a spy as he was too stupid. In fact, that could be taken as a backhanded compliment.)

I, a non-drinker, was toying with a Pepsi Cola when the Russian accused me of being pro-American. I answered that I hadn't thought of it that way. As I didn't like champagne there was not a lot of choice. Vladimir's answer was conciliatory;

"I am neutral. Look! Portuguese," pointing to his champagne as he emptied his glass. "I don't know how to be anything but neutral."

Donald's voice rose above the hubbub;

"Vladimir, you don't know anything. You are a product of the Revolution and were probably born in 1917, weren't you?"

The Russian's blue eyes frosted behind his thick spectacles.

"No, Colonel, in 1916. I had to prepare myself for the Revolution, like you will have to one day."

As the laughter swelled up, he continued loudly;

"You don't know anything yet." His eyes were steely and his lips pursed into a pretence of a smile. "You have it still to come."

We then went to eat. I was glad that the food was of better taste than the conversation and the party broke up at half-past 2.

We then drove back to the MOD to meet Major General Oudone Sananikone, the Director of Operations, an English-speaker. He was of a powerful family who had many fingers in many commercial dealings, so it was rumoured. I did not expect to gain much from the visit except, perhaps, to know where his office was. Any questions asked about operations were met with bland replies, not that I would have expected anything else at such a meeting. Donald surprised me by saying that his lack of definite answers was because he did not know what was happening; the only people who did were the Americans. I felt deflated but told myself that these were early days yet and perhaps our last visit of the day, the Americans, would be more down to earth.

There are few more impersonal and soulless buildings than an American embassy viewed from the outside if only because there are no windows to relieve the monotony of the stone pile. Designed to keep angry crowds from storming them they are strongly built, incorporating fireproof doors and certain delicate electronic devices. They also contain voracious paper shredders ready to dispose of sensitive material, with food and water to withstand a short siege.

We drove past the main, grim block, turned a corner and drew up at a low, single-storied also windowless building, the military element of the embassy. Orders for B-52 and F-111 strikes on PL and NVA targets emanated from it. Entering by a glass door I shivered in the cold, canned air.

I saw that all MRs and military activity in them were marked up on the extensive map coverage on Bailey's walls, in more detail than in our office. Donald tried to find out about NVA 335 Regiment that was reputed to be to the west of the Plain of Jars, in MR 2's area, which we were to visit, courtesy of the Central Intelligence Agency, on the following Saturday. I noticed that the American Colonel cleverly turned the question of admitting that there were some assistant attachés in the area "so we're only one step ahead of you but you Brits are good at counter revolutionary warfare, so maybe after your visit you can tell us." That pleased Donald, who continued to hold forth. The American was a model of tact.

That evening, after returning to my hotel from a farewell cocktail party given by the French attaché for Donald, I was very tired. I went straight to bed and, before I dropped off to sleep, I mulled over the events of a very full day. My head was in a whirl. I knew it was premature to make any reasonable comment, let alone come to any conclusions, but never had the start of any job I had previously tackled seemed so discouraging, depressing or inauspicious. I remembered teaching in the Jungle Warfare School that the communists used unconventional methods, never for one moment thinking I would come across such a mirror travesty.

I was still tired when I awoke next morning.

My first visit to a military region was that second day when we went to HQ MR 5. We drove along the banks of the Mekong, past the Prime Minister's residence, the Soviet embassy, the Czechoslovakian consulate, the Lao-German Technical College and, incongruously, a recently built bowling alley, much frequented by the Lao generals who found it an intriguing new game.

Our destination was Chinaimo Camp where, as well as HQ MR 5, HQ of the River Flotilla (hence my 'naval representation'), the RLA Staff College and officer cadet training school, a psychological warfare office, propaganda teams and other minor units were housed. The camp was in large, pleasantly wooded grounds and we drove past some burnt-out Soviet T-34 and T-55 tanks. Round a bend in the road a Guard of Honour was lined up ready to welcome us. At the top of some steps leading to the office, standing between the Laotian and British flags, stood the commander, Brigadier General Thonglit. The Laotian flag had the same motif as did the aeroplane I had come in, when was it…only thirty-six hours before?

The General spoke good English and made a plea for more help from Great Britain which he described as one of the Great Powers. He asked why it was that a country with so much Far Eastern experience was only interested in pulling out of Asia and leaving the smaller anti-communist nations to fend for themselves. Britain had so much and Laos so little. We had been successful in our Malayan struggle. He'd welcome more than encouraging words.

I stayed quiet as Donald made some remarks about Britain's decline and only spoke again when I was asked if I had any questions. I asked about several low-level tactical and training problems but, apart from polite interest being shown, no comment was offered. Indeed, the points I asked about were startlingly foreign to the General; this I later put down to their whole concept of the use of manpower in military operations and the training of them being utterly different from ours and probably not felt to be the concern of senior commanders.

We paid one other joint visit, to HQ MR 2, on the Saturday morning. Dressed in plain clothes, we were driven down the main road to Wattay airport. The French Military Mission – allowed for in the 1962 Geneva Accords for Laos – had its HQ off a side road.

On reaching the airport we turned into an entrance marked Continental Airways. This was one of the CIA's two airlines used to carry VIPs and 'case officers', men on contract with the US-funded Thai secret army and Lao Irregulars. The second airline was Air America that had the contract for troop movements of all such soldiery and their stores. We went inside and saw a number of Lao and Americans in an inner room busily engaged in preparing various details for the day's tasking. I only later discovered that these briefings included the positions of suspected or actual communist anti-aircraft artillery or missile sites, as well as areas to be bombed or strafed by USAF B-52s and F-111s. We were asked to wait outside until the case officer especially detailed to escort us arrived.

In 1972 there were no roads leading to Long Cheng, a stronghold of the Meo tribesmen, where MR 2 had its HQ. It lay southwest from the Plain of Jars. Air was, therefore, the only practical way to get there. No third country representatives such as ourselves could go there without explicit permission, very rarely given, from both Laotian and American sources. Such was the mistrust that the Americans held the British in that the visit was not confirmed until the last minute. We were joined by Cam West who had considerable rapport with the Americans as, at that time, the Australian government fully supported their involvement in the Vietnam war. I noticed a feeling less than warm between Donald and Cam.

The Beechcraft that was to take us flew in from the USAF base at Udorn in Thailand and stopped behind a large hanger and off-loaded some passengers. Almost concurrently, we scrambled inside and the 'plane took off. The haze that envelopes so much of that part of the world for part of the year had yet to develop so we had a good view of the countryside. Twenty minutes after take-off we were flying over a lake, dammed at one end. Skeletal tree trunks dotted the water and two small naval craft from the River Flotilla were tied up near the dam wall. The dam complex had been constructed under United Nations auspices with Britain chipping in. Millions of dollars' worth of timber was lost because nobody agreed on how much of a rake-off how many and who should get from it and it was left to rot in the water.

We flew towards a range of mountain that rose sharply to a height of 3,000 feet. The terrain grew more spectacularly precipitous with beetling limestone crags and thick jungle. In the valleys and on the lower slopes I saw where Meo tribesmen had slashed and burnt the jungle so that they could plant their dry paddy. I had seen the same in Borneo: more millions of dollars' worth of timber going up in flames each year. My mind turned to the times I had spent in the jungle. Would I ever go back, except if the embassy Beaver aircraft made a forced landing? I should ensure that we had survival packs in the machine.

My ears told me that we were descending as the pitch of the engine changed. The little 'plane was making a tactical approach by circling tightly downwards. I gasped as a concrete runway came into view with yet another high cliff of limestone at the other end of it. The 'plane straightened out, flew over a small hill with only feet to spare and was forced down at the end of the runway, the pilot fighting the up currents. Wired and sandbagged gun emplacements with 5.5-mm medium artillery pieces in them dotted the area. Civilians, dressed in black clothes with lemon, red or blue sashes round their waits and hanging down behind them like tails, were walking along a straggly dusty road. I saw six radial-engined T-28 training aircraft, used as fighter-bombers, H-34 helicopters and C-130 Hercules transport aircraft of the RLAF

The Beechcraft drew to a stop and we got out. There were a number of Americans about, dressed in civilian clothes of a style so close to being military that it was not hard to tell what they were; technicians, advisers and administrators. Uniformed Lao and Meo soldiers shambled about. The air was considerably cooler than down in Vientiane and I wished I had an extra sweater on. Our escort led us to a disreputably dirty jeep that had driven up to meet us. We clambered in and drove two hundred yards before turning right and on past two imposing buildings on which bullet and shell marks were easily visible. HQ MR 2 it was explained and, if we were lucky, we would meet the General before going back.

We were driven into an administrative complex and got out in front of a wooden hut that, like all the other buildings, had sandbag emplacements around it, "to keep us safe from incoming," said the driver. Told to go inside, we joined a queue of Americans and locals getting their 'chow'. I opted for a cup of coffee but Donald, despite an incipient weight problem, made a hearty meal of waffles and eggs. It was only as we tramped out did I realise that our fare had to be paid for in US dollars and was embarrassed as I had never thought to bring any with me.

Behind me Cam West gagged, "Don't worry. I'll pay for you. At least my country isn't bankrupt."

There was general laughter and the Americans joined in with similar ribald cracks about the British economy. I burned with humiliation as I saw that the remarks were made so easily, how much they were meant and how true they were.

We were taken from there to the control centre from where orders were given for the defence of the complex and for operational activity against the communists. It struck me as decidedly odd that this should be run by a handful of Americans when just down the road was HQ MR 2 commanded by an RLA Major General, the Meo Vang Pao. Introduced to the senior American adviser, we went into his operations room and were offered the inevitable coffee. A large map covered the wall on one side, with pins and chinagraph markings, blue for own troops and red for the enemy. Although we were asked not to take notes, Donald did just that.

I was intensely interested in the briefing. Major General Vang Pao was virtually king in those parts and his word was law. He was very popular with the Americans and, as were all Meo, apt to be volatile. The Americans worked closely with him 'as we are paying for it all'. There were also several assistant attachés who seemed to be responsible for the deployment, if not all other aspects, of several infantry and artillery battalions of Thai volunteers (which were still secret then but became common knowledge a year or so later) and a number of Irregular battalions, each of 330 men.

The large feature to our front as we flew in was pointed out on the map. "That's Skyline Ridge and there's an NVA company there right now." It was too early in the season for the normal offensive to start and it was thought that it might be a reconnaissance in force, but for what? Not important enough for the B-52s, it was being shelled with the 5.5s and strafed by the T-28s. The American adviser wanted to have a look so had ordered a chopper and offered to take us with him. Reading between the lines, the communist threat seemed more serious than conventional wisdom had it.

"I'll really show you something, much better than any of this crap. My bedroom," the boss said after the briefing. He opened another door and proudly showed us the room where he slept. I went inside and gasped. It was a small room, with only basic furniture, but every square inch of the wall and ceiling was covered with nude pin-ups from *Playboy* and *Oui* magazines. While no prude, I wondered how much this galaxy of lasciviousness kept his mind off other and more important matters.

Back outside, we drove down the one dusty and bumpy road either side of which were Meo men, women and children. They looked tough, stocky independent hill people, very like Gurkhas whom they resembled facially. We reached HQ MR 2 and there, on the doorstep, stood the General, a small man with a strong open face. I was introduced but he hardly bothered to shake my proffered hand, let alone look me in the eyes. "We're on our way to look at Skyline, General, are you interested?" the senior American asked him.

He was not, so we went on without him. Cam confided to me that Vang Pao was a strange man, moody and full of likes and dislikes, who worked a lot by dreams and omens. I was not to be put off by his terse manner and his unfriendly attitude. Apparently he had not hit it off with Donald so didn't trust him. It could take as long as six months before he would trust me. (It was a pity that he muddled me up, first with Donald and then with Cam, both of whom had upset him in one way or another, and it was nearly a year in both cases before he realised his mistake. Eventually we became very friendly.)

We reached the Thai artillery battalion lines and a liaison officer was there to greet us, speaking in American-accented English. As we walked through the lines I met a one-time student from a jungle warfare course and talked to him. Even had I remembered his name it would not be the one he was using there: the volunteers in the secret army had to use an alias – but I only leant that months later.

Shortly before noon we boarded a modified and armoured Jet Ranger helicopter, piloted by an American civilian and few up to Skyline Ridge. Below us a battle was in progress. Little puffs of smoke from the guns back in the main complex were visible, as were little spurts of dust and smoke where the shells exploded. There was no noise except for the thrash of the blades and the whine of the jet engine. The chopper circled continuously, standing off from a couple of T-28s that were pounding a hilltop with 50-kilogram bombs, synchronised with the fall of shells. I could make out a snake of figures moving, hour-hand slow, along the ridge towards the area that was being shelled and bombed – the attacking Thai troops. I thought I saw figures crouching in the target area but I was not sure as the vibration of the helicopter and the dust and the smoke made clear viewing very difficult. It was all a little unreal and I felt somehow that I was intruding yet inwardly chafed at being a spectator. I had to be objective and neutral, and I was finding it a hard lesson to learn. But the ingredients were interesting; Thais, Americans and North Vietnamese, with nary a Lao in sight or involved, except the T-28 pilots.

Back on the ground I thanked the pilot and in Vientiane late that afternoon I thanked our escort. Donald said that he was disappointed by what we had seen and been told about. I had found it fascinating but was as yet unable to put it into context.

I would visit the other three MRs by myself in due course.

On other days I attended ceremonial occasions that included medal presentation, traditional games, prayers and the opening of an international trade fair by the King. This period was known as Thad Luang, after the area where much of it took place. Thad Luang proper is on the northern edge of Vientiane and consists of the *wat* so named and a large Buddhist school. As though the builders had hesitated to erect anything else nearby there was a large open space in front of the *wat* and the school into which six rough, unmettalled tracks led, chokingly dusty in the dry season and clingingly muddy after rain. There were some shanties behind the temple where a group of catamites operated, silkily dressed either to allure unsuspecting foreigners or to cater for the tastes of the perverted. Always a menace, they were shrewishly vindictive when roused or when paid handsomely so to be.

Part of the festivities was a unique type of Laotian hockey, followed by some horse racing. It was the done thing for the members of the attaché corps to have a mild flutter on each of the four races, all bareback, twice round the area for the first two and three times round for the last two. There was another show of unhappy British/Russian relations when, before the first race started, Donald leant over to Vladimir Gretchanine and asked him if he would bet in pounds, dollars, roubles or the Laotian *kip*?

"Ah, this is a decadent western capitalist sport and anyway the pound is worth nothing," was his carping and uncompromising reply, unrelieved even by a smile

He turned to me and continued in the same vein: "When your country is truly socialist you will not need such capitalist props to society as gambling. You, Colonel, don't strike me as a man that gambles, rather as a man who works on certainties."

I turned towards the mocking Russian boor and coldly looked him straight between the eyes but was saved from answering as there was a great cheer as the first race started.

We had to attend some classical dancing. At this last I met one of Princess Golden Fairy's elder sisters, Princess Jasmine (or Marina, from the Lao for jasmine, 'mali'). If anything she was more lovely to look at than my tutor who had written to her, asking her to help me learn Lao if I wanted it. She gave me her telephone number and asked me to contact her after five in the evening, "as I am a working girl."

I was also present at a *baçi*, a uniquely Laotian ceremony of prayer and good wishes, given by their domestic staff to the Thursby-Pelhams. I found Donald a brainy man, quick-witted and something of an extrovert. His sense of humour was not understood by many, especially the Asians and impatience made him appear brusque to some. His wife was a timorous French lady who wore a martyred expression for fashion rather than for comfort.

At the end of our time together I put my thoughts to Donald. I told him I had acquired a certain amount of received wisdom but, as yet, no experience. In that first week it was difficult to pinpoint anything specific but first impressions were very different from how I had imagined affairs would be – and I was saddened at what I had found. It would not be too much to presume that His Excellency was the darling of the left wing and the despair of the right, thereby making my position an unenviable one. By being loyal to him, I'd never gain any American, Free World or right-wing Laotian confidences. If I were to be disloyal to him, not only would I offend my own code of honour but my disloyalty would count against me with all sections of the community in which I must work. If I showed I was against the left, which by definition, as a hater of communism, I was, I could justly be accused of representing the United Kingdom only to the RLG when I was the accredited military representative to the whole of Laos and that included the communist part of it. And anyway, I could not show myself pro-left because I wasn't. Nor was it an easy situation in which to show disinterest as I doubted that that would produce any results at all. "It's the hell of a problem and, quite frankly, one I'm surprised is allowed to exist by our Lords and Masters at home," I remember finishing my long spiel.

He agreed with me but I had no need to despair as the present incumbent would not last for ever. My own common sense told me I was to behave completely naturally, impartially, disinterestedly, sensibly and patiently. Then I should sniff the wind, be an opportunist and not have too many scruples. I was a target and all the others believed that they were my targets but, under the present circumstances, it were better to make haste slowly. I should take advantage of what I could and this was particularly so with my Asian background and Asian languages, seven of which I could use Vientiane. If Lloyd was the darling of the left, then I should cash in on it by cultivating otherwise difficult contacts. I should take a leaf out of their book. I was up against dedicated and ruthless political animals as far as the Russians and the Chinese were concerned and neither of them were allies.

Later still, Cam West's remarks struck me as especially valid: "Without putting too fine a point of it, you are a boy in a man's league," he wisely said. The Americans were keeping me at arm's length and I had no idea how long that state of affairs would persist. As regards the RLA, the generals would be much slower in making up their minds. I was counselled patience: "You have got to give them time to weigh you up and see how you react to your new situation."

I was urged to try to keep up to date with the various communist pronouncements, deadly dull though they were, and study the language they used. If politics was their god, then semantics was their godling. I was not expected to like or agree with them but I would have to talk to them at various times, at receptions if not in their offices and homes. I had my own recipe for dealing with them. They were, in a way, like wild animals: not to frighten them to start with and let them see I was not frightened of them. Throw them some food and keep still. They'd choose their moment to come and take it. Throw the next lot not quite so far, wait again. And eventually they'd take me as part of the scenery if not actually eating out of my hand. But until then, it was routine work, blandly studying languages, never criticising, never offering advice, playing hard to catch, appearing not over-keen to get involved, even nebulous.

A week after I arrived in the country, on 22 November, I moved into the DA's house, Villa Sinxay. It was over a mile from the British embassy and on the edge of the town. I was glad to be away from the hotel and delighted that I could look after the dog, Singha, that went with the house. At half past 2 the Thursby-Pelhams drove down to Wattay airport. In the VIP lounge a champagne bar had been set up. The outgoing couple booked in, weighed their luggage, passed through emigration formalities and went upstairs to receive their guests – the attaché corps and any members of the other diplomatic staffs who wanted either a free drink away from their office routine or to say farewell. There were no Russians or Chinese among those who came to see them off. The Australian couple, Cam and Joy West, came as did all the senior members of the British embassy. The American, Broadus Bailey, looked in for a short while. Some of the MMF wives came to say farewell and there were tears as kisses were pecked in Gallic profusion, the French being more emotional than normal when one of their womenfolk has married a foreigner. I gathered there was a certain amount of snob value attached to how many and who came to see off a departing member of the international community. On this occasion it seemed to me that the American attitude was perfunctory, the French shallow and the British bored but as I had not attended anything similar before I had no yardstick. I was relieved when the passengers were called forward for boarding Thai Airways Bangkok flight TH 533. I bade them both farewell and thanked Donald for his hand-over.

I waited until the aircraft was out of sight before leaving the airport building. The week between my arrival and now seemed far longer than seven days. As I drove back, the flag on the car fluttering proudly, my thoughts were mixed. I was now on my own, more than at any time before. Domestically, living alone in that house would take some getting used to and so would the entertaining when my kit arrived. On the work front, the new routine would be strange for a while yet and there were still many other attachés to meet in my own right, as well as visiting those remaining three MRs in the provinces. I rehearsed the advice given to me by Donald and Cam. However, I was ill at ease; I sensed that, with John Lloyd's troubled personality affecting relationships and the other attachés' reactions to Donald being less than positive, I was in for a difficult time ahead.

As I drove away from the airport it was just as well for my peace of mind that I did not know quite how hard and lonely my furrow would be to plough.

4

A Boy In A Man's League

My very first morning as the British DA I had to dress up in full ceremonial fig. This was for a commissioning ceremony – *Le Cérémonie de Baptème* – of military cadets by the King, at Chinaimo Camp. Fearful of being late and not knowing the intricacies of the 'time and space' problem, I arrived ultra early. The organisers made me welcome and led me to the seat farthest from the King's temporary throne. I was joined by the next senior in precedence, the American, whose wife, Betsy, was to sit next to me. As she was lowering herself onto the chair she did not notice that the end of my sash was inadvertently there so she sat on it. She half rose, brushed it away and asked to be excused for sitting on my tassel. We got on well after that.

Pleasantries and badinage were promptly cut off at 9 o'clock by the King' arrival. After the national anthem, speeches were delivered. I noticed how bored the other attachés looked but I listened intently, trying to follow what was said and understanding an encouraging amount. I took special heed when the King made his address as it was the first time I had heard anyone, except his nieces, using the royal Luang Prabang accent that I had been launched into. That finished, the parade proper started: the thirty cadets, drawn up in front of the King in three ranks and standing to attention, knelt down, took their hats off and were blessed by the monarch from his throne. They then rose to their feet and put their hats back on.

The senior of them went up to the King who put on his new badges of rank. That done, the Prime Minister, the Commander-in-Chief, the Deputy and three other senior officials went down to the squad. At the right of each rank was an orderly with a silver *baçi* bowl full of second lieutenants' badges and two dignitaries went down each rank taking the metal brooches from the bowl and affixing them in the new officers' epaulets.

Now officers, the young men swore their oath of allegiance. Hatless and kneeling, they chanted it in chorus, phrase by phrase, after the senior man had delivered it solo. A saffron-robed monk and his young acolyte came forward, carrying two *baçi* bowls, one for holy water and the other for unhusked rice. The monk, intoning a mantra in Pali, sprinkled them with holy water, using a sacred leafy twig, then scattered some rice over them. The acolyte, noticing that the holy water had not reached those in the middle, tugged his elder's sleeve and the monk moved to a flank, the better to reach his target. The King nodded his head in approval but a spectator saying, rather too loudly, that the poor little chickens had yet to be fed, broke the solemnity of the moment. The new officers stood up and put on their headgear. The march past of the colours, the band, the newly commissioned officers, more cadets and, finally, the local militia with the King saluting and spectators standing, concluded the parade.

Next afternoon there was another commissioning ceremony, this time of police cadets, at Done Tiu, to the north of the town. It took an hour and a half as each cadet marched up to the King who personally presented him with his sword of office. At both ceremonies I could see how much genuine respect seemed to flow from the people to the King and how interested and concerned the King seemed to be for his people. At neither function did the King pay anything but formal notice of the foreign representatives gathered to participate. It was always a surprise to me that this good and great man could not mobilise his obvious (even to me then) magnetism to weld his people together, so have a slightly better chance of defeating the communists. None of the foreign diplomats seemed seriously to see his long delayed coronation as the one supremely Laotian fulcrum for this to happen. The LPF, whose aim of abolishing the monarchy was so cleverly concealed, played their cards superbly cannily, hoodwinking all to the very end.

Both ceremonies were most impressive and had an atmosphere of quiet dignity and intimacy often lacking on similar occasions elsewhere. Both times there was the same hand-shaking routine with the other attachés, who now greeted me as an equal, and with the local officials, at the start and the end, when warm Pepsi Cola, *amuse-bouches* small eats, and small talk had to be suffered. I fixed up my outstanding 'new boy' protocol calls – the South Vietnamese, the Filipino, the Thai attachés, the Indian, Canadian and Polish representatives of the ICSC and some staff officers in the RLA. I was jolted back to a former existence that second parade when the Indian ICSC Brigadier, Suraj Bakhshi, told me that we had overlapped by one month when we were cadets ourselves at the Indian Military Academy in Dehra Dun in 1944.

Another facet of life to get used to was money. The *kip* was a fragile currency. Some goods had to be paid for in US dollars (£1 equalled $2.35) but, because the rules for diplomats were strict and a flourishing back market made the *kip* volatile, I was distressed to find that my pound sterling was, in effect, only worth 25 US cents. Monthly pay for the soldiers of the RLA was 200 *kip*, less than the cost of an airmail letter to Britain. Soon after I arrived the *kip* was devalued to 1,400 to the pound, it having been around ten only a decade previously, and much thieving ensued. Donald used to sleep with a loaded pistol under his pillow and the dog downstairs. I took the dog in hand and it soon loved me so much that it would want to sleep upstairs near me. I was never burgled, the only house in the road not to be.

Weekly reporting deadlines controlled office routine and travelling time. I had to send two telegrams to London every Monday. One, full of as many military details as I could glean from the Americans and the Lao (although these latter were, so I was led to believe, wildly inaccurate), went to the MOD and a much shorter version went to the FCO. This latter had to be vetted by the Head of Chancery – Robin Fearn, a much younger man who rose to ambassador – lest there be any political slants unwittingly included. I had yet to learn just how jealously the FCO diplomats guarded their prerogative as sole arbiters of what constituted 'politics' and what did not. I never forgot one of the very earliest drafts I had taken in to be looked at.

"I see that you have put that 'there is an air of unrest in Vientiane'. I had not noticed it. What do you mean by unrest?" The indignant man pointed to Singha who had followed me into the office and was lying down, his legs twitching slightly. Robin wrinkled his nose deprecatingly. "Is Singha suffering from 'unrest'? How do I explain it to London?"

I sighed inwardly, thinking that the man was in danger of knocking the nail out of sight. It was hardly a political pronouncement of the greatest magnitude but I said placatingly, "Don't worry, Robin. In my all too short time here I've already noticed some indications of this; an American deliberately jostled on the pavement near the Morning Market, a traffic policeman overreacting with a European driver and some school kids shouting obscenities at a French woman. There may be rational reasons but, from my Asian experience, I take them to be symptomatic of unrest. I'm not saying they're unusual for this place as I admit I have only been here a short time. [Robin had arrived three days after me.] I'm not saying it won't die down. What I am saying is it's here now. 'Unrest' seemed as easy a word as any to encapsulate my feelings without going into too much detail. I'll delete it if you feel strongly that the desk will be unnecessarily disturbed."

"Oh no, it's not that but we're untrained to make positive statements like that. You're so lucky you have to be direct in your profession. We've got to say 'there are indications leading to a belief that...', 'it is possible to discern a tendency towards...' and so on."

The incident showed the working of the trained FCO mind. It was as well to know their point of view even if that point was, to me, out of focus.

At 9 o'clock on Wednesdays the Australian ambassador, defence attaché and first secretary would come over to the British embassy to lend weight to the discussions. The

Canadian representative of the ICSC would also be present. A military briefing by the British DA opened proceedings, followed by a desultory resume by the others. This consisted mainly of peace-talks prognostications, snippet-snatching, cocktail party quotes, the airing of vague ideas of possible trends and the venting of various points of view. That over, Cam and I would compare notes over a cup of coffee in my office. We had struck up an early mutual liking. Cam West was shrewd enough to see how valuable my empathy with Asians would be, especially when American influence declined, as it surely would. On the second occasion, Cam asked me how it was all going.

I told him that they were very early days yet and I was just a green new boy. Even so, I felt so useless, only getting information at second or third hand, with standards of what I had seen so different from what I was used to, including some of Lloyd's ideas.

Cam said that his ambassador was 'only lackadaisically pink' and regarded the LPF (whom the BBC always described as 'pro-communist' as though that absolved them from any real leanings that way) and the North Vietnamese as naughty children who, just for the moment, wouldn't listen to Daddy. What upset Cam was that such men advised people at home and it was the tendency of the Man in the Ministry to be guided by the Man on the Ground. That was the origin of so many wrong ideas that led to wrong policy decisions and one reason why the communists had seemed to do so well since 1945, with the western world losing out for no apparent reason.

The British embassy, unusually, had its own aircraft, a British Army Beaver, whose pilot was also the assistant military attaché. Cam and I planned to fly together visiting units after I had paid my courtesy calls on MOD and MR HQs, not forgetting the Neutralists, by myself. I was longing to get out on the ground and actually see how much of the doctrine we taught at the Jungle Warfare School was being used here. Cam's enigmatic laugh and ribald comment about 'doctrine' showed what an optimist I was.

Listening to Cam I found that the contacts I had already made during my courtesy calls and at various social functions represented the majority of people with whom I would normally have to work and through whom I would detect tremors of developments. Although I felt swamped by their names and had difficulty in placing a lot of them, they were the basic minimum on which I had to build. Once they were consolidated I could afford to develop any particular relationship that appeared fruitful. But even so they were still only those who were to be found in Vientiane. There remained the other parts of the country I could reach, with the necessary permission or by invitation. These were the targets of my outstanding calls in the one-third of Laos that was neither in communist hands, known by the LPF as the 'Liberated Zones', nor being currently disputed.

What was difficult was trying to sort out the patchwork of parties, factions, groups and cliques that went to make up the intricately complex and confused situation, if only because nowhere else had I come across right-wing and left-wing Neutralists – it was to meet the right-wing brand in Vang Vieng, to the north of the Vientiane plain, nominally in fief to the Prime Minister and allied to the RLG, that I had been given clearance. The left-wing brand were, at that moment, not worth bothering about and inaccessible anyway.

I reckoned I would be a fool if I were to try and start off in any way except slowly and at a basic level, working from first principles: a firm base, a workable plan and a reserve – prerequisites in any operation of the conventional sort. In this game, nothing was gained by hurry, which was also suspicious. My firm base had to be my reputation, my conduct and relations with the 'home side', my method of living and impeccable credentials of exemplary self-conduct. My workable plan was simple enough: behave normally, develop contacts locally as well as in the provinces, noting, observing, thinking, searching – but for whom or for what? – probing, teasing, assessing, analysing, collating, reassessing, recognising, rejecting and then seeing what was left, all within the confines and constraints of duty, tact and loyalty, never taking anything for granted. I knew it would take a long time to recognise the pieces of the jigsaw puzzle but maybe even if it was only a piece of blue sky that I found it would enable someone else to fit it into and even complete the picture. It would take even longer to judge whether what seemed genuine was so or purposeful disinformation, whether it was complete in itself or only that which gave a clue to yet something else, be it a hint in a smile, a message in the eyes, an implicit warning in a tone of voice, a turn of phrase or a coded handshake. So much said by leaving so much unsaid. It would take time if only because concentrating on everything at once tended to blot some points out or to see them disproportionally. A nonchalant attitude, letting things sink in to be dug out later, examined, and then judged as useful or otherwise, was a wiser if slower course of action than brash and frenetic beavering. It would not be easy to start with; in fact I doubted it would ever be easy.

And what of my reserve? A reserve of what? I had nothing in the conventional sense. All I could do was to build up sufficient good will and trust for me initially to become known and tolerated, then accepted and finally sought after. I knew I was eccentric enough for Europeans to be chary of me at first blush but that, for Asians, was a bonus – eccentricity is regarded as a manifestation of inner strength and, provided a person is consistently different from yet rationally the same as others, he is not only accepted but welcomed. I hoped that the pattern of acceptability I would build up would pave the way for longer-term benefits while taking the sting out of the current and short-term disadvantages. Nothing spectacular but all based on sound tenets, it would do as a start. Meanwhile life had to be lived, accommodating the imponderable as best possible and sedulously following protocol.

Of all the visits I paid to the other attachés, those to the communists stick in my mind. The Soviet embassy, a couple of miles out of town, was set in large grounds, with two tennis courts and an area where receptions were held. My car drove slowly in and, by the time I was at the embassy entrance, Colonel Vladimir P Gretchanine had come to meet me. Of medium height, he had a kindly face with blue eyes – which became glacially hooded when any serious subject was introduced – behind thick spectacles, spoke English and had a penchant for the droll remark. Having welcomed me, he led me across a foyer, passed a screened corridor and opened the door of what I presumed was a room for visitors.

Inside it was musty, as though seldom used. On one side were a settee, two chairs and a table, all huddled together. The rest of the room was empty. On the far wall a picture of an evil-looking, bald and bearded man glowered down at us. The walls were a dull yellow and, what with only one window, it was gloomy. The Russian sniffed and, remarking that the room was stuffy, turned on the air conditioner. It rattled into inefficient operation, exuding a crowd of surprised mosquitoes. Outside was a banging on the roof. Replacing tiles, was the explanation.

I was invited to sit down. Vladimir sat beside me and moved a bowl of wilted flowers, thereby sending out another cloud of mosquitoes. The background noises of the banging and of the air conditioner made conversation hard to follow and any recording difficult to understand.

I asked the Russian who the man in the picture was and learnt that it was Lenin. Not an auspicious start. I told Vladimir that he was the first Russian that I had wittingly set eyes on (fortuitously forgetting that, twenty-eight years before, the Japanese had delivered one of his fellow countrymen, carrying delicious coffee, into my custody). Small talk followed. He talked more about himself than ask me questions; how he used to go climbing until a basketball accident hurt his foot; his love of travelling; his difficulty in languages; his university education in Moscow studying chemistry, having failed to become a scientist; how he did not like working in the ministry and that one of his tasks had been combing unofficial Western publications for the amount of information of the sort that was carefully guarded in his country. I learnt that when the Soviet Union started making serious contact with India there were only five people who could speak Hindi. In return I told him a little about my life in Asia, how I had been with the Gurkhas and when the Ibans in Borneo wanted to cut off my head. I wondered how much of that was new, as I had presumed that the Soviets did their homework but was surprised that my first year's invitations to their functions always asked my non-existent wife to accompany me. It was interesting to be told that, contrary to what I had thought to be the case, budding diplomats were not immersed in the culture of their target country before taking post; in fact, I was told that there were no Lao-speaking diplomats in the embassy and I did not query the statement.

A waiter brought in a tray bearing vodka, thick syrupy coffee, salted nuts, biscuits and toffee, and laid them clumsily, laboriously and without finesse on the table – no trained mess waiter he – and I was inveigled into drinking a toast, not to systems but "as officer to officer, as wartime ally to wartime ally, let us drink to Mutual Understanding". We leant forward to clink glasses. "To Mutual Understanding," I echoed and tried not to make a face as my tongue touched the liquid. I put the still full glass back down on the table and excused my teetotal habits. (More than two years later a West German attaché told me that I would never get anything out of the Soviets until I was a drinker. He would eat a pound of butter, drink the oil from several tins of sardines and a pint or so of milk before going to meet his opposite Soviet number. For the first fifteen minutes of a half-hour meeting toasts to one another would be drunk in quick succession. The next six or seven minutes would see the Russian talking coherently but with loosened tongue. The last few minutes would be incoherent prattle before the man passed completely out, with the German much wiser than before and still completely sober.)

Although Vladimir did not commit himself about the PL, the general situation or the current peace talks, he made much of wanting to meet me more often and exchange ideas. He gave me the impression of wanting normality and, after an hour, I left to go to the Filipino, Colonel Augusto B Derpol, where I was delighted to find only biscuits and Nescafé.

The next call was on the Chinese DA, Chen Shu-lin. Luckily my driver, Khien, knew where everybody worked so I was spared searching the tangled jumble of small roads and back streets where so many people had to be sought out. At the sound of the car two men emerged from the house and stood at the top of the steps. They were dressed in plain blue jackets, done up at the neck, and blue trousers. I waited for Khien to switch off and open the door for me. As I got out and went up the steps a clock inside the embassy of the People's Republic of China struck twelve, the time I had fixed.

"Good morning, M Chen," I said in French. I had been told that I had to address him as *Monsieur* as the Chinese army had no ranks. "It is most kind of you to welcome me." Chen limply took my outstretched hand. His interpreter translated and then relayed the answer. "You are welcome, Colonel. Please come in."

The room into which I was led was large and L-shaped. Straight ahead a beautifully lacquered screen divided the area into a sitting and dining room. There was another, not so pretty, screen to the right, round which I was led. On the wall opposite was the largest picture of Chairman Mao Tse-tung that I had ever seen.

The three of us sat down, Chen and I on the settee and the interpreter (an official of the *Gun An Jiu*, the Public Security Bureau, as the Chinese secret service is known) on a chair to my right. My fascinated gaze was riveted on the grotesque picture and, as I stared at it, I realised I must not appear brash, rude, critical or insensitive and that, by then, I had gazed on the Chairman long enough. I turned and looked at Chen and, if by instinct, I turned back to the picture on the wall, then back once more to Chen.

"I can't believe it: you must excuse me but the likeness of your Chairman and yourself is so uncanny I'm going to ask you if you are a close relation or not?"

As the remark was translated Chen's eyes gleamed with pleasure. He chortled with joy as he gave his answer. No, no, he was no relation at all but, when small, had been carried "on my father's back on the Long March that was led by our Chairman." Chen had seen him since, many times, but "I have never forgotten those difficult days. But for his greatness we would have all died a hundred deaths."

He asked me my age. I asked him his. Translated into the zodiac, he was a Dragon and I a Cow – I the more unlikely and less representational of the pair of us. More small talk ensued.

A waiter, smartly dressed in white, came in and placed one glass of beer and two fizzy orange drinks on the table. I put the orange drink in front of me and Chen took the other. The interpreter looked sadly at the beer, presumably originally destined for an alcohol-addicted foreigner, and longingly at the other two glasses.

As I was invited to take my drink another waiter appeared with a trayful of goodies – nuts, toffee, salty fish, a type of yam and some nasty-looking brown squid cubes. Six wineglasses were produced, the three larger filled with a red liquid, the three smaller with a colourless brew. Another waiter brought in three cups of weak, milkless tea, and placed them among the saucers and glasses. I asked Chen how long he had been in Vientiane and was told three years. He had come shortly before the British ambassador. "How is Mr Lloyd? He is counted as one of our friends; he understands our point of view."

Chen then took one of the toothpick slivers of wood from the tray, neatly skewered a particularly revolting-looking piece of solidified squid and, lifting it to my mouth, smilingly indicated that he was intent on feeding me. There was an air of unreality to this pantomime that followed so swiftly and unexpectedly on the banalities of small talk but I managed to show no surprise. I opened my mouth and Chen popped the delicacy inside. I munched nobly. What, I wondered, was protocol in this case? Did I have to skewer one of the pieces of yam or squid and likewise feed Chen? The decision was postponed by Chen lifting a glass containing the red liquid and proposing good luck, good health and good relations between us two men and our two countries. I took a tiny sip and involuntarily grimaced. It tasted foul.

I felt I had to take some initiative and still hung back from the sliver approach. Instead I bravely lifted the glass containing the colourless liquid and changed my original thoughts for a toast, "To the Dragon and the Cow" which might have gone down like a pork chop in a synagogue, to a craven "To our friendship, man to man, despite politics." My lips touched the fiery brew and I blenched like a gun-shy virgin.

Under those circumstances it was not surprising no serious conversation ensued, Chen not even committing himself about the peace talks, only pleasantries and more banalities with frequent pauses. I was asked if I had my family with me and countered by asking Chen the same question. No. When I tried to include the interpreter in the conversation, the response was such that it soon became clear that there were only two people party to the meeting, the interpreter not being one of them.

I asked Chen how many Chinese languages he spoke and was told six but, regrettably, no English, except 'Hello' and 'Goodbye' but nothing in between. Possibly we could combine to teach each other? I was given a Lao-language copy of *Quotations from Chairman Mao Tse-tung,* popularly known as the Chairman's 'Thoughts' that I had asked for at Donald's farewell party. I wanted to use it as a textbook.

"When did you first come across our Chairman's thoughts?"

I thought quickly. It would have been a gross error of tactics to have let on that I had studied them at the Jungle Warfare School in an effort to try and fathom some of the Chinese guerillas' rationale the better to slant our training to counter it.

Luckily a white lie and a lame answer satisfied him.

After thanking him suitably, I felt it was time to leave. Glasses, cups and half-empty plates were as eloquent as any watch. As I rose to go I glanced once more at the preposterously large picture, then at Chen. As the Chinese DA was shaking hands with me at the top of the steps, I was asked to think of myself as being able to come and talk to Chen at any time I wanted. "Just ring first and fix an appointment. Our doors, for you, are always open. We must exchange ideas. Remember also, the Dragon is a more reliable animal than the Bear."

The favourite pun of the Chinese when they spoke French was the similarity between *URRS* that sounded the same as bear – *ours*.

To round off the day I called in on the Polish delegation of the ICSC, where I met Air Force Colonel K. Piecychna (pronounced Pee-Ed-Chee-Na) who offered me coffee and an extra special Polish delicacy, wine a hundred years old. He asked me how I saw this whole area after a settlement. I gave him two answers: one Asian peasant mentality and the other my own idea of great power mentality. I suggested to him that the communist attack on South Vietnam was tactical, not strategic. Had it been strategic it should not have been towards Saigon, a 'dead end', but rather southwest across Thailand where, eventually, if the line were extended, Chinese and Soviet influence would collide. This added an unthought-of dimension to his thinking.

All I learnt when I visited the Frenchman, Lieutenant Colonel Jean Laboucheix, was that he was most upset by having been accused by Donald of cheating at bridge!

On the domestic front I did not start entertaining for some months as my heavy kit was shipped out eight weeks late and then had to wait a further month on the Bangkok docks. (I had a letter sent to me by the suppliers in London addressed to Bangkok, Chile, whereas the FCO Outward Bound Bag Room muddled Vientiane and Vienna, Laos and Lagos.) I found myself caught up in the social whirl straightaway. Functions were chiefly in the evening. I learnt *tenue confortable* meant long dresses for the women but short-sleeved shirts for the men; *tenue de ville* meant suits and *tenue de soirée* meant dinner jackets and black tie. I learnt that the irksome, finicky details of protocol order of precedence (in such matters as who sat where at table) prevented stupid squalls of temper by those whose diplomatic status was in advance of their mental stability.

On a broader front, I tried to pick out that which was obviously part of an accepted pattern and which were oddities. Some were risible, others not so. The Chinese became very excited when, at a ball held in the MMF on 2 December, they learnt that the French were celebrating a victory over the Russians and were horribly downcast when they found out it referred to Austerlitz in 1805. I noticed, for instance, that there were no Americans among the thousand-odd guests at a cheese and wine party held at the French embassy, and the difference in the way other attachés reacted to Cam West after the Whitlam government in Australia had changed their Vietnam policy direction – but was any of this what I was looking for?

At one large cocktail party I was asked to go and talk to a PL man. Two Americans would be watching, one at whom the surprised man would try to look at before talking to me and the other at who, in the crowd, would pay attention to us two talking. Thus, apparently, my 'target' could be identified as in the pro-Soviet group or the pro-Chinese group.

At another party, given by Broadus Bailey for the Japanese attaché from Bangkok, I was in a group of five: Vladimir Gretchanine (sitting next to me), two Americans and the Thai, who started talking about chemistry. "I know nothing about chemistry," I ventured.

Vladimir turned to me, stared fixedly at me with eyes malevolently hooded and magnified by his thick spectacles and said, very softly; "You know everything about everything. Your predecessor knew everything about nothing. Soon you will be learning Russian and when you go to Moscow, *I* will take you." He then continued talking normally with the others. I was mighty wary of him after that but he only ever said anything as direct once again: "You understand everything, everything. If you say you don't it is camouflage. Colonel Thursby-Pelham sometimes didn't understand, but you understand everything."

I continued to try and contact Princess Jasmine, to see if she could give me some Lao lessons as tentatively arranged but, when I rang her from my house, I always got the wrong number. In fact I could never get any number I wanted from my house and only used my office telephone. When I first went to meet her she was not in but one of her many sisters, the ugliest, who was working in the garden, gave me a cauliflower. 'The ugly princess gave the English colonel a cauliflower' ran risibly through my head like an example from an old-fashioned phrase book.

Not since joining the army nearly thirty years before had I felt so useless. Sure, the folk in the embassy were kind and helpful; sure, I was made welcome by the delightful couple who ran my house – a Thai, called Chok Di (Thai for 'Good Luck'), Villay, his Lao wife and their two small children – happy to have a single man with simple tastes to look after and relieved that I did not interfere in the kitchen. I felt a mental loneliness that surely must assail everyone new, especially when the job was so different from the open and shut, black and white of regimental soldiering I was used to. At first there was enough novelty in everyday life, the new country, the new language, the delightful people and the challenge of the inconcise nature of the post, to say nothing of learning my job, keeping me fully occupied. There was also travel in the embassy Beaver aircraft.

Two weeks after I became DA I started my visits to the provinces. It was with a keen thrill of expectation that I was driven down to Wattay airport, going round the back where there was a complex of hangers, workshops and stores. Several wrecks littered the periphery, making the place untidy. Of interest was a Soviet AN-2 aeroplane, nicknamed the Colt, in service since 1948 and the world's largest single-engined biplane. It was guarded by a couple of policemen, one of whom was asleep on a stretcher under the wing. Its main task was ferrying LPF personnel from Vientiane to their 'capital' in the northeast of the country, at a place called Sam Neua.

We were to fly to the royal capital, Luang Prabang, eighty minutes' flying time away, where I was due to meet the commander of MR 1. The journey was to be broken at Vang Vieng, base of the right-wing Neutralists, on the northern rim of the Vientiane plain. It was a novel experience to be in the cockpit of a small 'plane and I concentrated on all I heard. I listened in on the headset to the complex jargon of international and local air traffic, to the 'planes crossing zonal boundaries, to the monitoring of weather reports, to the clearances for landing and takeoff, to the restrictions imposed by artillery firing and the air-to-air conversations between the pilots themselves. It was not a world I was familiar with but I appreciated the orderly, methodical and disciplined code all air operations required.

Large jungle-covered hills with perpendicular limestone cliffs floated up and curved round to greet us as we approached the runway at Vang Vieng. I was startled to see a line of some twenty men on the town side of the strip, all dressed in a uniform of sorts. We taxied over to the near side of the airfield and Alan cut the engine. I undid my straps and climbed down onto the ground. I pulled my jacket straight, put on my hat, and looked around. Nobody came to meet me and the thought did cross my mind that it was somebody else the delegation was lined up for. But no: to my relief the end figure became detached from the rest, came over and introduced himself as the Colonel in charge of the Neutralist Vang Vieng Military District. Would I like to come and be introduced to his staff? It seemed that everybody who was anybody, and some who were not, were there. As well as military officers, I was to meet the police, a large contingent from the civil administration and a schoolmaster – all were Neutralists, so I was given to understand as I was escorted towards them. I went down the line, shaking everybody's hand, looking at each of them straight between the eyes, a smile and a word of greeting and thanks for their welcome.

Formalities over I was escorted a short way down the road, tarred but badly in need of repair, and led into a wooden-hutted military camp that housed the HQ of the Neutralists. These were not part of the RLA but called themselves by a French title; *Forces Armées Neutralistes*. To my further surprise they all, including the schoolmaster, mounted the steps of a building and sat down on seats arranged around an impressive but probably inaccurate situation map. A military briefing followed, general and anodyne, at the end of which various statistics were given, including, to my amazement, the farm animal population of the entire district, down to the last chicken. Had I any questions? My mind raced with wanting to know many details. How was it that so many outsides could be included in the presumably confidential briefing? Who formulated Neutralist policy and what was the chain of command? How did they manage for operational clearance on their boundaries with the RLA? Who had counted the chickens? – but, apart from checking some of their figures, said no, I hadn't any as the briefing had been lucid and comprehensive and I was still so new that I had nothing against which to compare it. Maybe another time?

I sensed their relief at my not wanting any more details and, after a pause, a cup of heavily sweetened black coffee (from the Bolovens plateau in the 'Panhandle', the southern and thin part of Laos) and a glass of almost colourless lukewarm tea were offered and a few minutes passed in pleasantries. After allowing enough opportunity for my hosts to take the conversational initiative, I looked at my watch and rose. I glanced round the room and tried to read their faces but their expressions were as bland and empty as had been their briefing. But could I expect anything else at this first meeting and what could I offer them except the courtesy of my presence which, to them, showed that the British government still rated the Neutralists separately?

We flew over some spectacularly rugged mountains on the 40-minute journey to Luang Prabang. At an average of 6,500 feet high, the highest was 8,054 feet. Dangerous flying in bad weather. The airstrip at Luang Prabang is some way to the northeast of the town but we flew down to above the town first, ears popping, to keep out of the flight path of the RLAF T-28s and C-130s that were keeping the tower busy. Six T-28s took off in quick succession with bombs in the pods under their wings and headed for the fighting farther to the northeast. Stores were being unloaded from one C-130 and another was waiting for a group of soldiers to emplane. I noticed a hill, the Phou Si (named after a mythical giant), in the centre, around which the town was built, with a temple at the top, glistening golden in the sunlight.

As we made our second circuit over the town I could pick out many more *wats* tucked away in odd corners and the royal palace at the foot of the hill. It was then our turn to land and, as we taxied to dispersal, a black car drove up to the small terminal building. Shallow craters made by NVA and PL mortar bombs pitted the aerodrome pan.

We were driven a short distance along the road leading into the town. We turned off left, passed a sentry who stared at the car without enthusiasm, and up a short incline. As the car stopped a Captain came out of the nearest office and opened the door for us, saluted as we got out and, in American-accented English, welcomed me to HQ MR 1. I was invited to meet the Chief of Staff, "who speaks no English, before meeting the MR commander, Brigadier General Chao Savang, the King's half-brother, who also speaks no English."

I was led to an office where the Chief of Staff, a small fleshy man, was sitting at an empty table, looking bored. "*Bonjour, Colonel, asseyez-vous*," he welcomed me, pointing to a chair. As the General was the King's half-brother, I wanted to know whether I addressed him as *Altesse, Excellence* or *Général*. I was told *Mon Général* was all I needed to say and to treat him like any other senior officer.

We went into the General's office, a small, dim room, with a large wall map hidden by a green curtain. At the table to the left of the room sat a large, squat, heavily-built man, who got up when I went over to the table and saluted him. He put out his large paw to be shaken and mumbled something inaudible. I was invited by the Chief of Staff to sit down at the opposite end of the room. A silence followed. I, using strictly protocol French, thanked the General for the courtesy of allowing me the privilege to come, as the new British attaché, and pay my respects. Another silence followed. The General stared at me and I saw his mouth open but discerned no noise. The silence continued. The Chief of Staff looked at the General, then at me. The General, with the slow movement of senescence or of debility, pressed a button on his desk and the Captain came in, went to the map, drew back the curtain and gave a briefing. There was no mention of the Irregulars, of which MR 1 was full, nor of Thais, who were also represented in fair strength. There was, however, a surprising amount of detail on numbers of NVA, PL and Chinese People's Liberation Army's road-building troops. As I listened to the list of figures, I wondered if they bore any relation to the Neutralists' chickens.

On the map was a road marked in red leading out of Laos to Dien Bien Phu in Vietnam and, looking at it suddenly made everything more real, especially as the fighting was much nearer than the road. I was not invited to ask any questions and there was another eloquent hush. I could not make out whether the General's reticence was due to a sore throat, a hangover, boredom or shyness. The briefing had included the still unfamiliar American and French army terminology and that, combined with the confusingly tongue-twisting Laotian names I had been subjected to, the heavily accented French, to say nothing of the pregnant silences – or were they merely stillborn? – and the fact that I was neither to be taken to any combat position nor to visit any soldiers, made the visit to HQ MR 1 unspectacular, unexciting and memorable only in its utter banality. As we were being driven down to the town I gloomily recalled my pious hopes of seeing something of the doctrine and the tactics used by the RLA against the communists were still as pious as ever and I glumly wondered if an acorn, waiting underground to germinate, felt as useless as I now felt. I knew I had to be patient but it was frustratingly hard going.

For the visits to the other two MRs in the 'Panhandle', 3 in Savannakhet and 4 in Pakse, we flew across Thailand which looked flat and uninteresting. Parallel with the Mekong and Route 13 (that runs from Saigon, through Vientiane and on up to Luang Prabang), and away to the east beyond some distant hills, was the infamous Ho Chi Minh Trail. Halfway between the trail and the western part of the region, in hilly country, the Thai secret army and the Lao Irregulars were in almost constant contact with the NVA and the PL.

If ever a war was fought by proxy, I thought as we flew along, it was here. With the USA backing Souvanna Phouma, the Prime Minister, and with the North Vietnamese, Russians and Chinese backing his half-brother, the Red Prince Souvannouvong who lived in the Sam Neua area, I felt it a strange, sad and senseless way of settling what had originally started as a family quarrel; nevertheless it was as real in fact as it was unreal in its many facets.

In late 1972 Savannakhet, the second largest town in Laos, boasted a French population of about a thousand souls. They were teachers, planters and members of the detached MMF as well as missionaries, a tin miner and retired folk. A flaccid, flabby Colonel, driving his own jeep, met me. HQ MR 3 was twenty minutes' drive away and, apart from an unprepossessing Guard of Honour drawn up for me to inspect, the standard of briefing was lower than that of the other HQs. The Brigadier General in charge was ill and nobody was authorised to say anything in his absence but, as the new DA had come all the way from Vientiane, they would give him a briefing. This scarcely mentioned the fighting but went into spurious details of square hectares of cultivated land, subdistrict boundaries, and US-financed fish farms. It had as little relevance to the war situation as the Church Lads Brigade had to Mounting the Guard at Buckingham Palace. The HQ staff was bored and I felt out-of-place and uncomfortable. At the end the Colonel hinted at Britain's parsimony, especially as she was a Great Power and the Co-Chairman of those Geneva Accords. For once I was glad that Britain had done no more than had been the case and I declined to be drawn. Even so, politeness costing only effort, I gravely thanked them for sparing me their time and left, being driven in silence back to the airport by the Colonel. Once more I was engulfed by a sense of futility and purposely being kept away from matters of any importance or significance – yet that was also significant.

At Pakse, MR 4 Commander, Brigadier General Soutchai, was a refreshing change in that he had earned his rank by military prowess (and American insistence) and not through family or political considerations. I stared at the ultra-large map, lost in reverie…I had to start from somewhere and what was that Chinese proverb? *A journey of a thousand miles starts with but a single step.* I was past my first step and, faltering though my progress might seem to me, it might not seem so to others.

I paid more attention to the briefing, this time concentrating on what was left out rather than that which was included. What I did not understand but felt was important was how come that twenty-eight years after this war started, the communists had not won if the right-wing forces were as bad as they seemed or rather the controlling staffs were as bad as they made out. Surely the communists were not as bad as that themselves? But if they were, was that one reason for the war still dragging on? Was it merely a question of one side being ruled by terror and the other by vested interests? I was still deep in thought as we flew back to Vientiane.

I rang Princess Jasmine's number before leaving the office after I got back that day and was greeted by a silvery voice at the other end, asking me why I had been so long in contacting her. I told her I had tried many times to ring her from my house after 5 p.m. but I could never make contact. Now I was ringing from the office.

51

She invited me round for the next day to her house, Haekham Villa, where I had been given a cauliflower on my first visit. I was driven there after office hours, along a road that squirted out clouds of the finest dust when trodden on. I told the driver to take car and dog (which now often came with me) back and that I would walk home. As the car drove away Singha looked anxiously back from the rear window. I walked up the concrete drive and, as I reached the front door, that very beautiful woman, Princess Jasmine herself, opened it. My heart leapt and missed a beat. She invited me in, asking where the dog was. "I hear you take him around with you. Don't look surprised – there are no secrets in Vientiane," and she laughed delightedly. "Maybe next time you'll let me get to know him?"

We went inside and sat at an expensively made dining room table. A painting of HM the King filled one wall. She asked me how she could help me and for the next hour I plied her with many grammatical questions that had been troubling me, glad that she used English when my Lao was not up to the task.

I put my notebook away when I sensed that she had had enough for one session. I thanked her for taking up as much of her time as I had. "Not at all. *Bo pen nyang.*" She asked how I was finding life amongst the Lao and hoped I was enjoying it. I told her where I had been and whom I had met. I added that I thought I had met all the senior Lao officials protocol required me to. She looked up and hesitated. "You are already well known in high Laotian society," she rather sweetly said. Even if she did not mean it, she need not have said it.

Next week on the Monday morning Mr Lloyd called me in and asked me where I had been at the end of the past week. I had, in fact, told him well in advance about my intended moves but there was no reason why he should have committed them to memory. The reverse would be more likely. I told him about going to Luang Prabang and the 'Panhandle'. He said in reply that he was glad I had not been up to MR 2. "I wouldn't let you go there and visit those hawks even if you asked. The PL would be most upset if they thought that the British DA and the embassy Beaver had been there." I said nothing and the conversation drifted into less contentious topics.

At 7 o'clock on 20 December I turned on the BBC World Service and learnt with surprise that the Americans, tired of getting nowhere with their peace talks with the North Vietnamese and the Vietminh, had started bombing Hanoi and Haiphong again. John Lloyd was so outraged that he was virtually beside himself.

Two days later saw the fiftieth anniversary of the Soviet Constitution, an occasion that was deemed important enough to invite the diplomatic community to the Soviet embassy in its honour that evening. I joined the queue of people being welcomed by the ambassador, the first secretary and the DA then drifted off into the crowd swarming with Soviet bloc representatives as well as other communist countries' minions. I found a thin sprinkling of RLA generals.

I joined a group of communists and brashly started using my Vietnamese to one who transpired to be the chief delegate of the North Vietnamese mission. He seemed intrigued so, emboldened, I started to say something before I realised I could not finish the sentence due to poor vocabulary. I started off "It is dangerous and difficult..." and saw his face freeze with wariness. I switched into French and said, "it is the poor who always suffer", which was Delphic enough for me to extricate myself without losing too many points.

I caught sight of Chen Shu-lin and went up to him. His Lao and French interpreters were with him. He asked me if I had met the chief delegate of the LPF in Vientiane, Soth Phetrasi? No, so we moved over to where he was and introductions were made.

"So you're the one?" Soth asked, quizzically and not unpleasantly.

"That sounds ominous!" I smiled to rob the remark of any offence.

"Not at all. Not at all. An attaché who speaks Lao is welcome by us all. Your prowess is well known already."

"You flatter me," I said. "I must pay you a protocol visit."

On the way out I saw General Kouprasith talking to the US ambassador. I explained how I had been talking to the North Vietnamese delegate before I knew who he was (as UK and the North Vietnamese did not have diplomatic relations this was a gaffe). The Lao smiled politely. The American, fat, sweating, drinking quickly and cigar-smoking, interrupted and said, "Aw, he's just a little shit" and immediately translated that into French for the General's benefit. We were both embarrassed. It was so like a scene from a bad novel it was a caricature from real life – but it was real.

I fixed up a formal meeting with the LPF and told the Lloyd about it before I went. He was delighted and, using my Christian name for the first time, told me that it would have been a dereliction of duty if I had not done so. Exactly on time, my flagged car turned into their HQ compound, near the Morning Market. A sentry at the gate gave me a passable salute. As the car drew up at the front door a waiting PL soldier opened the car door for me: sincere or not, it was a kindly gesture. The senior Vientiane representative, Soth Pethrasi, came to the front door as I reached it. We greeted each other and he led the way into a room on the right of the corridor. Easy chairs, backs to the window, were at one end of a long room, the other end of which had the unsmiling pictures of three founder members of the movement glowering down.

We sat down and a moon-faced girl in national dress brought us a fizzy drink. I asked Soth Phetrasi about the owners of the faces hanging on the wall and the history of the design on the LPF plaque. That led the conversation on to the life at Sam Neua, which, in turn, led Soth Phetrasi to talk about the old pre-1954 days when the enemy had been the French. Regardless of ideology, it was fascinating. I mentally equated what was described with the tactics I had taught at the Jungle Warfare School and whether the counter-ambush drills we advocated would have proved effective against some of the more suicidal Vietnamese attacks.

None of this was soldiering as I knew it but it had the attraction of being the other side of the frontier between knowledge and ignorance.

As a result of the resumption of the American bombing in North Vietnam the peace talks in Vientiane broke down. It was patently obvious that North Vietnam would never give up its quest for South Vietnam and the strong NVA presence in Laos spelled long-term doom there also. When Chen Shu-lin paid me a return visit a day or later he said that Laos could start making peace the next day, ahead of the rest of Indo-China "if only the Vientiane Lao would talk as sensibly as the Lao Patriotic Front does." Peace talks resumed a few days later after that and, before the end of the year, the bombing had halted. That did not mean, however, an end to terrorism, infiltration and land grabbing by the PL, backed by the NVA, as always.

At the end of the year the Beaver pilots/assistant attachés changed, Peter Shield relieving Alan Calder. Flying in Laos in a single-engined aeroplane was no sinecure. Terrain, especially in the north of the country, was high and jagged, with the weather in the mountains always a problem. Flying conditions were better during the cold weather (true for the whole area from the Khyber Pass to Hong Kong) when visibility was good. Thick haze, caused by the Meo tribesmen's habit of slashing and burning, and dust from the roads as much as by nature, built up after February. In late spring before the rains cleared the air it was not uncommon for cars to drive with headlamps on at midday and for aircraft to take off from Wattay airport with visibility only halfway down the runway. It had been known for two aircraft to be directed by the tower to land and take off on the same runway from opposite directions at the same time, so blind, or stupid, were the men in the tower.

The problems of maintenance, fuel and spares had constantly to be kept under review, the British Army in Hong Kong being our superiors although the machine was on loan to the FCO. Only by adhering to laid-down standards was the aircraft safe. Safe, that is, as far as the pilot's skill and good maintenance facilities could allow. Navigational aids owned, supplied and maintained by the Americans, were good and reliable but, even so, there were other hazards to contend with. Certain areas were restricted because of USAF intervention (B-52 and F-111 strikes) or artillery being used in the ground fighting. Going to the northwest of the country meant flying over Thai territory, which could be dangerous as the Royal Thai Air Force could be trigger-happy despite clearance having been obtained. Flying direct over where the Chinese army had brought anti-aircraft artillery to defend Route 46, running from Yunnan to Pak Lay, south of the River Mekong, was out of the question. Chinese Army engineers were then upgrading it. A civil aircraft had been shot down not all that long before. It had been covered with soil to prevent aerial photography. Permission for the Americans to photograph it was, somehow, obtained from Peking through the good offices of the British and, so the story went, an American 'plane was sent to do this. The crew was on tenterhooks. The pilot contacted the ground and, forgetting that he was still through to them, said over the crew intercom that he hoped the 'little yellow bastards won't shoot us down.' He was startled to hear a disembodied voice squawk from the earphones: "You velly lude man, one time lound only."

By 9 o'clock on New Year's Eve the road in front of the *hôtel*, as the Prime Minister's residence was billed on the invitation card, was jam-packed with cars as all those who had been invited tried to arrive on time. I met the reception committee in the large foyer and joined the group of attachés waiting to greet their ambassadors as protocol dictated. As I saw Mr and Mrs Lloyd coming up the steps in the queue I went forward and greeted them. After a pause I asked if they had any idea about when they would be leaving because protocol demanded that the attaché only left after his ambassador. I was told that I need not worry and not wait for them. I thanked him and, flippantly, wished them a happy and successful 1973, peace of mind and a generous tax collector to boot. Lloyd smiled at me but his wife – new, raw and unsettled – merely glared.

I wandered out onto the lawn and made a circuit of the tables. There were many French guests and I recognised scarcely any of them. They seemed entirely at their ease, jabbering away nineteen to the dozen. I overheard a number of them talking with Lao guests, all of them using French. I was fascinated, yet repelled, by their insensitive manner of taking what they saw as their superiority for granted. I had yet to become accustomed to living in former French territory and I compared French behaviour with the more phlegmatic British way of setting about things. Until they got to know me, the Indo-Chinese would think I'd react as a Frenchman or an American would. That was probably a grave disadvantage.

I came across the South Vietnamese attaché, Colonel Nguyen Huu Chi, and his wife, the latter attractively attired in ceremonial *Ao Giai*, long, split silk trousers and matching coat. They were sitting as near a charcoal brazier as they could to keep warm. It was never so cold in Saigon. I wanted to get to know him better and was glad when I was offered a seat with them. The Chis were even harder to entertain than was I, being vegetarians as well as teetotal. Mme

Chi gave me lessons in Vietnamese. Chi asked me what I thought of the King's *matinée* at the palace? I told him I was only a new boy and the novelty had yet to wear off but I could see it could become boring. I did not tell him my main problem had been how to shake hands as custom demanded with my hat under my arm, my gloves in my hand, clutching a glass and small eats, wearing spurs and a sword, and keeping upright on a slippery floor.

His answer intrigued me. He was always interested in these affairs, as I would be if my country was next door and at war. Sometimes it was for what people said and sometimes for what they did not say; for whom they talked to and whom they avoided. To keep up-to-date he tried to learn something new at each of them but he was not always successful. "Same as tonight: it is a dull man who can't get some advantage from a party." His perception was of value to me, so I asked him what he had learnt that morning. Apparently I was becoming part of the scene with many of the attachés but was an object of interest and curiosity to those missions that didn't have any military representation, such as the Indonesians and the North Vietnamese.

At a quarter to midnight the Prime Minister came onto the stage and gave a short speech of welcome with an optimistic New Year's message in impeccable French. From then on all the many Frenchmen kept on looking at their watches with nervous hen-like bobbing of their heads as the bewitching hour approached and, on the dot of midnight, dived on their wives with frothy kisses and then on any other female who, if not exactly going begging, was temporarily unoccupied by any other male. The Thai attaché murmured 'dangerous' as he kept a wary eye on his wife.

After a buffet of local food – I was hungry by then – I made my unobtrusive escape. 1972 had been a strange year, I mused as I went to the embassy to check the security as I was duty officer: a 107-day trek in Nepal; being in England longer than at any time in twenty-eight years; nearly getting married and now in this extraordinary country, Laos. I recalled the time in 1967 when Britain's 'East of Suez' policy had seemed the end of my service (with or without Gurkhas) after 1971 – the end of an era. But I was still in Asia, in a challenging job. I had so many blessings and I did not grumble, there were so many, many others with infinitely less. The immediate novelty had by now worn off and I was finding my way round a bit. Contacts were still tenuous and were exacerbated by the personality gap between John Lloyd ('dove of doves' who was generally thought to have lost any influence the British ever had) and his American counterpart, 'Mac' Godley ('hawk of hawks'. "Call me field marshal," he would say and, indeed, he held the power of life and death over more people in the country than any other man did). I hoped that my superiors in London had an inkling why my reports were so woefully thin, why I was still an outsider from the source of all hard information (the Americans) and that I was therefore trying to develop my Lao contacts. I must not brood; more challenges were yet to come. Those gone had already been entered into the ledger as plus or minus by whoever was the Great Marker. I 'grieved not for that which was past'; I was not a man with a future but a man with a present. The stage I was going through was an apprenticeship, as necessary as it was frustrating. An unobtrusive escape from the party was as good a way of ending 1972 as any other.

5
The Test

I soon had many opportunities to see startling differences from what I was used to and which needed understanding if ever I were to get to grips with the job. Although the chemistry of being an attaché had started to work, I was still very much in the embryo stage. One of the difficulties was that I only had the efficient Brigade of Gurkhas' background against which to judge what I came across and saw, so my military hackles were constantly ruffled.

Certainly in most armies to command a battalion is either the epitome of all military ambition or is a most necessary step in the quest for the upper reaches of the military hierarchy. The reaction of one Neutralist officer to being promoted to command a battalion was different. He had been voted by popular acclaim at what the charitable might call a promotion conference. The battalion was near Luang Prabang but the aspiring commander demurred. He told me that he had asked for a year on the staff in Vientiane first as he wanted to see the bright lights. This was not allowed and he was told to go and take over his unit straightaway. However, he did not go to assume command as ordered but fifteen days later, only after the old commanding officer had left. "It might have embarrassed him had we been there together," he explained.

Standards of military honesty were mutable. A Lao colonel reported to his American colleague that he wanted to transfer from the Irregulars back to the RLA. When reminded that the pay in the former was higher in the latter, his reply was that he was only getting 10 per cent of his soldiers' pay but were he to transfer back he could get 20 per cent, thus he would be richer. "To get him to talk openly about it shows how honest he is," his American colleague told me.

An ex-guerilla unit under training suddenly found some of its NCOs commissioned overnight. The unit boasted 524 souls of whom 396 were officers. Chaos reigned.

Imagination in planning did not seem to play a great part for the staff officers who arranged attaché programmes. I wrote in to get official permission for my first visit to the River Flotilla. I had already had verbal permission to go and my letter was confirmatory. Two weeks later I received a telephone call from a very perplexed Lao colonel. "Tell me," he implored, in very good English, "What Flotilla do you want to see and what river is it on?" I told him that, yes, it was the River Flotilla I wanted to see and the river, yes, was the Mekong. The colonel seemed relieved and said he thought that was what I had probably meant in my written request.

The Minister of Defence commented that the system in the RLA was wrong because it was French and 'they have never won a war'. The French said 'the Lao never do anything today that they can get someone else to do for them tomorrow'. A Lao colonel told me that the French had handed the country over to them as a darkened room: only recently had they found the windows to let in the light. An American said that the French gave the Lao just enough rice to keep them hungry and put just enough salt in their water to keep them thirsty. "Now that's real diplomacy," he opined. It was about that time that I heard the Prime Minister make a speech about peace in which he made an allusion to the five principles of co-existence, the *Panch Shila*. I overheard the French DA explain to his neighbour that *Panch Shila* was the name of a famous Buddhist monk in Tibet. Well, it might have been, mightn't it?

The Soviets, too, had their problems. Overheard at a Soviet party, when two Russians were in deep conversation discussing the problems they were facing with the PL: "The trouble with these Lao is that they break everything." Yes, there were some different perspectives to be taken into account.

In Vietnam the cease-fire came into effect on 28 January 1973, when the NVA and Vietminh were controlling large areas of the south. Initially, with US air support, the ARVN withheld attacks from the northern forces. Under the cease-fire agreement, all remaining American forces had to be out of the country within sixty days. After that fighting broke out once more and declined after a second cease-fire on 15 June 1973. In the first twelve months after the first cease-fire it was reckoned some 58,000 troops had been killed.

As for Laos, I wrote home on 7 February 1973, in disgust and in despair:

Over a thousand men were killed last week needlessly, on a false military assumption made by men who are not soldiers on wrongly evaluated Intelligence by men who are not soldiers. The heart has utterly left those who have been representing the non-communist world and the communists have won...28 years of war have not been enough for the non-communists to win and the past 15 years of US $315 million annually have resulted only in B-52 bomb craters and massive corruption. Harsh words...and the disadvantage of all generalisations doesn't devalue my observation by much. As you know, my life has been spent combating communism, in one form or another...at our [weekly] conference today to hear both UK and Australian ambassadors laugh at the difficulties now facing the Americans, and to hear them say that, although Souvanna Phouma had lost, the communists would behave themselves and not profit from their victory, chilled my blood. Those men, the men on the spot, advise their governments and unquestionably their advice is accepted. No wonder some of the things we, the British, do are as absurd and incomprehensible as they are.

That week's total of deaths was more than for the whole of 1970: 'call me field marshal', I thought grimly. In the short time between the two cease-fires, the USAF laid a curtain of steel, dropping, so it was alleged, more bombs than the total dropped during the whole of the Second World War.

The cease-fire in Laos came into effect at midday on 23 February and within fifteen minutes massive NVA attacks gained significant advances in many places, now that US air power was no longer a factor in the military equation. Although we knew that, basically, USSR and China backed the NVA and PL logistically as well as politically, any details that were forthcoming were always at second- or third-hand, fudged and unable to be verified. For me, therefore, they had an insubstantial and remote character, lacking substance. This feeling was also reflected whenever I talked to the communists. In another letter home I wrote:

It really is incredible what being a communist means. Anything that smacks of the Party Line has the same effect on them all: the shutters come down behind their eyes and the light is dimmed. Hackneyed phrase follows hackneyed phrase: blatant untruths are stuck to with limpet-like tenacity and direct question is brushed aside or ignored without any embarrassment.

I went around to the Chinese embassy of Friday (23rd) morning to fix up a Chinese dinner party. It was fascinating to watch the shutters lifted when a normal topic was broached. I was asked by the Chinese if I had read the Cease-Fire agreement and I shocked them when I said no, it was only politics and I was a soldier, not a politician! I told them the Leftists had, in my opinion, won and the Rightists had lost. How did I know that and why did I say so? My reply was that certain of my embassy had met Leftists who were smiling and others had met Rightists who were not smiling. He who wins smiles, he who loses doesn't. All the trouble in SE Asia, I was told, was because of the Americans. I countered this and said no. I was asked how could I say that and, if not the Americans, then who? So I said the French were and I was acknowledged correct up to 1954. It was all rendered less crisp than it might have been not only because my French is not as good as my English, but also that the interpreter wasn't translating accurately all the time. I know that as a number of little asides between them occurred now and then. However, I had not gone there to indulge in petty polemics but to invite the blighter to dinner.

We went into a list of countries, the representatives of whom would or would not be acceptable to him. Any country with diplomatic relations was the answer. How about Russia was my query. Down went the shutters. We have diplomatic relations with the Soviet Union, you may ask them if you like and we would attend. But surely there are some you'd like better than others? I asked. The answer was text-book! OK, I won't ask the Russians as it would be difficult and would restrict conversation. Up went the shutters,

'D'accord?' We then went into the menu: great interest shown at the one I had with me, written in Chinese. I said I would only ask 8, 12 or 14 guests, not 10 as the Chinese considered 10 unlucky. What nonsense: we Chinese are not superstitious. I was then gently upbraided for having, at a previous meeting told their DA that I believed certain Chinese characters had significances. You don't read Chinese: you have been told wrongly. You have been told wrongly about the North Vietnamese Army being in Laos, you have been told wrongly about the Chinese road in Laos, you have been told wrongly that a God exists (recapitulating odds and ends of previous conversations!). You have been wrongly told...and it all reminded me of my long and circuitous conversations with the [Malayan] aborigines. I only had an hour and 20 minutes of it ...All this is a far, far cry from yesteryear when a man with a red star on his uniform was a scrawny bandit in the Malayan jungle...

Despite all that, after seventy-nine days in post I found the chemistry of being an attaché had started to work and I was tapping sources that my predecessor never got near. The acorn had started to sprout.

She was sitting in the foyer of the embassy as I walked through to go to my office, a young Lao woman. She looked up at me and smiled. The doorkeeper told me in an aside that she had come to see me. As I went over to her, she stood up and demurely made the *wai* salutation, hands joined together in front of her, head bent slightly forward. Then, unusually for a Lao woman, she confidently opened the conversation in French.

"Excuse me for inconveniencing you, *Monsieur*, but may we have a talk?"
"Certainly, *Mam'selle*. At your convenience. Please be seated. I can spare you some time here and now."

She was dressed traditionally in blouse and skirt, with nothing on her head, wore no stockings and had on black, open shoes. The inevitable silver belt was around her waist. Her hair was tied up in a bun on the right of her head, signifying unwed status. She was not very tall and had delicate features, high cheekbones but, whilst attractive, was in no way pretty. She sat, clutching her black handbag, knees and feet tightly joined, feet flat on the floor. (I irreverently felt that she had a good landing position for a parachutist.) She cleared her throat.

"I come to hear that you need a teacher of Lao and so I have called in to see what we can arrange."

Suspicious, wary, worried and groping, I looked back on the few weeks that I had been in the country and, while I could not remember all that I had said, I knew what I had not. Apart from my acquaintance with Princess Jasmine, I'd never hinted to anyone that I wanted a teacher. I was learning Lao and revising Thai, Vietnamese, Cantonese and French. I had my own books, tapes and memory cards and I worked hard in my own time, four hours and day during the week and twelve hours on high days and holidays. My mind raced with intriguing possibilities and I stalled for time. I remember our conversation because I rehearsed it afterwards.

"Do you speak Lao with a northern accent?"
"*Non Monsieur*, but I completely understand it. Further I speak Thai and Viet."

Her use of only part of the word 'Vietnamese' to describe the language was not lost on me – a direct translation of what the Vietnamese people use to describe their own language.

"What dialect of those two languages do you speak? For my part I speak Bangkok Thai and Hanoi Vietnamese."

"I am the same, *Monsieur*. I speak Thai Issan, the Thai of northeast Thailand, and Saigon Vietnamese." She used the whole word the second time.

"I'd only get muddled, *Mam'selle*. It wouldn't be worth my while to have you as a language teacher."

I stood up but she remained seated. Was it a sleeping dictionary that she wanted to be? Generally, Asian women are much more decorous than their western sisters, certainly in public, so it was only when they flaunted themselves at a person were they libertine or acting a part. For sure, most single foreigners had their 'keep' and many single Lao women saw this as both natural and rewarding. However, in my case, I steered away from such liaisons as any ephemeral pleasure gained from them would, I was sure, invalidate any long-term benefits. I told her that before I decided one way or the other I needed to know more about her. Please would she tell me her name, who she was and her terms.

She was Mlle Kaysorn Bouapha. She lived in a house on the Avenue Circulaire and worked in the French Cultural Centre at the end of Rue Pong Kham. She had spent some of her early life in Saigon when her father, an advocate, was working there during French colonial days. As regards place and times of tuition, it would be done in my villa after work, from 5 to 6 o'clock each evening. We could practise Lao on two days, Thai on two days and, if I were willing to work on Saturdays, Vietnamese on two days. As for price, she would expect US$5 for each period.

I considered what she said before replying. She was so decisive in her manner that she might almost have been primed and if that was so, I felt I needed to know who had primed her, and why. Even if, which I doubted, I was wrong in my diagnosis, she might have some limited linguistic uses.

I had to get used to the various dialects so I decided to try it for a couple of weeks. It could not be every day as I would be travelling sometimes and have to attend some *soirées*. The penetrating look in her eyes as she came to thank me and bid me farewell warned me that something did not ring true. Having seen her off the premises, I went to make arrangements to have her traced.

Lessons started on the morrow. I had returned from a session with Brigadier Bakhshi about ICSC plans to patrol the disputed areas after a cease-fire, showered and clad only in a shirt with a sarong round my waist, sat in my upstairs study. There would be enough time to slip a pair of trousers on when the front door bell rang. I had decided that informality was required so, instead of having lessons downstairs, I would invite Mlle Kaysorn upstairs to where I had made a mini-language laboratory. Besides which, it was cooler and lighter to work in than downstairs and I could get advanced warning of visitors.

I was startled, therefore, when the first I knew of my teacher's arrival was when she came up the stairs, silently and unannounced. My room was walled only on three sides, the open side leading onto a passage off which were three bedrooms, a boxroom and a bathroom with a sitting bath in it. I had no choice but to rise dressed as I was. "Sit down" she commanded abruptly before going into every room on a tour of discovery. I waited for her to finish, nonplussed by the unexpected turn of events – at least I was ready.

Her inspection over, she came and joined me on the settee. Gone was the demureness shown in the embassy foyer. She sat down so close that we were touching all the way down, buttocks included. She looked at me, then at my feet (I was wearing thongs) and remarked that I needed my toenails cutting and if I would tell her where the scissors were, she would get them and cut my nails. There was an air of unreality about the situation. I declined her offer. She got up and went over to my desk and bookcase. She inspected my invitation cards. She looked at my books, my tape-recorder and my several language tapes. Having satisfied her curiosity she came and nestled up to me again.

I had three ways to play her: I could be formal ("Excuse me, but do you realise that we are so close together that even a piece of paper wouldn't go between us?" would sound pompous even if I wanted to say that); I could be very informal, lean over and squeeze her; I could leave the initiative to her. She took it by saying, yes, all was very nice, she approved and that we would now start our lesson.

She was an engaging and energetic teacher who knew her subject matter well. Her approach was serious as regards study but kittenish towards me. She had no sex appeal but, at first blush, few inhibitions either. I was amused yet concerned. Chok Di, shutting the door as she left the house, was grumpy at her having got into the house without his knowledge. His professional dignity had been damaged. He was also suspicious of her.

Meanwhile, I was resolutely barred from visiting anywhere sensitive and so the only military units in the provinces that I could visit were low-grade Lao ones, battalions called by their French names *Irreguliérs*, *Commando* and *Volontiers* that were kept well away from the fighting, as were the Home Guard, or *Force de Choque*. Most had to be reached by air. Some had landing strips of their own, others did not so the nearest flat ground had to do instead. One such was the village of Ban Nam Kheun, very near the remnants of the Chinese National (Kuomintang – KMT) Army, the, who had been there since 1949 and had long since only been interested in smuggling opium between Laos, Thailand and Burma – the Golden Triangle. Horses and children wandered around the only flat place near the village and had to be 'buzzed' once or twice to clear a space for the aircraft. The locals were Yao, who have their own language and script, as well as an exotic brew that was said to be made from the whiskers and powdered knee caps of tigers.

The soldiers of all these units, some in their early teens and others well into their forties, were apathetic, lacklustre and bored, with ancient equipment, poor pay (by then the equivalent of £3.50 a month) and uninterested officers. Dishevelled and dowdy, their sentries reminded me of so many 'blank files on leave'. I was told that even those units in contact with the enemy and wanting help from the Americans (air strikes, ammunition, rations, etc) seemed incapable of giving any details, even of where they or their enemy were. When pressed for details they would say, with a shrug of their shoulders, that they were not bothered by it. Why asked why, they passed it off as something they had learnt from the French. Broadus Bailey, responsible for organising their needs, bemoaned his difficulties and said to me, "John, I was fit to be tied!" And yet, by the time I was close to one unit I had asked to visit, it was in a battle but the commanding general flew from his HQ in the field, dressed in a flak jacket, just to give me a briefing. He gave me five minutes of his time and hurried off back to his battle.

This US assistance did not always come in for a good or fair press; the resumption of bombing at the end of December was denounced in no uncertain terms. However, when three hospitals in Laos, established by the Americans, were destroyed by the NVA and their staff killed, no condemnation was forthcoming. Photographs of the shattered buildings and other gruesome scenes were shown to the American press whose only answer quoted to me was; "OK, good photos, but we can't use them as we know our editors wouldn't publish them."

I was cagey of the press. An Englishman called Simms, working for *Time* magazine, visited me and, playing it cool, I said I did not know anything (which in one respect was true) in answer to a question of his. "Then you are bugger all good at your job," was his unflattering comment, to which I agreed whole-heartedly and disarmingly. He had the grace to look abashed and said that a senior (and of course unnamed) American with whom he had had lunch had mentioned my name as being a fellow who could tell him things. Another pressman started off by saying that he had heard I had 'little time for American or Lao intelligence' but I refused to be drawn.

I had learnt when working with the aborigines in Malaya and the Natives of Borneo that the way to adult acceptance was twofold; by language and making the children laugh. Now, in my spare time, I would take my dog on long walks when I found solitude in the quiet of the countryside. Carrying my language cards I set myself targets of words to be learnt. When I met the children I wobbled my knees and eyebrows and made mice squeak in their heads, and delighted them when I whistled, in a flute-like yodel, to my dog Singha. The children tried to imitate this, calling shrilly, 'looly, looly, looly', and *Papa Looly* soon became my nickname. This cry greeted me as I walked back that afternoon the children keeping pace with me until they had reached the limits of their 'beat'. As soon as the grown-ups knew that I was English, not French or American, they allowed me to practise my Lao on them, ever ready to correct my mistakes. To them I was neither influential nor important but I always had a friendly reaction.

The trace of Mlle Kaysorn Bouapha arrived, terse and to the point. 'One woman of that name was educated in the Patrice Lumumba university in Moscow. Collateral evidence is being sought. Meanwhile you are requested to try and find out who is running her. You are advised to remember one of the characteristics of a sleeping dictionary – it always opens at the same place.'

I was brought up to believe that a clear conscience was essential for peace of mind and that was my comfort now. I had been told by one of the English girls in the embassy that I was feared for my 'remoteness, ascetic qualities and cleverness'. I knew that my learning Lao, unusual abstinence (the three attaché 'B's – brothels, bars and boys – did not tempt me. However, one Australian told me he always told his whore he was English) and bachelorhood made me a conjecture to both right and left. I am no prude but I have an aversion to 'dirtying my own doorstep'. There were at least two areas where Lao agents worked for the North Vietnamese; the telephone exchange operators in the US and Australian embassies, and the brothels. (Interestingly enough, the only time I heard gossip, was when my mother joined me for my second Christmas and that was always from the wives.)

I knew my habits were unusual enough for me not to be fully understood by many but I believed I was respected. I had done nothing wrong so that it was not for what I had done that I was being targeted but to make me do something that otherwise I might not be willing to do.

It was only reasonable to suppose that my teacher had reported back to her controller. It was also reasonable to suppose that, like many Asian girls not used to associating with Europeans, she had mistaken polite bonhomie for subdued passion and she had been told to turn up the heat. Even before I had heard the result of the trace, I had not altered my approach to her during our lessons yet had noticed her more forceful techniques. For instance, one Saturday she turned up with a local delicacy, Vietnamese spring rolls, which she proceeded to dip in some sauce she had also brought, and tried to feed me as though I were a baby. I allowed her one attempt, in that I had been too surprised to stop her, before I prevented her from another shot. I gave her some red wine and she drank too much and nearly fell asleep at the table. Another time she brought me a pair of ludicrous, maroon-coloured, Thai pyjama trousers which I refrained from trying on there and then. She was so unlike any Asian woman I had previously heard about or come across – not that there had ever been similar circumstances – she *had* to be acting.

Even without these drawbacks I had decided only to keep her on for a limited time but I had been asked to find out, if I could, who was running her. I was torn between anger at being used and disgust that the girl was being run by the left wing. I did not particularly relish my rôle but had agreed to co-operate. The very same evening as I was told about her background I had a lesson. Whatever else might ensure I had to play my part and she was an insistent teacher.

I smiled at her insouciantly and bade her sit down. I tried an innocent-sounding approach. It was not long after the New Year. "I never asked you if you celebrated Christmas or do you feel that *Boun* [festival] *Noën* is no longer apt?" (Noën, not Noël, as the Lao were unable to pronounce final 'l's and 's's – or 'r's anywhere for that matter. I was Colonen Clod!) There was no hint of Moscow-inspired aversion to it, in fact the reverse. A radiant smile lit up her plain face making it almost attractive.

On no, oh no! In fact she had brought me a late present. She opened her handbag and took out a small book wrapped in gaudy paper, which she handed over to me. My heart sank as I had nothing to offer her in return and being the recipient of presents embarrasses me. I was embarrassed even more when I saw what it was – an RLA manual on counter-subversion with the security caveat *lab*, secret.

It was known I was a keen linguist and I knew that bachelor linguists were at high risk in the security stakes. I therefore presumed that her controller had thought I would commit myself linguistically as I had not done so sexually. I felt my face muscles tightening as I gave her back the book, unopened and re-wrapped.

I thanked her for thinking that I could improve my military vocabulary by bringing this to me but I had to return it. I told her I was not entitled to such a publication, only the RLA was. If they were to give it to me, in my office or in theirs, it would be perfectly in order. To take this type of material from anyone who was not entitled to it was a breach of trust, was against my charter, incriminated me and made me into an intelligence agent, if not a spy. My eyes bored into hers, making her drop her gaze in feminine confusion, as I told her to tell those who had given it to her to give me what I was saying.

She was sorry. She didn't know. Was I sure I wouldn't change my mind? She couldn't believe there was any harm in the book. She was sure I knew the material in the book already and it would be a great aid to my military vocabulary, she retorted, smiling winsomely at me. We got on with the lesson and I invited her to talk about what and where she had studied but however hard I tried to bring the conversation round I could get no indication of her having been farther afield than Bangkok and Saigon.

It was dark by the time we finished and I was so angry by then that I was determined to do some acting of my own. I took her into my bedroom and, having undressed her, laid her on the bed. Let's see who the better actor is this time, I thought savagely, determined to take her as near the point of no return as I could. But she was cold and frightened, so I let her dress and wash her face. She was a rotten actress.

When the Soviet attaché paid his return visit I found him bland. If I had thought I would get any clue about my language teacher I was disappointed. We talked about Russian literature (he had read Bernard Shaw) and he pointed out that a Christmas card of snowy Scotland I had in my office was like his Pamirs and Urals. If I took the conversation close to 'politics' his eyes, open and clear before, became blank and utterly unresponsive. I quoted Mao Tse-tung's dictum of 'politics is war minus bloodshed and war is politics plus bloodshed' and said that the breakdown of the peace talks in December was the end of a scene; the signing of the peace agreement would be the end of the act, but the play would never end. He agreed with me decisively and also predicted further fighting after any agreement had been signed in Vietnam and Laos. Coming from him I did not doubt it.

After the cease-fire I was accepted by the Americans at the same level as my security clearance warranted and not treated like a pariah, which was most satisfactory. Sadly, it was not all that long before US sources dried up and then trying to read the military situation in the country was difficult. Cam West and I both got hold of snippets and we thrashed them out, mulling over them and trying to make sense of them.

Not quite so momentous as being accepted by the Americans but equally satisfactory, I found out why I could never telephone anybody from my house: the dial had been set in such a way that it activated the wrong numbers. Subtract one and the system worked for all digits less the smallest – one! Clichés of sublime and ridiculous crossed my mind.

The Americans took me to Udorn to show me their 'casualty resolution', how to recognise a cadaver. I was startled to hear the camp radio blaring out periodic warnings to men about to go back to USA at the end of their draft service: "You caan't haave de-marb with a blarb on your narb," a message of degrading unsubtlety. I hoped that those Thais who had some command of English might misunderstand the accent and take the message as an esoteric US Air Force war cry of encouragement.

The party for the communists passed off successfully, especially as the Chinese were not superstitious at seating ten at table. Lloyd was there as a friend, not in his representational capacity. He was embarrassingly glowing about me in a speech he made: I made Asian friends, had a deep knowledge, spoke many languages, had a great future and I don't know what else. Even though he was a declared atheist, he had several Christian virtues mixed up with his unchristian beliefs. Anyway, with that and the American clearance, I walked on two inches of air. In a letter home I wrote...*Let us hope it will not be a case of the higher they go the harder they fall: I don't think so.* One of the LPF delegates told Lloyd that he was the only non-communist European they could trust and who could comfort them. At least the speaker was a declared communist as opposed to an undeclared fellow traveller.

Simon Hutchinson, my desk officer in the MOD, paid me a visit. We had known each other since we were both policemen in Borneo during Indonesian 'Confrontation' and liked each other. Simon, badly wounded in the Malayan 'Emergency', had a dry sense of humour and a high sense of duty. I laid on a programme for him that took him to places that had been forbidden to the British before. One Irregular commander paid me a pretty compliment by saying that Laos would have been a different place if it had had my service all along. At my parties Simon met in person many folk who, till that time, had been but names on paper. As usual I found myself the butt of heavy-handed wit at my abstemious habits and my single status. As one of the Americans so delicately put it; "What is life without drinking, smoking and poking?" or, in mixed company, "No vices, eh?", which I took in good part and smilingly replied that the absence of vices did not necessarily bespeak the presence of any virtue.

I thought I would be unable to see Simon off at the airport as I had an invitation from the Prime Minister to a *Pique-Nique* on the bank of the Mekong. I told Simon I'd call it off and he thought that would be wrong and tantamount to refusing a sail in Ted Heath's yacht. The refrain *A picnic with Souvanna Phouma* ran through my head like a nonsense jiggle! But that, Simon's understanding of the situation and John Lloyd's comments showed that the acorn had indeed started to sprout.

Violations of the cease-fire accords by both sides, but chiefly by the communists, were on the increase. At times the fighting was intense and there were many casualties. Sensitive areas were not confined to the demarcation between the two zones of influence. The few RLG enclaves in communist territory were equally prone to being attacked. One such was Bouam Long, where I visited on 20 March. Very few foreigners had ever been there.

It was difficult to get to being 4,000 feet up in the mountains. There was a small landing strip of red gravel but turbulence and uncertain weather made its use tricky. It had an appearance and character all of its own. It was a series of Meo villages joined into one fortified base and garrisoned by Irregular troops. The shacks where the villagers lived and the military buildings were indistinguishable from the outside. Each house was littered with the discarded paraphernalia of military occupation; jerry cans, sacking, cardboard boxes, strips of parachute cloth and tins flattened to make roofing. Next to each house was a patch of growing poppies to provide the opium without which the Meo seemed incapable of living. Whether the shacks were soldiers' quarters or not was immaterial; women, children, pigs, chickens, curs and men all carried out their various duties and functions with the age-old rhythm of a tightly-knit community. The men: were they husbands or soldiers or both? The womenfolk: were they wives at home or camp followers in an army that remained static? All was a jumble that defied normal criteria. Surrounding the enclave were thick strands of wire and a series of observation posts and defensive positions. Gruesome relics of the last determined NVA attack still draped the wire in some places; skeletons, tattered bits of clothing and old pieces of equipment, all an awesome travesty of the garden scarecrow. Beyond the wire, outside the enclave but reaching almost up to the rim of the defensive position, were countless large bomb craters that bore mute, sombre and stark testimony to the efficiency of aerial power used with pin-point precision. No troops in the world could stand firm against such an onslaught and peasants of Uncle Ho's army were no exception.

Around the centrally-situated airstrip the ground rose steeply. Dug deep inside one of the hills was the HQ of the military units commanding the enclave, where we were given a slick and detailed briefing. It was a far cry from those offered by bored unit commanders far from the fighting that had been my bland and tame staple hitherto. The strange, stupid and savage war that had engulfed such a beautiful place with such nice people seemed more senseless than ever – and the communists who could not leave anyone with their own ideas in peace seldom seemed so evil. I returned to the vapidness of Vientiane in sombre mood.

To maintain the balance, I needed to throw another party, this time for the right wing. I wanted to invite Princess Jasmine and, when I put it to her, she suggested that I invite the Minister of Defence. Rather than ask him 'cold' I fixed up a meeting, having first asked John Lloyd if one so humble as a DA should go and see him. "I wouldn't bother with him, he's mad and a hawk," was the uncompromising answer, but I could go if I felt I had to.

I fixed up a meeting which was not easy: the Minister looked after Finance in the morning and Defence in the afternoon. It was a morning visit so Khien drove me to the Ministry of Finance. It was a mistake as the Minister had gone to the other ministry, especially to meet me. I was late as a consequence. His office was separated from Jubilation's by a room occupied by the secretaries of both men. I was shown in, saluted him and apologised for being late.

Prince Sisouk na Champassak was a tall, well-built, good-looking man in his early forties who had married a French woman and was the father of two of the most beautiful girls imaginable and one boy. He had held diplomatic posts in India and the United Nations, and was fluent in English and French. He got out of his chair, came round from behind his large desk, offered me his hand and bade me be seated in of the two comfortable chairs by the far wall. He sat opposite me, looked me straight between the eyes and said; "Welcome. Your Ambassador is mad, a pacifist and no good for Laos." It was a tricky situation. To agree with him about my own Ambassador's state of mental health and politics would have been consummately disloyal. To have said 'no' would have been a partial untruth, so both 'yes' and 'no' were out. What price being a diplomatic soldier? "Thank you, Your Excellency, for saying that. There is now no need to mention it again." I hoped that I, personally, was unscathed and uncontaminated.

He asked me about my service in Asia and I told him enough to get him interested in me. We talked about the continuing military violence and Sisouk railed against the iniquities of the NVA's presence and their virtual colonisation of eastern Laos. He asked me if I knew the Laotian saying: *The day a Lao is born is the day he starts to hate the Vietnamese.* I did not. Where had I been and whom had I met. I told him in outline but he did not seem satisfied.

"Have you been to PS 18?"
'No sir."
"Have you been to Whisky 3?"
"No sir."
"Why not?"
"Because this is the first time I have heard of them. I don't know where or what they are."

He grunted something about being early days yet but that he was surprised. He told me that Jasmine had told him I was going to ask him to dinner and that he would accept. "Thank you for coming to see me. I don't suppose it's the last time we'll meet. I'll have to choose my moment..." and his voice trailed off as though he were talking to himself. He held out his hand as a sign of dismissal. I shook it, saluted and left him. I smiled at the two secretaries in the outer office and made my way downstairs to the car that was waiting for me under the portico. At least my invitation had been accepted. Sisouk was interested in me and I had neither been snubbed nor branded as an English dove – maybe that in itself was enough for one day.

April came to Vientiane, hot and dusty. The time set by the cease-fire accords for the formation of the Provisional Government of National Union (PGNU) passed like a damp squib. I continued with my language study and walking with the dog. I found the local cold storage sold dog biscuits. It was prophesied that the Khmer Republic would fall three weeks after Saigon and Laos shortly after that. The Prime Minister snubbed the Soviets. The Swiss gave two tons of fondue cheese to the refugees who threw it away as 'the soap didn't lather'.

The report by Simon Hutchinson on his visit reached me and fully vindicated the method I had tackled the messy, unpalatable and sensitive situation I had found on my arrival and was still with me. With neither of the Lloyds keeping their mouths shut, he blurting out secrets to journalists and at cocktail parties, to say nothing of both being anti-American in front of Americans, my official life was a misery but that had found no echo in my official reports. The fact that Donald seemed to have offended most of the attaché corps was never fully expressed but Simon was no fool and his report was a model of glowing delicacy, understandable by those who knew how to read his words and bland to those who did not.

I also had a letter from MOD UK by the same bag which gave me considerable peace of mind, something I had not had on the work side for several months. In brief, my unhappy position was now understood far better than ever before. London valued my reports (and my very being there) and wished they could help – but they couldn't. I knew they couldn't help the situation my end, which was only due to last another month or so anyway but, paradoxically, by their realising they couldn't help me, they did help me because all the reports I had written, all the activities I had undertaken and what little petty successes I had chalked up were now seen in a far more realistic light because they now realised just how hard it had been. I slept more soundly that night than for a long time.

Before that letter the fight had gone out of me work-wise and there was no spunk left in me. I had the vision of cities all over the world having attachés scurrying around, all pretending to be busy, all eating far too much and most drinking far too much, and to what avail? It was a gloomy thought and I mentioned it to Cam whose sensible answer was that we would always try our best in any job we did – which, of course, was very true.

I held my right-wing party and, at the end of the meal, I stood and welcomed my Lao guests – two princes, two princesses and two commoners – with all their tongue-twisting titles and names. I hoped that, in the future, we would see a growing trust, liking and friendship in Lao and British and, for the benefit of my other guests, Australian relations. I translated it into English and we then drank a toast. Nothing contentious was said and I adjudged the evening a success.

New Year's Day, *pi mai*, 2516 (Buddhist Era), the Year of the Buffalo, fell on 13 April and I flew to Luang Prabang with some of the embassy staff observe it. It was a day all Buddhists had been looking forward to, when all would enjoy themselves in a prolonged *boun*.

From early morning there was excitement in the town. It was hot before the mist had cleared and when it did the heat would hover around 40° Celsius. T-28 fighter-bombers would take off on their routine missions to warn the ground forces of any communist advances from their positions in the hills a few miles to the northeast. In previous years there had been shelling and mortar attacks during such holidays, with the communists patrolling even as far as the King's orange groves to the southeast of the town. Nobody wanted this *boun* spoiled.

Before dawn His Majesty the King had gone to worship at the royal *wat*, surrounded by elderly, saffron-robed, shaven-pated bonzes, who in turn were flanked by similarly clad and shorn acolytes. Here the prayers had been for a speedy end to the 28-year-long war which had split the country so tragically in two, the kingdom reunited, a return to their homes for the refugees and to their families for the many men under arms with, finally, in confirmation that Laos was an independent, sovereign state, the coronation of His Majesty, King Savang Vatthana.

The late king's sovereign power, the last gift of the defeated Japanese at the end of the war in 1945, had been revoked by the returning French soon after. At all previous new year celebrations since the late king's death fourteen years before, the scriptures had been read and the divinations foretold by the abbot, now stiff-backed and a little hard of hearing, but renowned for his knowledge of the omens.

King Savang Vatthana had yet to be crowned because it was well known that *the king who is crowned when the wild buffaloes are trampling the grasses of Laos will be the last crowned ruler of Laos.* Now that the cease-fire had been signed, would 2516 BE see him crowned and unite Laos against the communists? Certainly there was a day for it already printed in the Government calendar for the coming year and the LPF had never publicly come out against it.

After the reading of the scriptures the King had offered fruit and sticky rice to the senior bonzes and then walked back to his palace while outside, in the town, spectators gathered for the procession of virgins, hoping to catch more than a passing glance of them.

Despite the unsettled conditions there were tourists in plenty. Small boys caused havoc as they squirted and sloshed water mixed with some tiny sticky seeds over everybody and those girls who, for one reason or another, did not qualify for a place in the virgins' procession, caused more havoc by coming up behind unsuspecting folk and tearing their clothes off their backs.

The procession itself started off as numerous individual trickles of virgins, bonzes, musicians and jokers from the many *wats* scattered around the town. In front of each were eight pretty girls walking in front of a ninth, and prettiest, who sat on a model buffalo carried by four stalwart youths with glistening, rippling torsos, with larger models draped round a motorcar. Behind the girl on the buffalo came the virgins, six abreast and maybe four or five rows deep. The heat, the noise, the excitement, the water, all seemed to have no effect on them as they walked demurely along with heads held high, tantalisingly nubile. Their long, jet-black hair, in a bun on the right of their head, signified virginity, and a thin gold chain and a comb kept the shiny tresses in place. They wore silk blouses of peacock blue, emerald green and damson red, their trim little figures scarcely discernible. A silver belt around their waist held up their skirt, more subdued in colour than the louder tones of the blouses, each with a strip of brightly coloured, intricately designed needlework round the hem. Bare-legged, they wore sandals with low heels. Their oval faces had high cheekbones; all noses deliciously and delicately snub. Their brown eyes gazed with unfocussed indifference, almost disdain, as they passed through the ever-thickening crowds of spectators with their raucous applause and ribald comments.

Behind the virgins came the bonzes, their saffron robes girdled and folded over their left shoulders, their shaven heads darkly stubbled. In their midst, carried aloft under a large orange umbrella, came the head monk of each *wat*. Behind them came the musicians, who played flutes, drums and giant xylophones carried on poles.

In the rear came the jokers, some stripped to the waist covered in yellow dust, others with soot-covered faces, dressed any old how. They sang and danced, twirled and pirouetted, veered, jinked and shuffled their way along, throwing water over the crowd who joyously responded in kind. As the last of the jokers passed some of the crowd joined them, while others waited for another procession to pass, replenishing the water supply for their own and the jokers' buckets.

A wide avenue runs all round the Phou Si hill and on one side a steep path from the *wat* at the top joins it in front of the King's palace. The royal *wat* that the King visited earlier on was the destination of all the little processions which were so routed that the trickle became a stream, then a torrent and finally a flood of moving, pulsating, tramping, dancing, singing, banging, happy, torn, wet people with their own quiet patches of virgins and bonzes making the rest of the commotion more concentrated.

They squeezed into the courtyard of the royal *wat*, the earlier ones being forced toward the walls, where there were intricately carved fabulous beasts, gold-leafed pillars and large bells, a wonderful riot of bright colours. Finally there was no more room nor anybody else to come and gradually silence fell, with even the jokers restrained.

From inside the *wat* the hushed crowd heard the quavering and plaintive threnody of prayer. It became subdued then ceased and pent-up emotion welled out with a long audible sigh and excitedly people spoke among themselves before drifting away.

By early afternoon all was quiet again and the crowds of the morning had dispersed. It was strikingly hot and humid, with a few low clouds. The rains proper were still some weeks away. The ground was parched and very dusty.

Suddenly, at about half past 4, there was a sharp roll of thunder and a short but violent dust storm. As it died away there was a single rifle shot, then another and a third. Peter Shield immediately told the embassy families to stay indoors and he saw a man come a window across the road and fire his weapon into the air. Within a few minutes the noise of rifles and machine-guns firing was heard all over the town. Traffic and pedestrians vanished and the army appeared at street corners in the town and on the outskirts. An officer, talking into a radio, passed by with a platoon of soldiers. Tension mounted while, in their hotel rooms, little groups of diplomats counselled among themselves, feeling a tinge of induced heroism, in all likelihood composing telegrams for their ministries at home. The firing died away and life slowly returned to normal. We learnt that it had been in aid of scaring away the wind devils to prevent rain that would have spoiled the rest of the day.

By 7 o'clock, dressed in ceremonial uniform, members of the government, local dignitaries, senior members of the army and the foreign diplomatic community started to arrive at the palace for the culminating ceremonies, when they would be presented to Their Majesties before a procession of lights from the Phou Si *wat* at the top of the sacred hill, a long drawn-out presentation of Laotian classical dancing, based on the ancient Hindu classic of the *Ramayanas*, and a buffet.

On foot or by car they converged on the gates of the palace. There those in cars got out and joined those on foot, leaving the police to sort out the traffic chaos. They passed the young sentries of the King's bodyguard, dressed in red trousers and white jackets, and armed with long, old-fashioned rifles nearly as tall as themselves, and went through the gates into the ornate palace grounds. Members of the Protocol Department guided them to their rightful places; only those privileged few to be presented to the King and Queen went to the palace itself. The majority of guests had to go to one side where there were chairs and tables set out in the open ready for the night's entertainment.

Once at the palace the diplomats were confined to the verandah that flanked the large reception room. There they moved around slowly with the polished and insincere shallowness of their profession. Accompanied by their womenfolk they smiled, bobbed, bowed, shook hands and passed empty pleasantries or veiled and cryptic comments – ambassador to ambassador, first secretary to first secretary and attaché to attaché. I noticed the pointed ignoring of Russian and Chinese, the hauteur of the French, the cockiness of the Australians, the brashness of some Americans and the diffidence of the British. (I was still easily, but inwardly, irritated at so seldom being taken for an Englishman, always American or French – neither the flavour of any month. Overseas French were condescending and haughty – though for the life of me I have never learnt why as there was no comparison with the standard the British had left even impoverished India, to say nothing of rich Malaysia, with what the French had done in Laos.

The French lagged miles behind – and too many ugly Americans had debased their image, thereby neither 'tribe' presenting themselves in a particularly good light.)

I asked General Kouprasith Abhay what he did when the firing opened and maybe was not sure what it was all about. He had done nothing at all as, being asleep, he had heard nothing. His wife had told him about it later. "She knows better than to wake me up just because firing is heard," he said, moving off to meet somebody else. The French DA who overheard that sniffed disparagingly. "I was a lieutenant in 1946 when we French came back to Indo-China after the war. Then the brave general was an idle sergeant. Still should be just that," he added disdainfully.

The guests were called in to the large audience chamber and formed up in protocol order of seniority, Lao guests on one side of the room and the foreigners on the other, to meet Their Majesties and the royal family. The French ambassador, having been longer in the country than any other head of mission, so the doyen of the diplomatic corps, was the first foreigner to meet the royal entourage as well as giving the loyal address. Next to the French representatives were the South Vietnamese. No North Vietnamese was present. In all, there were fourteen groups of diplomats, some of whom had come from as far away as Bangkok, as well as representatives of the UNO and the ICSC.

The curtains at the end of the room were drawn back and the royal party came in from the throne room opposite. King Savang, tall and dignified, wore a white coat with a white collar and, as usual, the red and yellow sash of the Order of the Million Elephants and the White Parasol, First Class. His lower limbs were encased in purple cloth that was wound around his body, drawn between his legs and tucked in at the back. His Queen wore the same type of dress as the virgins had earlier on the day but with colours more subdued. Behind them came the Crown Prince and Princess, the King's brother and wife (Golden Fairy and Jasmine's parents) then lesser luminaries. So commanding was the King's presence that he dwarfed them all.

At the King's approach the Lao made obeisance, the King touching some of them on the shoulder. The foreign males inclined their heads and the women made a curtsy as His Majesty passed them. No word was spoken. The royal group regained its place in front of the curtains.

The French ambassador took some notes out of his pocket, cleared his throat and, in a sonorous tone of voice, began to read them.

"Sire", with a sibilant gurgle, "it gives me great pleasure to have the honour and humble duty of offering to Your Majesties the sincere and loyal greetings of all my colleagues of the diplomatic corps, on behalf of our national governments, for a happy New Year..."
The polished and graceful phrases rolled on and on. The King nodded gravely from time to time, especially as the Frenchman came to the end of his speech with "...a return to homelands and of menfolk and a long, successful, prosperous reign of Your Majesty.

The French ambassador stepped back in to line, put away his notes, joined his hands together in front of his body and looked pleased with himself. Doubtless it would look fine in the despatch that he would be sending the Quay d'Orsai, even though he personally may not have believed much of what he said.

The King then made his address in faultless French. He looked around and started to speak.

"*Altesses, Excellences, Mesdames, Messieurs; la reine et moi...*" he continued, "thank you all for your presence here tonight and the loyal address of welcome and warm wishes for a happy New Year that you have extended to the Queen and me..."

As we were all streaming out after that a little Lao lady stopped me and asked, in Lao, if I was Colonel Cross? She was Golden Fairy's mother and knew I had had tuition from her daughter in London. "She taught you well, didn't she?" She asked maternal questions of solicitude, at the same time saying how nice it was for us to have met.

From the Phou Si hill temple opposite the palace came a beautiful procession of candle lights, maybe six hundred, all aflutter as their holders, small boys, negotiated the many steps downhill. In front was a dragon, borne on a stretcher, that opened and closed its mouth and turned its head most realistically. The line of twinkling specks reached the bottom of the hill, crossed the road and walked down the palace drive where, on arrival in front of His Majesty, all in the procession prostrated themselves. They got up and the dragon was put into a pool of water, as a fire precaution. Three hours of classical dancing followed, enacting scenes from the dawn of history: this time with Shiva, Vishnu and Garuda, and the buffalo with its escort of pretty girls.

At 11 o'clock we went upstairs where there was a sumptuous buffet. I introduced myself to Golden Fairy's father, this time talking in French as protocol dictated. I told him that I had urged his daughter to write to her parents but she said that she was too lazy to! The American ambassador requested royal permission to send his air attaché away to organise a B-52 strike on Tha Vieng, away to the southeast near the Plain of Jars. This was in response to an NVA attack on government positions there. I left shortly after midnight.

Sunday lunch on 22 April with the Indian ambassador and Mrs Rao was a pleasant and relaxed affair with only a few other guests. My host and hostess were as charming as all Indians can be when they stop trying to imitate Europeans. I withstood some good-natured teasing about my single status, had a nice meal and, in due course, walked back to my villa. The front door was open and there, on the floor and the chair in the hall, were two enormous temple rubbings of Angkor Wat. Who had brought them? I went upstairs to get out of my tidy clothes, passing Singha halfway up on the landing, lying grotesquely on his back. I heard the noise of the air conditioner in the main guest room. I presumed that Chok Di had left it on after cleaning up. I went to switch it off after I had had a shower and a change. I opened the door and stared in disbelief as I saw Mlle Kaysorn Bouapha lying in bed. I went quietly over to her and she pushed back the bedclothes to reveal her nakedness. She seemed bemused and drowsy, if not drugged.

Till then we had remained on no more than good terms. I had found nothing out about any communist leanings; I had been to her home and met her family. I had found out that she was the cousin of the staff officer, Colonel Hinphed, whom I had met in England and with whom I had kept a close relationship. I had asked her for a tape of Laotian songs and she had brought one. I had never asked her for anything like this.

Was it a trick? Was it blackmail? Did she think I would be unable to resist her? Then what? I decided to play safe. "What are you doing like this?" I asked, perhaps superfluously. She mumbled something about two presents, the temple rubbings and her. Her cheap shoes and clothes lay in a heap by the side of the bed. All the pent-up emotions and uncertainties of the past weeks throbbed in my veins and I looked at her hungrily for a long minute. My urgency did not, however, communicate itself to her; she seemed to wilt. Lust turned to anger, to disgust.

I left the room, got dressed for a walk – I had to think this one out – and called Chok Di, who seemed agitated. I told him in no uncertain terms to ensure that she left the house and was never to be allowed in again. I called Singha who, gladdened by the chance to go out, bounced up at me with joy.

My feet led me towards a rice swamp, wide and deep. I started to cross it, feet instantly filthy with black mud, bare legs scratched by coarse grass. But it would have been easy to have made her yours, you nearly did! Are you chicken? one part of me queried. Yes, I suppose I am. It's not so much that I've always been averse to dirtying my own doorstep, the other part of me answered, but it wouldn't have done you much good. Arguing with myself, I sent Singha on in front. Where he did not have to swim, I followed. When I saw the dog swimming, I tried another tack. Who was trying to make my life a misery? Was this a test and, if so, who would say whether I had passed or failed?

It was a situation that defied normal experience and I rebelled at being thought seducible. I believed there were those who would like to have a conduit through whom they could reach me. There were those – the KGB the most likely –who were paid to solve puzzles or even try a little recruitment. There were also those of the home team and host country. Was I an ally? Was I thought to lean the way my boss did? I knew I was a puzzle: I did not drink, so didn't talk in my cups, had no penchant for pederasty, was not engaged in black market activity nor illegal currency conversion – just the reverse in fact. I spoke a few Asian languages: I fitted no pattern that was a familiar one. Was it to that end I had been approached? My innate suspicion had warned me in good time. This was a strange game I played, even though I was only on the sidelines.

I continued across the swamp, trying to burn out my anger, returning a long way round back to the house and, as it was growing dusk, an anxious Chok Di met me at the gate. Dog and I were covered in glutinous, black mud. Chok hosed us both down. The woman had left.

"You cunt! You rude cunt! I'll never invite you to my house again. I'll invite the PL instead. They're the only ones with any manners." The shrill, nasal voice of the British Ambassador penetrated the large room where the Indian Ambassador was giving a farewell reception.

Everybody turned to see what was the cause of the outburst. Pale with indignation but saying nothing was Prince Sisouk who had just told Lloyd that he was unable to come to a dinner on the morrow as he had been called to an important meeting. He had probably learnt that the other guests included the Labour politicians Michael Foot and James Callaghan on their way to Hanoi.

(They were refused visas. At a small lunch party at the Lloyd's they had heard an American 'plane break the sound barrier. Once back in England both men said how dangerous it had been in Vientiane with PL artillery shelling them.)

Lloyd repeated himself loudly, pointing with outstretched finger at the outraged but silent Lao Minister, took a step backwards and lost his balance. He fell into the arms of the Soviet Ambassador who was in the act of making his farewell. There was an appalled hush, quickly followed by nervous talk to cover the embarrassment everybody must have felt. Barry Denny, the First Secretary, was on hand and took Lloyd's arm, guided him to his car and told the driver to take him home.

I had never heard such angry tirade at a civilised gathering and felt deflated, not only because of what had been a public humiliation of the British but also because I saw my carefully cultivated relationship with Sisouk as a dead letter. That, coupled with the affair with Kaysorn

71

of twelve days previously, made me wonder just how far I had got in the less than the half year I had been in the job. Sure London had said that nothing of substance was expected for the first six months but now it looked as though, starting afresh, it would take at least that time, if ever, to mend fences that had broken down. All the language study and the visits, the building up of contacts, were on no value if trust evaporated. How much, I wondered gloomily, would the night's incident set me back?

Three days after that a conference for the four Heads of British Missions in Indo-China took place in our embassy which Lloyd chaired. Present were the British Ambassadors from the Khmer Republic and South Vietnam and their military staff. Because Britain did not have diplomatic relations with North Vietnam our only representative in that country was John Stewart who was accredited to the Mayor of Hanoi. My task was to give a military briefing to start with then 'just be in attendance'. I listened in for the whole of the two days of discussions and was shocked at the low standard of the Ambassadors' ideas on the developing situation, their inability to be constructive and the poor quality of their verbal content. At times such as this my doubts and fears of those who advise the decision-makers came once more to the fore and our decline, muddled thinking, equivocation and, on occasions, duplicity, all fell into place. The tier above those at the conference could not have been in much of a different mould. The many social requirements, the parties, the politenesses, the charade of diplomatic living seemed to have sapped them of original thought, clear-cut ideas and intellectual vigour.

The evening before they left, a party, cocktails and small eats on the lawn of the Lloyd's residence, was held so that the three other Heads of Mission could meet local and foreign dignitaries. The LPF delegation in Vientiane were there, all four of them. The right wing was scantily represented. Standing by himself in the shadow of a tree where the lights hid his features, stood General Kouprasith Abhay.

As I glanced at him my progress with the army over the months flashed through my mind. Although my initial visits to military units had been vague and ephemeral in content, at least I had been expected and full courtesies had been observed. From that time on, however, it was as though the military did not want to know me when I visited the army in the field. Though I did not know enough to be able to say whether it was normal or not, I found it disturbing. After I had 'joined the club' the Americans had fixed up those visits that were of military significance, such as to Bouam Long.

I went up to the General and asked him if I could get him a drink. He looked at me, turned away from anyone who could see his lips as he spoke and said, very softly, "Colonen. *I* sent her. You have passed the test." A pause, then, "Yes, I will have a drink."

Momentarily stunned and scarcely able to make the mental switch so firmly had I been rooted in the idea of a Soviet ploy – but, after all, Kaysorn was Colonel Hinphed's cousin and the Colonel was the General's closest military adviser – I murmured my thanks, mind still reeling, and called over a barman. I did not say anything ever again on that subject and, from that time on, visits were always granted speedily, were always known of well in advance and became more and more intriguing.

Not even the degrading rudeness of Lloyd's turning away from the General each time he tried to make his farewell and facing the four LPF leaders who had gathered around him (and who were as embarrassed as all of us who saw this) militated against me – unlike the case of Lloyd's crass insults and public humiliation of Prince Sisouk. Even without this example of atrocious British behaviour, it was not surprising that the royalists had had to make sure of me.

Plate 1. The *Yamagishi Butai* surrendering to British Forces (1/1 KGV's Own Gurkha Rifles, 100 Indian Infantry Brigade, 20 Indian Infantry Division) in the French Barracks at Thu Dau Mot, Cochin-China, in November 1945.

Plate 2. The author inspecting an 'Honor Guard' of the Royal Lao Army at secret guerilla camp PS 18.

Plate 3. By the side of the Mekong River in an armoured boat of the River Flotilla.

Plate 4. Headquarters, River Flotilla, Luang Prabang.

Plate 5, Whisky 3. Inside a guerilla camp

Plate 6. Brigadier General Soutchai's own force at Pakse, MR 4.

Plate 7. Welcome at Vang Vieng, Neutralist stronghold on the Vientiane Plain, November, 1974.

Plate 8. Meal in ex-guerilla camp, MR 4, November 1974.

Plate 9. Looking east over Pathet Lao territory near Sala Phou Khoun.

Plate 10. Guard of Honour, MR 4.

Plate 11. Briefing in Done Hene: Australian DA, Colonel Cam West and British Head of Chancery, Robin Fearn.

Plate 12. KMT camp in northwest Laos.

Plate 13. At the border of Royal Lao Government and Pathet Lao territory.
In the foreground: unknown American adviser,
Colonel Cam West, Brigadier General Soutchai and the author

Plate 14. The border.

Plate 15. The author on tour, November 1974.

Plate 16. Meeting villagers.

Plate 17. HM King of Laos inspects 'Honor Guard', Vientiane.

Plate 18. Major General Kouprasith Abhay, Deputy Commander-in-Chief

Plate 19. 'Rogues' Galley': the attaché corps. From left to right Canada (ICSC), UK, China, USSR, UK, USA, 2 Thais, Australia, France, USA, China, USA

Plate 20. Two Pathet Lao sentries at Sam Neua.

Plate 21. HBM Ambassador, Alan Davidson, with the Red Prince, Souvannouvong, in the Lao Patriotic Front HQ, in the caves at Sam Neua.

Plate 22. Outside the large protective baffle at Sam Neua.

Plate 23. Pathet Lao at Sam Neua.

Plate 24. Pathet Lao at Sam Neua.

Plate 25. Signed copy of a photograph of the wedding of Princess Marina Rangsi and His Highness Prince Sisouk na Champassak.

Plate 26. *Papa Looly* on patrol.

The Acorn Grows

Prince Sisouk was coldly furious. At the line-up of attachés at the National Day parade on 11 May I was the only one he did not shake hands with. Nor did he at the annual International Show (given by the foreign community) on 18 May. I was a non-person in his eyes. I had no idea how to remedy the situation.

Luckily that did not seem to effect my enhanced status with the RLA. On a visit to the south Cam and I went to Xeno, the home of one of the two Strike Divisions, the 'Scorpion'. We were first taken by helicopter to Done Hene, once the home of an officers' school, with not a building left standing and wanton desecration of all Buddhist shrines. A briefing and tour of the position and the ruins at Kengkok, another completely ruined town, followed.

A white ICSC helicopter flew in our lunch – boiled and sticky rice, fish, buffalo, spiced sausages, salad, sauces, tangerines, custard apples and red wine. What a meal and at what expense, in a country where six months before the end of the financial year it had the equivalent money that the Japanese needed in half an hour's trading on their stock exchange. The comparison was even starker when this was in a town, razed by fighting, where two American nurses had been seized by the NVA and burnt alive in a wooden house. The refugees, destitute and in rags, watched covetously as we foreigners fed ourselves like fighting cocks.

Farther south we were driven by General Soutchai in person to the front, on the Bolovens plateau (famous for its coffee that was still available at 80p a kilo: one beneficial result of the B-52 strikes was that the blast of the bombs had pruned the coffee bushes), 4,000 feet above sea level. The air grew cooler and the signs of war more as our convoy of four vehicles slowly climbed the road, battered by bombs, shells and mines. There was thick undergrowth on every side. Empty cases and barbed-wire were everywhere, while steel helmets, tanks, lorries and battle positions were only a little less in evidence. It was beautiful hilly country.

There was a secret Thai battalion at the front and we got out of the vehicles, walking through their positions to a couple of barriers, beyond which was a one-way ticket. On the far side soldiers in foxholes watched us, a PL flag limply hanging over the nearest position. We were closely guarded. I met and spoke to some of my ex-Jungle Warfare School students.

At HQ MR 2, General Vang Pao himself met Cam and me in his jeep and we were taken by helicopter to the other Strike Division, the Cobras, in the front line. The General invited us to spend the night, the first non-political people to be so honoured other than those benighted by adverse weather conditions. At Borikhane in MR 5 – a village overrun three times since the cease-fire – I was taken to talk to nine PL 'ralliers' who had given themselves up the day before. The younger was sixteen with four years' service and the elder twenty-two with eight.

As the right-wing military representative of Co-Chairman of the 1962 Geneva Accords for Laos, I again visited the LPF HQ in Vientiane to discuss demarcation lines, future plans and my driving to Luang Prabang, through territory controlled by PL. (Why should a mere cease-fire alter the conquering communists' successful policy of nibbling land grabs?)

Before sitting down I examined some knives in scabbards that hung in clusters on one of the walls. When I was there before I had ignored them, but being interested in national knives, I now asked about them. Soth Phetrasi smiled, got up and, going to the wall, took one down and gave it to me. Of feather-light aluminium, it had, on the blade, an inscription: *debris d'avion U.S. Air Forces: abattu au Laos: Front Pathet Lao 1970.*

It was a difficult moment. Decline this unusual gift of part of a shot-down American aircraft, it could be taken as a gesture of disapproval: accept it, would it not put me in the same category as Mr Lloyd? Face impassive, I examined it and made to go to the wall to put it back. I was intercepted and told to keep it as it was now mine. Acquiescing, I thanked him for it.

When he was out of the room one of his minions told me that Soth 'liked, respected and trusted' me. I was worried lest, with all my contacts on both sides of the political divide, I was being looked on as 'running with the hare and hunting with the hounds'. Eternal vigilance was a prerequisite not to jeopardise confidences. I planned to talk this over with General Kouprasith and this I did later.

Kaysorn would not take no for an answer and gatecrashed to offer me some bath salts. Chok Di told me he thought she had fallen in love with me. Lack of progress with Sisouk still irked.

In late June Cam and I drove to Luang Prabang. Originally unmetalled its entire length, except in the towns, some attempts had been made to control the nose-clogging, gut-rotting, all-pervasive dust by laying a tarred surface in places. I had driven part of the way before and knew that the sun became uncomfortably hot; keep the windows open to benefit from what breeze there was and immediately a film of clinging, cloying dust formed everywhere, getting thicker and thicker. Have the windows shut and it was like an oven. In the event we flew to Vang Vieng, where my landrover was waiting for us, met our RLA escort and drove off north.

I recalled my first visit at Vang Vieng, complete with inventory of farm animals and chickens. (Everybody there was pleasant to me nor did 'I lose my dignity as a DA' as Jean Laboucheix did the first time he stopped there to relieve nature. He was set upon and debagged by three young women when he was in mid-stream. *J'ai perdu ma dignité comme attaché militaire Français*, he told me sadly, shaking his head.) The driver had a leg-stretch and a bowl of soup. We drove on while the temperature was still comparatively cool. The land began to close in as the road reached the foothills.

The vehicle slowed down sharply as a refugee village, shielded from view, came abruptly into sight round a bend, the road the children's playground. I had always admired the way Asian children could play anywhere; the slums of Bombay, the backwoods of Borneo, the mountains of Nepal and here, with utter unconcern of the world around them. Their toys were stones and sand, bits of brick and wood, water and earth: nothing to go wrong and nothing that went wrong, so unlike their spoilt and pampered European counterparts' generosity of gadgetry and superfluity of sophistication, with subsequent frustration accompanied by peeved tantrums when the inevitable breakages happened. Was this one of the underlying reasons why Asians, masters since childhood of improvisation, were so hard to beat in the context of guerilla warfare in jungle terrain? A fascinating theory, I mused, as we gathered momentum, leaving the village behind.

We drove through a narrow defile, presaging hilly country to come. So like the Malayan and Borneo jungles where we had won. Now the communists were winning (fighting was still flaring up and we seemed to be drifting from one political non-event to another) and the Americans were feeling a cooling of relations between what? Client and crimp? Although it was hard to blame the Americans for the lack of a firm political base in Saigon, Phnom Penh and Vientiane, here it redounded on me by my being turned to for advice, comment and confidences more than had been the case in the past – and, from Sisouk, answer came there none.

The road straightened out at Muong Kassy, the last large village before the main mountain range. We stopped, Khien for his morning meal, Cam and I for a glass of tea, a roll of sticky rice wrapped in a banana leaf and a stroll. It was a one-street village with an airstrip built as a bulge in the road to the north. A pilot landing there always had to circle the strip once or twice before landing to ensure there was no oncoming traffic. Takeoff was even more risky because oncoming traffic could not be seen. A bridge crossed a river and, up a short rise to the west of the road, was an army camp, holding a *Battalion Volontiér*.

As well as the nondescript soldiers it also housed three decrepit armoured fighting vehicles that the French had driven there about twenty years before. The place had an abandoned air, heightened by a burnt-out hulk of a tank the PL had managed to drive that far during one of their many probes in the late '60s. It looked an impressive kill but the 'battle' had been a fiasco. One of the French tanks had been induced to move out of the camp under its own power as a PL-driven Russian T-34 tank had approached from the north. On seeing the other tank, the PL driver had tried to reverse so as to make good his escape but he had stalled his engine at the very same moment that the French tank broke down. The PL crew jumped out and surrendered. The crew in the immobilised French tank had then fired and, at a range of 30 yards, had managed to hit the other, which then burnt out. Thus is military history written – in bullshit and quick-drying ink.

But then the soldiery of the royal army was not entirely to blame. The way they were recruited was savage, reminiscent of the bad old days in England of press-ganging. A road block would be set up near a village, sometimes on a feeder road, other times on the main road, and all men and boys from the ages of twelve and, say, forty, were forcibly held: bus loads, taxi loads, travellers in bullock carts and pedestrians. They were taken to a training camp and desertions of up to half during that first night were common. The French had laid no foundations on which to build a national army, unlike the British had so successfully in India. Lao senior officers, NCOs when the French left in 1954, had been catapulted into positions of great responsibility but with grossly inadequate training and experience. They knew no better. I was reminded of the Drill Sergeant's prayer: 'Dear God, send me some soldiers. Wooden ones would do'.

The road had started to wind its way up the mountain side and was closely flanked by tall jungle trees. I found myself lost in thought as the vehicle lurched round the sharp bends. I had taken full advantage of the Beaver, making new contacts and revitalising old acquaintances as more and more places were visited. For the most part it was neither exciting nor glamorous but well worth the effort. I had yet to get to those mysteriously code-named places that Sisouk had so tantalised me with. Would I ever now?

The view from the top of the high ground, at around 4,000 feet up, was breathtakingly grand, despite a haze, as, wave-like, ridge and ridge of greeny-blue jungle, flecked with brown and studded with white perpendicular limestone outcrops, stretched back into the distance and disappeared into obscurity. Nearby, on a small plateau, were an artillery unit, a few armoured cars and some infantry soldiers that formed the garrison of the strategically and politically important road junction, Sala Phou Khoun. It was strategic because it was the only place that could control road movement between the three capitals, the royal at Luang Prabang, the commercial at Vientiane and the communist one at Sam Neua away to the east. Politically it was important as it was the only piece of real estate that had belonged to the LPF after the 1962 cease-fire that was now held by the royalists. Had there not been some massive B-52 strikes, immediately followed by a complicated heliborne assault by troops and guns shortly before the cease-fire, it would still surely be in communist hands. There was not much depth to the position where, an American had told me, the RLA were 'hanging onto by their finger nails'.

There were the remains of the one building, the *sala*, or rest house, built in the thirties by an enterprising Frenchman, where travellers could rest themselves, their porters and their horses before continuing on their long route to anywhere else. Now it was a battle-pitted, roofless skeleton, with crumbling, graffiti-covered walls. We drove up into the camp. Being on the borders of three military regions it either had an excess of orders or no orders at all. One result of the rush to get reinforcements in quickly was that Thai secret army soldiers, Meo Irregulars and ordinary RLA soldiers were, unusually, mixed up. Some were hatless and long-haired, for all the world 'coffee-shop cowboys'. Some were wearing a strange medley of plain clothes, other wore uniform with garish flashes haphazardly stitched on their shirts, all underpaid, underfed and inefficient. It was an unhappy mixture as the terms and conditions of service of the three different sets of soldiers caused jealousies and other complications the overall commander could well have done without – even had he realised they indeed existed.

Visitors, except Americans who arrived by air, were so infrequent that we, wearing other types of uniform not normally seen in that neck of the woods, were accorded more than our ration of stares. A Captain came to meet us. He took us round his camp then offered to take us round the area in a helicopter.

Route 4, the road that led away east to Sam Neua and eventually Hanoi, was but a track, hardly discernible in the long grass. Row after row after row of large bomb craters, similarly shaped and spaced with mathematical precision, provided the explanation for the inability of the PL, backed by the NVA, to hold the position. Away in the distance a PL flag fluttered.

Back on the position we had a quick look at two 5.5-inch medium artillery pieces, congratulated the Captain on how well they were camouflaged, thanked him for his programme and drove off to visit a second camp. The road wound its way down the mountain and the jungle fell back leaving enough room for small rice fields, homesteads and animals. The monsoon held off and it was dry, even dusty in places. Nearer to Luang Prabang ugly clusters of shanties where hapless refugees lived marred the natural dignity of the countryside. We took the road that led past the American-donated fish farm, the King's orange groves and elephant stalls and, once past the ice factory, we were in the town, one of the prettiest in Asia. On the journey back I thought of a way to contact Sisouk.

On my next session with Princess Jasmine I bluntly told her that nowadays Prince Sisouk seemed to view me with disfavour. I could only put it down to my having made a protocol mistake by using commoner Lao instead of royal Lao to him when I gave a welcome and a toast at my party so he was understandably angry with me. I would be most grateful if she could find out, discretely, and let me know. Sure, come round in two weeks.

For my first attaché lunch in July I decided that the easiest method would be to sit at card tables, soup ready on the tables and the rest buffet. Arranging the tables was interesting: I had to remember who spoke no French, who spoke no English and who was not on speaking terms with whom. At one table I had Australia, US (air attaché), Philippines and Canada; at another were Poland, USSR, US (army attaché) and India; and at the third were France, South Vietnam, Thailand and myself, so I could keep the Thai, who had neither French nor English, happy. We finished up with fruit salad and the two Asians at my table were fascinated and not a little horrified when the Frenchman leaned across, took my glass and poured the water into his bowl, adding some of his own white wine. He lifted the bowl to his lips and slurped the mixture down. As he had eaten six potatoes in their jackets, I expect he was thirsty.

That was boorish: the next attaché function was a crisis. At a French party, the American had approached the Chinese. As the two countries had no diplomatic relations then they could only speak on neutral territory. The USA was keen for any contact possible, so Broadus Bailey suggested that Chen join in the attaché corps function and host a luncheon in honour of Colonel 'Buzz' Curry, the retiring US air attaché. Chen Shu-lin had never joined in any attaché function.

He was, by then, the doyen but was not interested so Broadus approached the next senior, the Soviet Vladimir Gretchanine, and asked him to lay on and host the party. This Vladimir did but, instead of issuing invitations as acting doyen of the attaché corps, he had sent them out in his own name, as the Soviet attaché. To ordinary mortals that might not have been of much consequence: to the Chinese, who also got an invitation, it was a grave insult. Chen Shu-lin broke all precedents and rang Broadus and told him that America had insulted his country. Broadus came round to ask me to fix it.

I rang the Chinese embassy and fixed a meeting. Twenty minutes after arriving I was allowed to broach the reason of my visit. Chen's face darkened as I explained my mission. No, he would not accept that Vladimir had made a mistake in sending out the invitations in his own name. It was an attempt to belittle him, Chen. "Vexing indeed, dear colleague, but I have an idea. If I can get the Russian to retract his invitations, would you be willing to send out new ones?" I saw Chen wavering so I dangled a bit of bait. Would he agree to the party if I persuaded Vladimir to finalise the arrangements? After a long, long pause he gave a grudging affirmative.

I left and went to the US embassy and asked Broadus to let Vladimir know I was coming, then drove to the Soviet embassy. Once seated in the visitors' room he narrowed his eyes as he heard of my problem and how touchy Chen was. He heard me out and smiled bleakly. "Of course, it is well known that the Chinese is your friend." But our countries were allies during the war so he would do as I suggested. It would be much easier for the arrangements for the meal to remain as ordered. The other man could arrange for the seating plan, with my help, and collect the money for the present from the rest of the attachés.

Even so the Chinese was not ready to send out the invitations until he had received permission from Peking. The time it took to get the answer was, so I understood, the first occasion ever that the speed of Chinese radio communications could be measured accurately – far quicker than previously thought. While we were waiting for the answer Vladimir came round to my house, worried lest Chen put him in an impossible situation and asking my advice. I put paid to his fears.

The actual meal was good and the mood expectant, especially when Chen rose and made a long speech through his French interpreter. At the end he thanked us all for coming, the British for helping him in the arrangements, the Americans for showing concern and the Australians for helping with the seating arrangements (I had declined to and felt that such a task would enhance Sino-Australian relations) but with no word for the Russian who sat glowering at the end of the table. It was all a waste as 'Buzz' Curry did not speak French and no one interpreted for him.

Then came the incredible sight of the Wielder of the Little Red Book [of Chairman Mao's 'Thoughts'] presenting a semi-religious *baçi* bowl to the coordinator of the B-52 and F-111 raids on communist-held territory: desultory applause followed. 'Buzz' Curry then asked Broadus Bailey to interpret his speech of thanks into French. Broadus's American accent made Jean Laboucheix look positively choleric but that could have been because he had, once more, eaten too much. As the speech was not translated back into Chinese that too was lost on the person to whom it was mainly directed. Vladimir drifted over to me as we left. "I've done all I'm going to do. Your friend can pay the bill."

The tailpiece came the following Saturday when 'Buzz' Curry gave a party at the RLA officers' club at Phone Kheng. Chen Shu-lin was not there but Vladimir was. He came up to me and said he could not see my best friend. My answer was that I did not bring my dog to parties.

77

Jasmine told me that Sisouk was not angry at anything I had said (which did not surprise me) and that he would welcome a visit (which did). I fixed a date. Just before setting off I was in Lloyd's office when the Third Secretary came in to say that 'Your Excellency might be interested to learn that the latest rumour is that Sisouk has got a divorce from his French wife and is going to marry Jasmin'. I winced at the sneering comment about such a union, left the two men digesting the rest of the previous night's cocktail party gossip and drove round to see Sisouk.

No sooner had I entered his office he got up from behind his desk, came round to me and burst out excitedly that he was going to get married soon. Did I know? I feigned ignorance and offered my congratulations. I was motioned to sit down and he sat opposite me. I was asked to guess who his wife-to-be was. After a moment of apparent contemplation of all those who might be eligible, most of whose names I did not know, I gave my considered answer.

"That is a very difficult question, Your Excellency," I started and went on to say that if I were looking for someone who matched his social status, was very beautiful, had character, was good with all types of people, knew how to talk well, could speak English and French, knew when to keep silent, would be a companion at home, could discuss matters with him, had a sense of humour – here I racked my brains to think of any other attribute not already mentioned – wouldn't mind if he had important people to look after at a moment's notice, "um, I think the only person I know who could measure up to all that is Princess Jasmine."

The effect was dramatic. Sisouk got up, came round to me and shook my hand. "You've guessed my secret, you've guessed my secret," he burbled happily. I waited a bit and then said it had been a long time since we last met and I was happy to be able to pay a courtesy call on him again. Had I yet been to Whisky 3 and PS 18 I was asked. I told him I had not and that I still had no idea what or where they were. "Tell the Commander-in-Chief that he can take you there with him at any time." I felt I was so near to a breakthrough that I had the temerity to ask Sisouk if he would personally tell General Bounphone as it would save much bother.

He took the suggestion and told his personal assistant to send for the General, there and then. Waiting for him to come I tried to recall the links in this royal marriage. Sisouk was a close relation of the rapacious Prince Boun Oum, head of the old southern kingdom of Champassak and hereditarily antipathetic to the northern kingdom of Luang Prabang. Princess Jasmine, on the other hand, was a northerner and the marriage looked like being a merger, at long last, not only of the southern and northern kingdoms of history but of all three, with the third kingdom of Xieng Khoang, centred on the Plain of Jars and the fief of the Prime Minister, already being tied to Luang Prabang with the marriage of his son to yet another of the King's nieces. Was it significant that, at this juncture of history, the three ancient kingdoms were now nearer to national unity than ever before? Would this lead to the long-delayed coronation taking place? Would this unite the people against communist domination?

There was a discreet knock on the door and the lard-covered General, Jubilation, came in. I stood up and saluted him. He came over and punched me in the chest with a throaty cry of 'Commando!'. Sisouk bade him sit down and told him to take me to the guerilla units at PS [Pakse (landing) Site] 18 and Whisky [I never knew why] 3 and that I had *carte blanche* to go anywhere at all in Laos with him. I thanked Sisouk most sincerely and the C-in-C took me away to his office for another talk.

Bounpone told me frankly that he thought I would do much better on my own, going on to say that people did not show him everything and I knew what to look for and what to say. People were very interested in my background and what he would like was that I came and told him if I found anything I thought he ought to know about after touring these places. And who said that that fickle lady, Dame Fortune, never smiled?

The rest of the month was spent in escorting John Lloyd round the provinces on his farewell visits. Everywhere I went I was welcomed and found a genuine warmth awaiting me from civilians and soldiers. I attended a number of farewell parties to the Lloyds in Vientiane and heard more cant and toadying than had been my lot ever before.

In my own right I flew to a remote part of northwest Laos, Xiem Lom, where there were Thai secret troops and Lao Irregulars. Before I was DA the Beaver was not allowed below 5,000 feet or within five miles of the camp and here I was, in uniform, spending the night there and giving my views on communist revolutionary warfare, and its counter, to both Thais and Lao. In Vientiane I also visited the Staff College, the MOD training cell, the River Flotilla, the 'Psywar' and the Joint Operations Centre. I had a private dinner with Sisouk at his house. I prepared the 1972-73 annual report for London (one wet season to another, not the more normal calendar year).

The Consul General in Hanoi, Tim Everard, first broached the idea that I be accredited to Hanoi. In a letter home I wrote

...a weight is being lifted off my shoulders, 271 days after I arrived here: our man is going. Such is our self-delusion that we never believe others are glad to see us go, or that we have been an embarrassment or a failure... His going has allowed me to come of age... The constraints of tact, shame and loyalty have been hard.

Despite the cease-fire in Vietnam and Laos, in the Khmer Republic the USAF dropped a whole load of bombs on villages mistaking them for NVA sanctuaries. It was about that time when a Lieutenant Phông, of ARVN, on an attachment to the South Vietnamese embassy in Vientiane, was anodynely introduced to me by Colonel Chi. He was, I suspected, an intelligence agent. On our third or fourth meeting he said he had reason to believe that the airfield in the southern Laotian town of Attopeu (in PL hands for many years) was being upgraded to take the latest version of Soviet MiG fighters. Saigon was very worried: his request, put with diffidence, was could I arrange a U-2 'spy plane' to check this out?

I sensed an unusually devious channel for the request being put thus to the US authorities but I said I would try and oblige. This I did: the report was negative. Phông was very grateful and felt he 'owed' me. Had I heard of Office 95 he asked. I hadn't so he told me about it.

In the remote, jungle-covered hills east of the small town of Dien Bien Phu in North Vietnam's Military Region 959 was a secret camp containing Office 95. The mystique of '95' was that the chief Vietnamese representative worked in Room 9 and his LPF opposite number in Room 5. It was responsible for planning, co-ordinating and directing all activity of a clandestine nature: this included subversion, sabotage, the running of intelligence and counter-intelligence networks, disinformation and brazen strong-arm tactics, all of which were designed to further the revolution by exerting political pressure wherever necessary. It had tentacles all over Laos, especially the eastern part of the country that was dominated by the NVA and through which the Ho Chi Minh Trail had been built. I still thought Phông was an intelligence agent, but whether single or double was uncertain. However, I took his information on trust.

I was up at a quarter past 5 on 20 August and half an hour later heard what sounded like a short, sharp burst of machine-gun fire. My suspicions were confirmed when I heard more bursts from the direction of the town. So, of all days chosen by some desperate hothead to mount a coup, the day the new ambassador was due was it. Rumours had been flying around for some time, with the weather vane of speculation gusting from left wing to right wing as scare followed false alarm followed rumour. John Lloyd had been scathing when I had discussed it with him, talking about 'these damned silly American-backed fat cats, what have they got left and who would back them anyway?' I was asked what my 'general friends' said when I 'so rashly' drove up the road to Luang Prabang? Didn't they realise their cause was as good as lost? And how about those misguided men whom you say you met at the road junction – couldn't they see sense either?

I told him that I had not discussed such issues and went on to say that, as it was their quarrel, not ours, I was sure they respected my non-meddling. The more I saw of it, the more I felt that if everyone pulled out, including the North Vietnamese, and left the Lao to themselves, they'd work out their own solution if not their own salvation. There were too many foreign meddlers altogether, in my opinion, fighting each other by proxy.

By then evidence, albeit indirect, suggested that the North Vietnamese were in Laos for keeps. Sure they would withdraw armed men but those would be replaced with others disguised as Lao whose duty it would be to colonise, intermarry and establish an indisputable and irremovable presence. More NVA troops had arrived in Laos recently and were busy constructing feeder roads, main roads, an occasional airfield, camps as well as having perfected a Ho Chi Minh Highway as opposed to a mere trail, or trail system. And there was nothing anyone could do about it.

Lloyd agreed with me and he said he was pleased with the way I hadn't been up to MR 2 and 'hadn't encouraged those trigger-happy hawks like Donald Thursby-Pelham seemed to...' and I let carry on, half talking and half thinking aloud, without committing myself in any way. The phrase 'with friends like you why bother about enemies?' passed through my mind. And yet, in the same breath, he said that we had had a very fruitful relationship and I had been no worry to him. Indeed, his confidential report on me was a good one. What a strange mixture he was!

Mr and Mrs Davidson, the new ambassador and his wife, had elected to travelling overland by night train from Bangkok to the Thai border town of Nong Khai, crossing the Mekong and landing on the Laotian side at Tha Deua. They were due at about 7 o'clock if the train ran on time. Commonwealth Heads of Mission, who were supposed to meet each other on arrival, smiled wryly when they heard this as it was too early for most of them. I too had to meet him and had warned Khien to collect me at 6.30. It was still not full daylight and there was another burst of automatic fire and the unexpected noise of an aeroplane flying abnormally low. Something very different from usual was happening.

As soon as my car arrived I drove off to pick up Peter and Wendy Shield. I told Khien to drive carefully and be ready to take any evasive action necessary. At a small ordnance depôt troops were standing to, armed and wearing battle helmets yet civilian life seemed no different from normal. Driving past the Prime Minister's *hôtel* I saw General Kouprasith standing by the front door, an armoured car nearby. Ready for the takeover, I thought, remembering his well-known wish to be the next prime minister, or just covering his bets?

It was no business of mine. Just beyond the Shield's house, a machine-gun, placed on the verge of the road, fired at a T-28 aircraft with RLAF markings that flew out of thick monsoon cloud and within its range. Farther on, at Chinaimo Camp, there was a bustle of military activity and a strong smell of cordite. So HQ MR 5, General Kouprasith's power base, was the target. To prevent Wendy from worrying Peter and I said out loud that it must be an exercise. I decided it was better not to stop and ask the local commander what was happening: I had higher priorities and trigger-happy RLA soldiers were better left on their own. My flagged car with us in uniform inside was our best protection. At the border town of Tha Deua a worried-looking official was twiddling the knobs of a portable radio. "No news," he said sadly. "They've gone off the air."

The First Secretary, Barry Denny, arrived later than the others and told me that a renegade air force officer, Brigadier General Thao Ma, had seized Wattay airport, at the same time as taking control of the national radio station. His men wore blue brassards. We decided that, as soon as the Davidsons had arrived and the briefest of introductions made, we would drive back in fast convoy. Normally such a situation as the present one would automatically seal the Thai-Lao border. There was no river traffic, an ominous sign. The crump of bombs to the west and the far-off stutter of machine-guns moments later reached us as a small motor boat was seen coming across the river with a European couple as passengers. As it neared the bank the Chargé asked us to make a line before he went down to the edge of the river to welcome the newcomers.

Until the new ambassador had presented his credentials to the King he would have to leave the Chargé in control of Britain's interests. Only after having been accepted by the Head of State could Mr Davidson do any official business. Any delay was tiresome and periods of up to six weeks before accreditation took place were by no means rare. What was as rare was Lloyd's replacement arriving only eight days after Lloyd had gone and, rarer still, credentials were to be presented within three days. It was almost as though Britain was apologising for the past man and the Royal Lao Government was signalling its understanding.

Introductions were soon over, reassuring remarks and brittle jokes helping to cover the new arrivals' concern. We drove back as fast as safety allowed, reaching the embassy without any incident. On Davidson's table was a letter from Lloyd hoping that he did not arrive during a coup. We put our coup drill into action, including sending a message to the BBC to tell British residents to stay indoors.

Peter Shield went to the airport to check the safety of the Beaver and found a throng of blue-brassarded men. After some difficulty he was allowed to go into the area where the aircraft was and ensure its safety. At the same time an American diplomat, Mr John Dean, was telling a group of rebel soldiers and airmen at the side of the runway that the USA would in no way help them in their quest to overthrow the government. Meanwhile Broadus Bailey was in the Prime Minister's residence, keeping him informed of events. Souvanna Phouma was 'cucumber cool'.

It was all over by midday (we sent the BBC another message). It was a dismal failure – a *coup manqué* – the non-event of the year. Of the two aircraft that the rebels had managed to put into the air, one had been hit by small arms' fire and had burnt out on the airfield as it tried to regain base. That was the one I had seen. The other, piloted by Thao Ma himself, crashed on landing just as RLA troops reached Wattay airport. I gathered that Kouprasith's orders were ruthlessly obeyed: the rebel leader was dragged out of his 'plane, despite being wounded, and driven in a closed car to Chinaimo Camp. After a short drumhead court-marital, he was shot, as he had been told would be the case when he tried a similar coup in 1966. Most of the 250-odd dissidents who took part managed to fade away. Those who were caught were believed to have been shot, despite whatever other reports were issued.

A typically Laotian touch was added on the following night: a number of dissidents who had successfully fled over the river to Thailand crossed back to claim their pay and were promptly arrested. I went to LPF HQ a day or so later to find out their reactions to the coup. I was unable to see anybody as all were inside at a meeting chaired by the Soviet ambassador.

Alan Davidson was a 'horse from a different stable' in every sense: physical, mental, in temperament and interests (he wrote books on 'neutralism' and 'fish and fish dishes'), and he was teetotal. He was delighted, he said, to let me get on with what I wanted to do and only tell him if I thought anything was of importance. In that monsoon-laded atmosphere a fresh breeze blew.

Three days later Davidson and his senior staff flew up to Luang Prabang where a member of the Protocol Department, who had flown up the day before to arrange the ceremony with the palace officials. Travelling in the same RLAF Dakota were the staff and food (bought in Bangkok) for the British party who were to be accommodated in the government hotel that was only used on special occasions.

At dinner that night the Lao protocol chief, a tall, urbane man, who had served in France and Britain as ambassador, joined us. Garrulous on pre-dinner whisky, babbling during the meal and incoherently maudlin after it, we were relieved when he tottered off to bed.

Although billed to leave the hotel at 10 o'clock for an 11 o'clock audience, by a quarter past 10 nothing had come to fetch us and we started to fret. The telephone was out of order. I told a couple of battered taxis outside to remain in case they were needed. It had been a struggle for the embassy staff to get dressed in time and the ambassador found his medal ribbon bar loose. I was called in to organise its repair which, after much cajoling, was affected by a prettily winsome Lao chambermaid.

At ten to 11, to everybody's relief, three protocol cars and four police outriders drove up. The fact that we had been given a time an hour earlier than necessary disconcerted the protocol officer and the King's ADC not one whit. *Bor pen nyang* – we were ready, weren't we? We were driven off, police outriders' sirens shrieking and red lights flashing. As the cars stopped at the palace a guard of red-trousered, white-coated soldiers saluted. Out we got and ascended the steps of the ornate waiting chamber. Hats and gloves were taken from us. We passed remarks in subdued tone, the atmosphere a trifle tense. The large doors were open to a passage across which thick curtains hid the throne room.

"Will you come this way please, Gentlemen," a court orderly asked us, in French. We formed up in single file to enter the presence. Alan Davidson was in front, flanked by a protocol officer and a ministry of foreign affairs man. Robin Fearn, Head of Chancery, flanked by two court officials, followed him. The rest of us were solo. When we were ready, the curtain was drawn back to reveal His Majesty, King Savang Vatthana – an indefatigable, gentle and cultured man – sitting on his throne with the Crown Prince, *Le Prince Héritier*, to his rear right. The Queen was not there. We all bowed, moved forward six paces, bowed again and waited for the King to stand up. Davidson asked the King if he might have permission to present his credentials. Permission was given. Davidson walked another three paces towards the throne, bowed, took out his prepared speech and began to read his message of loyalty in a firm voice. He handed the King two letters, both addressed to H.M. The King of Laos, and two flunkeys bearing two silver *baçi* bowls, moved to the King who put both letters (I know one of them started, 'Sire, my brother') in one bowl, took his address and his spectacles out of the other. The King read his own address in a low voice, gave back paper and specs to the flunkey and took three paces forward. He shook hands with the new ambassador, congratulating him, and they talked for several minutes.

"May I introduce my staff, Your Majesty?"
"*S'il vous voulez.*"

That over, we went out in reverse gear, I careful not to trip on my sword scabbard. We were given a *vin d'honneur*. We signed the Golden Book, *le livre d'or*, and went outside for photographs. By then three platoons of soldiers had been formed up as a Guard of Honour, complete with our two countries' flags. We stood to attention while the national anthems were played. The new ambassador received a salute and was asked permission for the soldiers to dismiss once we had walked past them. We shook hands with the palace staff and motored back to the hotel with our police escort.

After changing out of uniform I went in search of the River Flotilla HQ, as I was planning to sail downstream with them the following week. I combed the river front for an hour, asking folk where it was. It started to rain. I reached the military hospital at the other end of the town and asked the sentry on duty to direct the driver of a motor trishaw to take me to the Flotilla HQ and I was taken to where I had started looking for it.

We stopped at a shack at the waterfront. On a rude verandah a woman gave suck to a babe and an oaf lazed nearby. Where, I asked, was the Flotilla HQ? A small, wooden notice with a once-white anchor imprinted on a once-red background, so faded as to be scarcely noticeable, was pointed out to me. So here I was! I asked to see the boss and the oaf, grumbling, pulled on a green uniform shirt and bade me follow him. We splashed our way up a muddy lane and came to a house. I took my shoes off, went inside and saw a figure of a man asleep on a sofa under a fan in the middle of the room. My guide awoke his Commanding Officer (for so he was) and left. Politeness made the officer put on his shirt – I saw he was a major – and he offered me a chair. I explained who I was, what I wanted, what had so far happened and asked what I needed to know. Satisfied, I left him some fifteen minutes later.

My river trip down the Mekong was an attaché first. An hour after we started we drew into a small riverine village and the Major invited me ashore. We walked into a world unspoiled by modern influence, except maybe a little education. Houses on stilts, a *wat*, good-looking, smiling people, chickens scratching for food, a few dogs and some pigs. We went to the house of the headman, a venerable old fellow who bade us be seated and offered us coconut milk. "Welcome to our village," he said with simple dignity after I had been introduced. "It is an honour to welcome a *farang*, a foreigner, especially one who does not want to change what has been ours for generations."

At a second village I was told that "You *Angit*, English, have shown the world how to manage people. The Americans only play at it and the French don't believe in it."

On the second day my boat broke down and had to be towed for several hours. We crunched over some rapids, drifted through an area controlled by the PL some of whom were laundering their clothes and bathing at the edge of the river. The crews were brave enough to engage in shouted banter with them from the safety of their boats. A PL supply boat with NVA advisers visible on board passed us close by. With no room or time to hide I sat down on the deck, back to them and hoped I would not be noticed. It was against just such an occasion that I had decided to wear my old Gurkha Parachute Company red beret which was the same colour as the crew's headdress, rather than my staff blue beret.

That night I slept in an RLA camp at Pak Lay, the first foreign attaché for twenty years to visit the place, was shown the greatest hospitality and asked back. Peter flew in on the morrow to take me back to Vientiane.

In September the FCO wrote ...*please thank Colonel Cross for his excellent report...read with great interest... Cross has certainly outlined in a readily digestible form the many military contenders in Laos...* and my conclusions were sensible. I took a Lao language exam and passed with 84 per cent: Princess Jasmine was on the board and said, "You know, you weren't really very good. You are much better when you come round to me."

The King's half-brother in MR 1 gave me a confidential briefing – *what* a change from my first one. The protocols for setting up the PGNU were signed on the 14th instead of on 23 March. For this the Scorpion Force moved up to Vientiane from Xeno to reinforce the town and guard against trouble. The soldiers, in uniform, went into the town where they forcibly sheared the locks of any long-haired male hippy tourist they met and sold their formation signs for as much as 100,000 *kip* (just over £66) a badge. The next night they had to wear plain clothes.

The end of non-communist rule in Indo-China was in sight. All that remained was how and when the change would be made. What intrigued me was would there be a resistance movement, a government in exile or in hiding and, if so, would it be organised by the Old and Bold or by Young Turks, inside the country or outside it? By September 1973 I had visited over sixty places in royalist Laos and had thought up a project I would put to London: monitoring the Young Turks. I found myself in a position that was exceptional, if not unique, by having a competently fluent Lao capability and an aeroplane. I had already established a pattern of weekly visits, the C-in-C had asked me to get around, I was welcome wherever I went and it had the added merit, in my eyes, of being interesting, challenging and unusual. I should be able to build up a reasonably accurate idea of thought trends over the months and, who knew, make some definite use of it. I cleared it with Davidson and was delighted when London agreed. Some time later I was again extended in post and serious consideration was given to my being accredited to Hanoi – there was no other contender.

On the evening of Thursday, 11 October, I was surprised when an LPF car drove into my villa. Unusually there was only one man in the back. He got out and I invited him in as his driver turned the car round. The Neutralisation Contingent was to begin its airlift from Hanoi next morning and the first two 'planes were due to land at Wattay at 10 o'clock. "Please, as the Co-Chairman's military representative, come to the airport and see them in." The Russians were flying in the Vientiane Neutralisation force and the Chinese the one to Luang Prabang.

The telephone rang and it was Jean Laboucheix. Was his English colleague going to the airport? Would the representative of Her Gracious Britannic Majesty go round by way of the French embassy so they could go together? *Oui. Merci. A bientôt.*

All was abuzz at 10 o'clock at Wattay airport the next morning. The visitors' gallery was full and, on the forecourt of the terminal building, a large crowd of communists had gathered: apart from the LPF there were Russians, Chinese, North Vietnamese, Poles, Czechs and the Soviet-leaning neutral Head of the ICSC. As far as any Indian right-wing interests were concerned, only the army representatives had any, the politicians had none – left wing was the prevailing fashion and paid better political dividends.

The Frenchman and I were the only two non-communist foreigners. Jean Labouchiex had orders to represent the Common Market – a bizarre idea at the best of times – and keep with me but, being very protocol-minded, he was sulking as he had been in Laos longer than had I. I was in uniform but he was in plain clothes with a homburg hat pulled over his eyes and a shabby mackintosh, and reminded me of an out-of-work jobbing gardener. As the sole representatives of the so-called Western world, we don't make a particularly inspiring couple, I thought.

By a quarter to 11 no 'planes had arrived and people were starting to look at their watches. The word spread that the time announced the previous day was not for the 'planes landing but the time the first of the two aircraft was due to take off from Hanoi (the strip at Sam

Neua was too small) where the Neutralisation Contingents had mustered for processing before flying down south.

At a quarter to 12 a cry went up as the noise of an aeroplane was heard and five minutes later a Soviet AN-21 landed and taxied to as near the terminal building as it could. The propellers stopped and the crowd surged forward and a policeman tried to prevent people from getting too close. A young, sallow-faced, bearded French journalist pushed his way forward but was stopped by a policeman. The Frenchman, now regarding him as an unrepresentational nuisance, shouted something insulting at him and those in earshot laughed. The foolish journalist made as if to strike him and was seized by two other policeman who had come up behind him. They carried him off, protesting. The French DA spat in disgust: "Some pig from the newspaper *Humanité*. They're all the same, that crowd."

The rear compartment opened, revealing rope-bound stores. A full five minutes elapsed before the side door opened and two PL guards emerged, blinking, to the top of the portable steps, completely unnerved and unprepared for the heroes' welcome they were getting. They quickly popped back inside. The cheering stopped. There was an incongruous and unrealistic air about it all.

Turning to Jean Laboucheix I told him to look at the crowd. I saw them as a flock of mechanical sheep. They were told to cheer the first 'plane in so they cheered the rice or whatever the stores were and the sentries. The powers that be in the north could have made an impression of efficiency but, no, they preferred to muddle along with bureaucratic inefficiency. They paid lip service to social democracy as being the people's wish but when it came to the crunch and the people would wish something with a touch of panache, what happened but a shambles? Among that group of representatives, only our two countries were enlightened enough to be able to have the political elasticity to withstand and accommodate to the pressures of what the majority wanted. "That should be what the word 'democracy' means. This disorganised bumbledom and political mockery is a far cry from anything like that," I finished up.

Before the Frenchman could answer my unusually long and uncharacteristically bitter diatribe, a voice lashed me from behind. "Colonel, the quicker you stop meddling in politics and stick only to counting soldiers the better." I wheeled round and saw the Czech Chargé d'Affaires angrily pointing an index finger at me. He said he felt insulted by what I had said, claiming that his country was a democracy also.

I brashly answered that there were democracies and democracies. It was interesting to ask what sort of democracy any country really was when it was recalled that the only time there was true democracy was in ancient Greece where they had slaves. "The cynic will say that the only true democracy we can find is in an ants' nest."

A stony silence followed. The Frenchman's lips pursed a silent 'bravo' and the Czech said something I did not catch. I realised I was getting nowhere at all letting off steam and upsetting such people. I had not appreciated what effect this crowd of gibbering puppets I was with would have on me. But realise I must, and quickly, as the AN-21 standing in front of me on the tarmac represented a turn of the page of history, without fanfare, without flourish. The victors were here and now in the capital city of the vanquished – despite all the material and other advantages the Free World, as it called itself, had poured into the armoury and coffers of the vanquished. I had read *Street Without Joy*, the book written about the French defeat in 1954. The AN-21 was merely the conventional, modern client-carrier of the unchanged, unconventional tactics and tenacity of only a generation ago. Let there be no mistake about that.

It may have been then that the truth about the way the communists operate was finally brought home to me: the truth is that is no truth, or rather that untruth is used as a weapon on a scale that we in the West do not seem to realise. It is wrong, indeed, to turn round, certainly in public and very often in private, and say that all communists are liars. Nevertheless, after repeated pronouncements at one level produced completely different situations on the ground, it was hard to draw any other conclusion except that the Great Lie was as great a weapon as any other – and greater than most. It was for that reason that anything one such as I could provide to help those in London solve the jigsaw puzzle of communist intentions was so important.

Swallow your pride, you fool, you are now in the enemy's camp for all intents and purposes, I told myself. I turned to the Czech. "Your Excellency, you are quite right. From now on it will be the soldiers getting out of the next AN-21 that I count." Thoughts were too private for the freedom of venting as though they were public. I'd also have been wiser to have checked who was listening to me before announcing my political theories. That day was a good one to start such a precaution in earnest.

The Czech seemed suitably mollified. He moved off and left us alone. The Frenchman congratulated me with a Gallic shrug. Banalities ensued as we waited for the second 'plane to arrive. The troop-carrying AN-21 came in forty minutes after the first but it was an anti-climax. Of seventy-eight passengers, seven were women. The men wore civilian clothes or uniforms of a nondescript green in equal numbers, representing functionaries and soldiers, however those not carrying Kalashnikov rifles or Makarov pistols were believed to be policemen. Counting these people as they streamed by had a mesmerising effect.

At a quarter to 1 I dropped Jean Labouchiex off at his embassy and went back to my villa to take the dog for a hard walk to work my frustrations out of my system.

It was not only the Czech I very nearly had trouble with. Sometimes I had wondered whether the Chinese were so subtle that they appeared nebulous and naïve rather than naturally normal. I had an altercation with Chen Shu-lin, later on in the month when he paid me a visit, after I had spoken to him without thinking. He always came with his French-speaking interpreter, never with the Lao-speaker.

I was on the embassy steps waiting for the two men. I led them through the foyer, along the corridor and into my small office that only had two comfortable chairs. I invited him to sit in one of them and his interpreter in the other. I had the choice of sitting behind my desk or on it, legs dangling: I chose the latter. The conversation started off with the normal platitudinous pleasantries; the weather, the ambassador's health, my dog (which accompanied me everywhere, including my office) and other banalities. Mr Chesney, my clerk, brought in coffee and biscuits, Chen having declined the offer of whisky.

Chen suddenly asked me what I thought of the Arab-Israeli war. I had no knowledge which side any Chinese policy favoured so played safe. (It was pro-Arab: when a Chinese diplomat went, by mistake, to an Israeli party in Rome given to mark Israel's twenty-fifth anniversary as a nation, he was recalled to Peking within twenty-four hours of it being found out. On another of Chen's visits to me the Israeli attaché, based in Bangkok, came to see me as I was escorting Chen out. Chen looked at the Israeli's badges of rank, did not recognise them and started chatting merrily. When he found out who his new acquaintance was, he became very angry. He broke off in mid-sentence and demanded to be escorted to his car. The next Israeli diplomat to visit me had been temporarily beleaguered by the Black September gang in Bangkok and brought with him a whiff of big-town tempo. Recounting a conversation he had had with his captors he said he had asked them if they had enjoyed Bangkok. "Oh yes," they said, "wonderful. We have been here five days and have had ten massages already.")

I told Chen that I hated it when any larger country bullied a smaller one: Egypt and Syria against Israel, India versus East Pakistan and, unthinkingly, China against Tibet. The effect of such a tactless remark was instantaneously obvious. Both Chinese were angry, not so much at the implied condemnation of two of their allies but at the slur against the Middle Kingdom itself.

There followed a 20-minute tirade. Chen held his head low and severely berated me, petulantly, keeping his voice subdued. After a while I felt that much of what was being said was for future use as far as the interpreter was concerned. He was, after all, an intelligence officer and even were he not, righteous indignation had to be shown. No communists were ever at peace amongst themselves.

"I came to be friendly but you are showing unfriendliness. Why do you have to raise this question?"

"It wasn't a question but an answer: an example if you like."

"If you are not friendly I'll get up and go. I won't come to your party you have asked me to if you are in such an unfriendly frame of mind."

"That's up to you," I said, wishing I had not been so impetuous and now bored with his tantrum.

"How can you say," and here the word that had offended was at last uttered, spat out almost, "*Tibet* is not China?"

"Of course it is different; different customs, different clothes, different language, different religion. Surely that's enough to start with?"

Breathlessly not missing any opportunity to gain a point, this last remark was countered by "Religion? Religion? How about Northern Ireland?"

"Sure. How about Northern Ireland? Our Prime Minister has said that it's up to the people. If they want to stay where and how they are, they can. If they want to join the South, they can. They've got the choice. Seems to me we're more for the people than you lot are."

Chen, jowls aquiver, rose up angrily from his chair, took two paces towards me, drew back his arm and swung it forward to slap my face. Suddenly, before the stroke connected, he tried to withdraw his hand, realising the enormity of his action. In vain: the impetus was too much and his outstretched hand hit my cheek, though not very hard. He sprang back, appalled by what he had done. I made no move. I sat there, swinging my legs, smiling at the, by now, thoroughly confused Chinese. "I came to be friendly..." he said, stopping in mid-sentence. The interpreter, hawk-eyed, watched us both.

I saw a collision course and decided to steer away. I put out my hand. "I'm sorry if I overstated my case. Forget it." We shook hands: relief shone from Chen's face and, very shortly, calm was restored. He left soon afterwards and, as we bade our farewells on the steps of the embassy, all seemed normal. I realised it was a stupid thing to have said but, paradoxically, by having slapped my face, the Chinese had lost face – on points. He made up for it by telling me, in January 1974, that the Chinese had captured five Soviet spies under a bridge in Peking, a week before the news broke; and the Chinese government's congratulations to Mrs Thatcher on being elected leader of the Tory party. I passed both points on to London, but the embassy diplomatic staff discounted both, as it was not they who had been told.

87

In November: there were rumours of the King's imminent coronation; I was recommended for a further extension in post; my overriding impression from monitoring the Young Turks was one of unrelieved gloom; the PL moved into a building opposite the embassy so posing a security risk; and I found myself hating communism more and more – I was always being asked by the Russians when I was going to start learning Russian. I learnt that the LPF called me their 'special colonel' as I was a Lao speaker, was unlike other Westerners, nor did I ever try to tell them what to do as east Europeans were prone to. Wherever I went I was seldom shocked but was constantly horrified. I also visited another 300-square-mile government enclave.

Despite an acute fuel shortage, General Soutchai took me in his helicopter to Kong My, deep in communist-held territory. We flew over the 'Sihanouk Trail' in the 'Panhandle' and saw communist supplies being taken down river to the Khmer Republic. The whole area was peppered with bomb craters. The countryside was beautiful, with the Bolovens plateau as a backdrop; thick jungle and six spectacular waterfalls. The whole village came to greet us. We wandered about meeting the people, Rhadé tribesmen – whose teeth were filed to a point – and the soldiers before having a military briefing and a *baçi*.

Standing at some microphones General Soutchai addressed the villagers, having to have an interpreter. He pointed me out as being the British DA but I thought no more of it until a government public relations official, who had flown in with us to show a film that evening, also spoke and, echoing some of the General's words, turned to me and invited me to speak to the crowd. It was then that I saw everything that had been said to date was being recorded.

It struck me that if the General needed an interpreter so did I, so the purpose of making me speak was not so much for the villagers but for a wider, even a radio, audience. Now was the need for a guarded tongue, so I merely said that I was happy and honoured to visit them, how I had been in Laos a year that very day and how I had learnt to like and respect all Lao and that I hoped for peace. I spoke for a modest three minutes and was applauded politely. The General came bounding over with a beam, a handshake and congratulations.

That should have been enough for one day but I was lucky to visit a secret army camp in Thailand where I had a full briefing (my opposite number in Bangkok knew nothing about the place so my report to London started by saying it was from 'an unnamed but impeccable source', otherwise I would have been guilty of 'poaching'). We were flown both ways by American helicopters, a must unusual show of trust, entirely due to Peter Shield's influence. Back in Pakse that evening General Soutchai invited us to his house for dinner. One of the guests was another of my one-time jungle warfare Thai students. The conversation was very fruitful.

I wrote home:

...in its way it has been a challenging first year: an utterly new job and a not-so utterly new language (my knowledge of Thai helping me considerably), a new country with new actors, personalities, heroes and villains, but the same old communism. [In Britain there was a serious miners' strike at that time.] *I feel I am garnering the fruits of 28 years' service in Asia pre-Laos and the fruits of the 29th in Laos. Pride, we are all told, comes before the fall so I must temper any thoughts of success with humility...I've relied on myself to a greater degree than often, if ever, before – but again only in certain aspects. No part of my life has been as hard as those hungry and forlorn Abo[originese of north Malaysia] days, but I had my soldiers to sustain me. Here, an alien, I've only had myself. I've recharged my battery by my solitary walks yet relaxed in the polyglot and cosmopolitan crowds. I've been to church more times than ever since I was at school and I now realise how barren is the Western world in its lack of faith in something good to thwart and counter the evident evils of communism and the insidious soullessness of socialism...And, during this year, I believe I've maintained my standards and that I haven't let me down...I hobnob with generals, ambassadors, ministers, princes, being greeted with smiles.*

Was there no sensible Asian solution for Asians? I later wrote home that it was hard work to be happy, concerned, intelligent, interested and quick and 'one can play the professional idiot only at certain times'.

I was told my return visit to Pak Lay, despite an acute fuel shortage, in an RLAF H-34 helicopter, had been sanctioned. The pilot, a very smooth major, bade me sit up in front in the co-pilot's sea, a great thrill as I had only been up for'ad in a cargo heli three times before.

An hour after take-off we arrived at Pak Lay where I was given a military briefing, but instead of going on our journey, we adjourned to a little riverside café where we had coffee and soup, both good though unexpected. There was a holiday air, no one fussed or fretted. We were now a larger party, civilians and military. After my last visit I had written a letter of thanks in Lao to the local government chief and he professed himself delighted with it. It inspired him to go along with us. An hour later we continued on our way.

Our second port of call was a company base, set up on a barren hill top, overlooking a small village. Most of the soldiers had been there a year which, under those conditions, was a long time. I wandered around, introducing myself and chatting to the soldiers, the first foreign attaché ever to have there (and to the other places also). The next leg of our journey was over some wild jungle-covered mountains, travelling west, over Sayaboury province, until we were some three or so miles from the Thai border. We must have flown over a number of PL and possibly some guerillas belonging to the Communist Party of Thailand. These men used the western part of the province as a sanctuary and were reinforced by ethnic Chinese from Yunnan in the north as well as ethnic Vietnamese from refugees who had settled in northern Thailand. An unworthy conglomeration. However, from our vantage point, all was serene.

At the third stop we strolled through the military camp (one regular officer and one regular NCO for a platoon's worth of Local Defence Volunteers) before going to a village set in fresh and lush country. "This," said the pilot, "is Laos. The people have their own rice, fruit, pigs and poultry. Why do the PL want to change it all? Ideology cannot be changed by force of arms." As we strolled back to the helicopter he told me that any time I wanted to use him to see real Laos he would be sincerely delighted to take me. I asked him about the fuel shortage. "Not for you," he said.

At the last village we sat in the house of their local leader and were offered Scotch whisky by a pretty young girl. I was given a coconut to drink from. While the Lao chatted I wandered around and made the children laugh. Back at Pak Lay once more we had a meal in the same riverside eating place as before. Liquor flowed. By the time we left the crew were drunk and the pilot, likewise, was not nearly as steady as he had been on the outward journey. It all it was an interesting day but I was glad to get back to Vientiane in one piece.

In December I visited Phnom Penh (when combat engineers tried to blow up a bridge nearby one night. How glad I was not to be working in that saddest of countries, where opposing armies had the ugly names of FANK and GRUNK) and Saigon. I had been in the attaché's house for five minutes when I was called to the telephone. A one-time Guiding Officer with ARVN students at the Jungle Warfare School – and who had been present when the unfortunate Gurkha was kicked in the mouth – somehow knew of my arrival and wanted to meet me. I was taken away for a meal and a chat. When I reported what I had learnt to the DA he was amazed. In his nearly three years in post he had never come across such raw and useful intelligence. "I only deal with the tactical battle," was his slightly sniffy rejoinder.

One morning I was driven to where I had so innocently trodden in 1945 – though not as far as where the Japanese used their 'secret weapon' against the Vietminh hiding in the ditch waiting to ambush us as the fighting was too heavy – and recognised not one whit of it. Where once had been peaceful villages in bosky countryside, now barren and dusty emptiness; where once had been a pleasant and clean Saigon, now a packed and jostling city. Not only was there pollution from the smog-laden stench of over-crowding and too much traffic (despite another desperate fuel shortage) but also from the insidious fear of sabotage, rocket attacks and what was yet to come, to say nothing of the veneer of American sub-culture that shattered morals and morale. Harsh words in a harsh environment. In effect I was in a new country but the age-old Asian preference of being left alone by all governments was ever obvious. But it seemed that the inhabitants were stuck with an unwanted, inapposite, twentieth-century democratic crusade from the New World or colonisation in the name of a misplaced, mismanaged and largely irrelevant, outdated, nineteenth-century political philosophy from the Old – and could do nothing about it.

Back in Vientiane I asked General Kouprasith why it was raining so unseasonably for December. "Because there are two Augusts this year," he said, in a tone of voice usually reserved for children who have not done their homework.

7

'Table Companions are Easy to Find . . .

1974 was a troubled year for the royalists and a good year for the communists as their influence gradually increased over parts of Laos not already 'liberated'. Unheard of previously, students rioted, their leaders being off-duty PL soldiers in plain clothes. Similarly unheard of were strikes, manipulated from the Soviet embassy. Land grabs caused casualties and desertions with a lowering of morale at soldier level a constant. Nothing ever seemed definite: I still could not make up my mind whether I could the better compare the situation in Laos with Chinese boxes or peeling an onion; there was always something smaller inside but was there anything in the very centre?

On 12 February four of us from the British embassy went to Sam Neua, the LPF stronghold, at the long-delayed invitation of its Central Committee. Everything in the communist world seems, at least on the surface, to be done by committee. While this may have the virtue of not necessitating any one individual to 'stand up and be counted', it certainly has the vice of extreme dilatoriness in any decision being reached. Since the last Frenchman left Sam Neua on 3 April 1953, nearly twenty-one years before, there had been one occasion when the non-communist world had been invited there, the British some ten years previously.

Sam Neua is a small provincial town on Route 6 in the northeast of Laos not far from the Vietnamese border. Too far to be administered from Vientiane, it used to be within the sphere of the French authorities in Hanoi. A quiet and sleepy place for many years, the war of 1939-1945 had passed it by. Only infrequent French armoured columns probing into the area from Hanoi between 1949 and 1954 shattered its tranquility. Even the cataclysmic upheaval at Dien Bien Phu (not all that far away) that culminated during the octave of Easter 1954 only sent ripples not waves that, on the surface at any rate, soon petered out as the defeated remnants of the French colonial army dismally concentrated in Hanoi after a foot journey of unutterable indignity. One senior officer wrote how he and another were handcuffed back to back the whole way: movement of any sort, eating and sanitation a perpetual, waking nightmare. Thereafter the many thousands of North Vietnamese who 'voted with their feet' as they elected to go to the south were essentially a Vietnamese problem, not a Laotian one. Some French vestiges remained in Sam Neua, an indifferent infrastructure, an educational system of sorts and an embryonic civil service.

Prewar there had been, for many years, the pull from Indo-China to Paris for the very bright student or the playboy son of the very rich. Also making the journey was a steady trickle of hopefuls who, if they did not imagine that the sidewalks of Paris were paved with gold, at least felt there might be an otherwise impossible chance of personal enhancement. Ho Chi Minh, later to become legendary and win immortal fame by kicking the French out of Indo-China and the Americans from South Vietnam, was in the 'hopefuls' category. In the 'playboy' group was Prince Souvannouvong, later known as the Red Prince, the youngest of more than ten sons of the pretender of the ancient house of Xieng Khouang, and half-brother to the future prime minister of Laos, Prince Souvanna Phouma. In his student days in Paris studying to be an engineer, the Red Prince fell in with a slip of a Vietnamese woman who had burning patriotic feelings for a homeland without French power – she was also an ardent communist. She was to be a guiding light and, at the same time, a goad to the Prince, whom she eventually married. She was shrewd enough to see that he had strong connections in his own country and even, maybe with dim, embryonic thoughts of Hanoi's hegemony over Indo-China, that he was her catalyst. Had he been even the second son she might have eschewed him for another, whatever her carnal thoughts for him were – and some Frenchmen with whom I talked averred that she never had any for anyone. If revolution is to be fomented and brought to a successful conclusion, it were better done through someone who had no chance whatsoever of obtaining supreme power legally. It made a person more fervid. Prince Souvannouvong had no chance of legitimate kingship.

When it was decided that the left-wing element of the Laotian nationalist movement should go it alone, Sam Neua was chosen for a base. It had the geographical advantages of being within easy striking distance of Hanoi and being far enough away from the royal and commercial capitals in Laos for communications to be tenuous. When massive American air attacks laid waste acres of surrounding territory it had the tremendous advantage of providing bombproof shelters as it was in limestone cliff country riddled with caves. Inside them it was tedious, uncomfortable and cheerless but life could still continue with little damage to the LPF cause. Indeed, it often enhanced it. Eastern Europeans, subservient to the Soviets, meddling Cubans and fence-sitting Swedes all saw the many surrounding bomb craters, some of which were later used as fish farms, and the shattered remains of Sam Neua town as sure and encouraging signs of little people being bullied by a vicious and wicked superpower, and emerging triumphant.

Political London wanted to know about such matters as how long did the LPF want a Co-Chairmanship to stay in force and, until it was disbanded, on what scale were its powers and writ envisaged. Guidance was to be given about, for example, the future level of British diplomatic representation, trade and aid for rehabilitating bombed areas. Davidson thought it likely that the LPF would portray the British as lackeys of the Americans so he told Robin Fearn to search the archives for instances of when there had been a divergence of opinions between UK and USA. One interesting snippet was unearthed: the Red Prince used to like the *Observer* newspaper, so a recent copy was procured to be given to him to show him that the British had long memories.

Military London wanted me to keep my ears and eyes open about a number of diverse matters: numbers and types of equipments, vehicles, weapons; state of bridges, roads and runways; state of alertness, morale and training of the officers and soldiers (if I could tell them apart); storage capacity for fuel; medical and hospital facilities; generating capacity, as well as anything else that might be of conceivable military interest.

The British team consisted of Alan Davidson, Robin Fearn, Peter Shield as pilot and myself. As far as Luang Prabang, where we refuelled, the flight was routine but the second and longer leg was hard work for Peter. The weather was dull and landmarks few. He had to be meticulous about flying over communist-held territory. His flight plan had to include a whole new set of radio frequencies, zonal boundaries, altitudes of both airfields in the Sam Neua area, approach angles, call signs, local hazards, fuel availability and alternative airfields (all in Vietnam) for a diversion in case of bad weather. Clearance was given for Nong Kang, the strip north of Sam Neua, so any deviation would mean landing somewhere we had not been cleared for. Peter flew by the seat of his pants and we arrived spot on time.

There was a tin hut at the end of the runway where a small reception committee waited. We drove along a dusty road, past bomb craters and wrecked vehicles, troops marching in formed bodies, defensive positions and barbed wire. We drove under a large triumphal arch erected to welcome a Hungarian delegation that had left many weeks before. It was comforting to see that the communist Lao were not unlike their right-wing brethren in some respects. The road left the plain and wound up towards a narrow pass between two limestone precipices towering above us. We got out and were taken up a path to a great cliff, walked round a vast stone baffle – a yard and a half thick and thirty feet high – that was shielding the entrance of a cave that was to be our home. It was very cold inside.

There was nothing to do that first day. It was cold and boring inside, not so cold and boring outside, where we were allowed to walk two hundred yards in one direction, always guarded. The discussions the next day were stilted and at times bordered on farce. Any point of substance Davidson asked, such as plans for elections, policy for the religious minorities, the transfer of any prisoners of war, zonal boundary markers, composition of government, their concept of neutrality, use of and payment for the Co-Chairmanship, these and many more were parried with inanities. Why, for instance, had the Vientiane side kidnapped one of their men when he had stopped behind a bush *pour faire pipi*, why had an RLA soldier been rude to one of their men and why had the Vientiane side repeatedly violated the cease-fire agreement and the accords? It was heavy-handed and puerile.

Foreign troops (Thais, Vietnamese and Chinese) and American advisers were mentioned once – suggestion, protest, accusation, denial and studied ignorance filled the air. Each side knew that the other side had a valid point and knew the other side knew. For our hosts it was a struggle between their being converted communists, so telling lies as second nature, and natural Lao imbued by their two age-old precepts of survival: behave well to your enemies of today as they may be your friends of tomorrow and be wary of your friends today as they may be your enemies of tomorrow; bend and you survive, break and you die. (A third seemed to be never do today what you can put off till the morrow or get someone else to do for you.)

At last the morning session came to an end. Even after only twenty-four hours I found the claustrophobic atmosphere of the caves and continuously being guarded as though prisoners irksome.

Our visit to the hospital that afternoon was cancelled ('no electricity') so we were taken to the cave that held the shop. On the way there I hung back and spoke to some of the soldiers who seemed delighted to be spoken to.

I was asked what fraternal country did I come from and when I said I was English I could see that, for them, that was only a language. They did not associate 'English' with a country. That started them talking. I learnt that they were not allowed to marry before they were twenty-seven years old; that, in their early twenties, they had been uniform about eight years; that they did not draw pay. By then my absence from the group was noticed and a functionary came hurrying back to take me away. The light of interest in the young men's eyes died.

In the shop some soldiers were deciding which of the shoddy goods they could have in exchange for their good-conduct vouchers: shoes, writing materials, books, a few items of clothes, torches – not much else. I tried to get an LPF *kip* to match it with a standard *kip* but this was not allowed.

Some senior members of the central committee joined us at our evening meal. The talk at table was in French except for an aside to me, in Lao, by the man on my left, that they had been afraid of me because I spoke Lao but had had good reports of my impartiality so had realised that we could help Laotian unification. That was why we had been invited.

We were then taken across to the cave opposite, the Central Committee cave, for a cultural show. The audience was already seated and gave us a slow handclap as we were ushered in. Above the stage a large banner proclaimed the LPF's slogan; 'peace, independence, neutrality, democracy, unity, progress'.

Songs were stereotype communist party propaganda, with catchy and lilting tunes, and politically slanted words. There were pæns of praise to their great victories over the American imperialists and the shooting down of aeroplanes by ordinary soldiers, eulogies to the heroics of the peasants and the fraternal aid of their socialist allies. There were dances by beautifully dressed young girls who sang about 'welcoming solidarity at local government level' and that 'the brightest star in the red sky is the signing of the peace accords'. One song had verses that praised the new spelling for the national language and another glorified elections. I remembered the spontaneous songs of love and separation, happiness and village scenes that the Gurkhas sang, so lively and vivid, not this dreary nonsense. Songs were the one way that sentiments near to the hearts of all could be the property of all, taken for granted but part of the fabric of everyday life, listened to if not actually sung by the World and his Wife, not this weary muck. Who could, in all honesty, believe it? Mind you, I further mused, some of the Western world's songs were inane...

My weasel-faced companion, with the unlikely name of Souk Vongsak, asking if I liked Laotian culture, interrupted my reverie. I could truthfully say that I liked the dancing. Souk was related to minor royalty. Now he preferred to sample the delights of an Asian communism in Laos, not realising that communism in this context meant the elimination of the Lao for Vietnamese benefit. What else? There was enough land for all peasants to own what they cultivated, no proletariat, no industrial base and no known raw materials and the whole thing was make-believe. The monarchy was also based on a myth but it was liked and respected and picturesque, not drab and mind-bendingly boring. Buddhism suited the people, not communism nor even Christianity. Communism, for all its fine principles, seemed to make its adherents suffer a life of purgatory in order to satisfy a chosen few at the top and deny individual dignity to the rest of the people. But this is not unique... Pay attention, I told myself.

We were taken up to the stage and made to dance. The girl who had announced the items was she who had performed in an LPF film I had seen in Vientiane. During the dancing I went up to her and told her I had liked it but that I liked the real thing better. Demurely she lowered her eyelids in maidenly pleasure.

The whole evening's performance was an exercise in surface-skating protocol; not too little, not too much – reminiscent of Buddhist philosophy and a once-famous advertisement for shaving soap!

The next and last morning we had a stiff, formal meeting with the Red Prince and some members of the politburo. Davidson told the Red Prince that although we were a small embassy we were good. He turned, pointed at me and said that I was the only attaché in Vientiane who spoke Lao, who got out and talked to the people and so we, the British, understood the real feelings of the people. The Prince smiled and said *Ah, le polyglot*. Photographs were taken and Davidson gave him a copy of the *Observer*.

From then on some of the points that had received scant attention on the previous day were given an airing but, as we had learnt to expect, the LPF merely followed their party line. We were asked to supply medical comforts for the refugees.

The thought struck me forcibly that the middle-piece cadres in the 'Liberated Zone' were entirely devoted to the cause, if only because they had never known any other. Like millions of other featureless functionaries throughout the world, they were doomed to the treadmill-like monotony of constantly coping with trivia despite the grandiose eloquence of superiority every system sired.

The meeting was over in an hour. We took our leave and drove to the outskirts of what had once been a thriving provincial capital. Here we were allowed to move around for more than two hundred yards and take any photographs we wanted. Not a house standing, nor was any habitable. Strangely the *wat* was the least badly damaged building and therein was a saffron-robed bonze. Outside were some soldiers and, in the knowledge that I was away soon, I was particularly cheerful when talking to them. I made them laugh. A casual observer might have thought such fraternisation unworthy of the occasion but would have been wrong: the mere ability of someone from the western world, vilified though it constantly was by communist propaganda, to make free, easy, sincere and uncensored contact with the young of the other bloc, and without another to check what was being said, was worth many hours of indirect propaganda. And anyway, it was the leaders and not the led that imposed the deadeningly bleak, unsmiling face of unimaginative officialdom everywhere.

The differing mentality between the two sides was neatly demonstrated a week or so later. I had requested a flight in a T-28 aircraft (after all, I was the Air Attaché), a small trainer turned into a fighter-bomber. Apart from the fuel crisis, the Prime Minister had forbidden all flying so that the neutrality of Vientiane should not be disturbed. The RLAF Commanding General therefore said 'no'. He was then shown a signal from Phone Kheng authorising my flight as a special case.

I met the pilot at Wattay airport and we walked to the aircraft. The pilot found the aircraft's tanks empty. Eventually a bowser came but it too was empty. Another was requested and we were given three hours' fuel. I was given a jacket, a flying helmet, told to sit in the back and was briefed on what to do in an emergency and which knob to pull to jettison. I was asked where I would like to go. Anywhere, for an hour or so, was my answer. Having cleared a flock of goats from the 'apron', we took off, flying at 2,500 feet, performing acrobatics, quick flips and looping the loop. The pilot practised dive bombing, pulling up and out vertically. It was all strange to me and I was glad I never satisfied a schoolboy hankering to be a pilot. I appreciated the gesture someone in the ministry made against the Prime Minister's strict orders!

After our return from Sam Neua I was in great demand by the RLA to tell them what it was like, what was said and what I thought of the future. Senior officers still believed that the LPF meant what it said but were intent on trying to thwart being swamped by the opposition.

The Director of Intelligence was Brigadier General Tao Ly Lidiluja. An American favourite, he hated communism, had a penchant for cowboy films and had commanded the 'Scorpion' Strike Division at Xeno, where there was a residual French presence, including a French doctor. Tao Ly's proud boast was that he could speak no French and as the French doctor could speak neither Lao nor English, it was indeed fortunate that he was blessed with good health and a sound constitution. Small and lithe, he was in stark and refreshing contrast to so many of the lard-covered robber barons also of general rank. I felt I should try and cultivate him but found it hard to arrange a meeting. I eventually managed to meet him when he was visited Vientiane, at the house of one Jim Sheldon having cadged an invitation. I had to endure the inevitable home movie and we hardly spoke to each other. But at least contact had been made.

We only met up again when he was in his new job and fretting for the field command he had once held. After I had told him about the Sam Neua visit, he asked me about the background of the cold war in Asia between the two communist giants and how Vietnam came into it. Luckily I had done my homework and from then on a close relationship started.

Once again General Vang Pao ignored me, this time for nearly a year until he discovered that a tactless remark made by me was a translation of what Cam West had asked me to ask, not what I had said. Accordingly I was invited up to Long Cheng, made very welcome, eulogised in public at a large party, met another ex-student from my Jungle Warfare School days with the still-secret Thai troops there and gave the General a briefing of the Sam Neua visit. From then on I could go to Long Cheng any time I wanted. The Americans wanted to keep tabs on what I said but, with no Thai or Lao speakers, the man detailed for this task admitted his defeat to me.

After Cam West left, his replacement was Colonel Colin Khan, an unimaginative man who had made his name as a brave soldier in Korea. Colin became friendly with his Soviet counterpart, Colonel Vasilli Soloviev who had replaced Vladimir Gretchanine. During the children's school holidays, they had each other's family round for meals. Colin saw that Vasilli's daughter wore a crucifix and presumed that the family had leanings towards Christianity so would be more likely to reciprocate plain talking if not confidences. Soloviev did open up and probed hard. Due to their Vietnam connection the Russians looked on the Australians as a link with the Americans, so concentrated on them. Much hard drinking till the small hours took place on more than one occasion, as Colin told me when he came round to my office for black coffee the next morning. I am not saying that Colin spoke out of turn but, being a suspicious person, I suggested to the security people that the crucifix might be a ploy. Discreet feelers were put out and four cases of similar Soviet initiatives towards the Australians who were friendly to the Americans were reported in southeast Asia. The Americans kept their distance after that.

A lighter note was struck by the wedding of Sisouk and Marina, although the communist press reviled it. I remember it well. The bride looked ravishing. She was dressed in a pale blue, long-sleeved blouse, made of silk with floral designs. Her skirt was dark blue with golden embroidery in the shape of diamonds. She wore thick gold bangles and a long, thin, red-gold necklace that was curled twice around her neck and, bandolier-fashion, twice around her body. A shawl, also dark blue, had the diamond motif in golden-red thread. It was nine inches across and was draped from in front, round over the left shoulder, under the right arm and back over the left shoulder. It ended in the form of a net. On her head was a strange hat of cupola mode made of red cloth studded with gold and with a golden band around it. The hat rose some six inches about her head and was topped in a rounded bobble.

The bridegroom looked equally striking. He wore a lavender blue silk coat with a high collar. In front were six golden buttons. Round his waist was a 2-inch-wide belt of golden cloth with diamond-shaped golden buckles. He also wore two golden chains, one over his left shoulder and under his right arm, the other over his right shoulder and under his left arm. Both chains had the diamond motif around the top and bottom of his high collar and around his sleeves. For trousers he wore normal baggy national dress that tied up in a tail under the belt at the back below the jacket and came three-quarters the way down his legs. He was bareheaded. Both wore European-style shoes; hers golden, his black.

But for me the nicest part of it all was that Princess Golden Fairy flew out from London and we got on even better than before. Later a Colonel Somneuk Siharaj offered to be an intermediary for us to marry. I wish now I had taken him up on it.

One of my many visitors was the famous author, John Le Carré, who was in search of material for his new book, *The Honourable Schoolboy*. We spoke at length about Laos, he listening intently and asking many questions. I offered him to go anywhere, within reason, in Laos, in the embassy Beaver and he went away thanking me and saying he would get in touch with me. He never came back. I found him a quiet man, with an ability both to listen and not to reveal any new ideas in his questioning. I was fascinated to see a whiff of what I had told him in the text and I wrote to him after I had read it and said that I had been worried at his non-appearance. We kept up an erratic correspondence and he offered me some sound advice if I wanted to 'write the big one'.

Another, sadder, visitor was an American, Miss Nancy Huberth, who thought I could help her get into contact with her brother, one of eighteen Americans held as prisoners by Sihanouk's men in the Khmer Republic. She came straight to the point. She wanted to contact the anti-government forces in that country. She had heard that I had 'very good relations with the North Vietnamese' so she wanted me to give them a letter from her. She had not contacted her own embassy.

I declined to go to the North Vietnamese as we had not yet established diplomatic relations with them and I knew I would get a rebuff but I would be very interested to learn who thought my relations with them were 'very good'. It was difficult to help her but, in the event, I put her on to Lieutenant Phông but, alas, he too was unable to help her.

On 3 June, sixty days after the formation of the PGNU (which only ever applied to the royalist section of Laos) by when all foreign troops were to be out of the country, Vientiane was flooded with reporters who wanted to ensure that that was the case. How they expected to find out by wandering around Vientiane I did not discover. I was visited by representatives of Reuters, the *Daily Mail* and the *Washington Post*, more out of curiosity than for corroboration.

Morale among RLA officers I spoke to sank lower and lower until, by July, it was rock-bottom in some places and frank comments of fears of there being 'no decent peace' were frequently made, nor was there any faith in the future. I had not come across any potential Young Turk among the secret parts of the army, not even the people who taught assassinations. Before the end of the year the PL were included in most military parades, even those for the King.

On the political front one most significant event was the return to Vientiane, after a 10-year absence, of the North Vietnamese ambassador. It was by uncomfortable chance that the South Vietnamese man was the doyen at the time, so had to step down. Nevertheless, the two were always next to each other at official sit-down functions, with granite faces and growled greetings.

By now, say it who shouldn't, the relevant parts both of the FCO and the MOD thought I was doing a good enough job. The FCO wanted me further extended in post: the Chief of the General Staff, General Sir Peter Hunt, personally told me (on a visit to Bangkok) that he would not withdraw the Beaver despite the 'aviation' people in London wanting it back in UK.

Davidson and I went up to Luang Prabang, he to meet the Red Prince who had moved there. I asked Davidson if he would ask if I could have permission to visit the PL battalion in the royal capital. This the Red Prince gave but no notice was taken of it (rather like at the previous April's party for the Queen's birthday with PL sentries persisting in entering the grounds of the residence when protocol forbade it. The RLA generals complained to me. I went to expel them but they took no notice of me. I then asked a very senior LPF official if he would tell them to move out but no notice was taken of him either). At Luang Prabang I walked round the town and struck up a conversation with PL soldiers who were most suspicious of me. I paid the LPF HQ a visit – the first foreigner so to do – held a 70-minute conversation with them and was asked back. Among other points I championed the Americans and the Thais, and I deprecated Sam Neua's 'black' propaganda. This prompted Davidson to send the FCO, and other interested embassies, a telegram on our return. I also called on the King's half-brother, the MR 1 commander, who bluntly said that Souvanna Phouma had to go because he 'was now a PL'.

Despite the fighting being officially over there were continual skirmishes, patrols, interdiction probes, assassination missions and propaganda forays, with the PL being much the worse offenders. The secret camps of the Irregulars had to be maintained and I visited them.

Instead of the sad, hapless, lacklustre creatures of the conventional army here were soldiers who had a purposeful robustness and who emanated a dedication of a high standard. In Whisky 3 I had an hour-long briefing about training methods, operational techniques, combat lessons and current offensive actions by both sides. I was presented with a bloodstained PL flag and was invited to look at the facilities, which included inspecting a new batch or recruits and a passing-out parade where I was asked to present the prize to the champion shot. I was very impressed although it was impossible to know what would happen during 'those last few yards'.

(Many spurious PL flags were made in Udorn, Thailand, and sold to the gullible men of the USAF. Three years earlier they were selling for US$150 a time. Those treated with chicken's blood actually fetched US$200 each.)

I was due in PS 18 around 10 o'clock the next day but, when the Beaver landed at Pakse to touch my hat to General Soutchai first, I was given an invitation card from Prince Boun Oum to witness some boat races at Khong Island, General Kouprasith's home base. Khong Island is only just north of the Cambodian border and boasts the world's widest waterfalls. Soutchai was there already. I remonstrated as the dress was formal and I was in jungle kit and taken away in a helicopter. At Khong I gave the crew a 3-hour deadline.

A pavilion had been erected on the waterfront. The great, brown Mekong flowed majestically by, over a quarter of a mile wide. My heart sank as I saw a galaxy of brass in serried echelons behind a throne on which sat the vast hulk of the Inspector General of the Kingdom of the Million Elephants and the White Parasol, His Highness Prince Boun Oum and his hardly less large wife. Two of the million elephants, I thought sourly.

General Bounphone jumped up, punched me in the chest and shouted 'Commando!'. I was led to the Prince and Princess and had to sit with them. She twitted me about not having visited them recently and so gallant was my answer that she went all coy and giggly, reminding me of a hippopotamus with hiccups.

At last it was time to leave. I excused myself and roused the crew but the helicopter would not start. There was a small donkey engine in the machine's body and Peter Shield could hardly believe his eyes when a cigarette-smoking crew member tried to start it. Eventually a large spanner was produced and the starter motor below the pilot's seat was hit hard thrice and the engine started.

At Pakse we jumped into the Beaver and landed in a remote and roadless area with only minutes to spare before sundown. I was invited to inspect a Guard of Honour that had been waiting there since 10 o'clock. It was then a quarter to 6. I felt sick inside and apologised for being so late, the first person ever to do so, apparently. After a meal I was introduced to and questioned in depth by all officers in camp on many points: the visit to Sam Neua, communist intentions, jungle warfare tactics, my own experiences, were some among many others.

Next morning we had a briefing in front of a large map. The Major let his hair down and told Peter and me of his troubles: besides training men for clandestine operations in MR 4 with an insufficiency of everything, he was also responsible for such tasks as monitoring the Ho Chi Minh Trail. The latest situation report from one of his teams made gloomy reading; infiltrated six weeks previously, no exfiltration plans had yet been formulated as no chopper pilots would fly that far without unauthorised danger money which he could not pay, having no slush fund. One of the small group of soldiers committed on that task had died of starvation. Radio batteries were almost exhausted. Should they wait for a chopper or surrender? They were too weak to walk out. Could they know when to expect an answer?

I asked when the Major hoped to get his men out. "Yesterday," he said, "but I was told there were no choppers after all, despite being told that I could expect one." Was that the one reserved for Peter and me, I wondered, hoping desperately that was not the case.

I visited many other secret camps, where I spent nights and had long talks with the staff talking about the Sam Neua trip and aspects of jungle warfare. I always had a riveted audience, went to bed tired and liked to think I never divulged a confidence. Unlike one Commonwealth attaché based in Bangkok and accredited to Laos who talked too much, particularly to the Indians. Like some flowers at dusk, all his openings were softly and unnoticeably closed. We suspected, but had no hard evidence, that all reports sent to New Delhi also went to Moscow.

One interesting sidelight on how the RLA and PL managed affairs took place in the northwest of the country, not far from the town of Ban Houei Sai on the Mekong. One small village, a day's walk from the town, was divided down the middle, royalists in the south, communists in the north. There was no friction; they used the same water supply for drinking and washing – which is what both lots were doing when I visited the place. The RLA troops had had no pay for six months and the officer in charge spoke about it to his opposite PL number who suggested that he go to Ban Houei Sai and complain to his HQ. The RLA man objected that he could not leave his post.

A compromise was reached. All the RLA soldiers would go to Ban Houei Sai and demand their pay. During that time the PL would occupy the RLA camp. If successful the PL would accept pay for as many days as the RLA soldiers were away then go back to their own camp. If however the RLA delegation was unsuccessful the whole lot would join the PL on their return. Pay was allowed and the PL did move back, five days' pay the richer. It was only later that I learnt that the two opposing commanders were cousins. Chen Shu-lin's reaction was to laugh and say that he could not understand the inscrutable Lao!

At a party given by the Czechs I met the left-wing neutralist (a typical Laotian exercise in terminology) commander, Kaysone Boupha, and wondered if the trace of my teacher Kaysorn Bouapha had been muddled up with his records. If so it would explain the inaccurate report I had been originally given. I would not have met him for many months otherwise and I took the opportunity of telling him that I would be asking him to an all-Laotian faction party in my house. Such diplomatic get-togethers as at the Czechs had their uses.

This party, which I had started planning at the end of May for ministers and senior military officers was, in its way another first. The PGNU was, by then, composed of every 'odd' ministry being headed by a royalist with his deputy an LPF man and every 'even' one headed by an LPF man with his deputy a royalist, with only Health headed by a Neutralist. It was most complicated as both sides had to get permission and, before this was given, wanted to know who the other side's guests would be. A month later, by the end of June, it was time for the next stage. This was personally writing out all the invitations in Lao myself (to the guests, proof of my sincerity and, for me, a precaution for them 'not understanding French' so disregarding the invitation). That done I personally took them around to the guests' offices where they quizzed me on various matters. As the guests were mostly senior men it took a long time.

The party was a success in as far as most of those invited came. For administrative convenience we sat at card tables in case seating arrangements had to be speedily changed. Three of the LPF rang earlier on in the day to say they could not come. Those that did come had more aplomb than the RLA (I was surprised when one general told smutty jokes of schoolboy standard) and it took some time for the atmosphere to thaw. To give a canine analogy, the 'ring sniffing' phase lasted a long time. I only had two at my table, the Deputy Minister of Defence, the left-wing Neutralist Kaysone Boupha, and the RLA Director of Psychological Warfare, Brigadier General Etam Singvongsa. As neither would speak to the other I relayed their conversation, a tiring and unnecessary chore. At the end of the meal I rose, went to the other side of the room and made a short speech, ending up with the toast to 'Peace, Independence, Neutrality, Democracy, Unity and Progress'.

Both sides rushed to clink glasses with me, crying 'with British help', thinking that I was on their side, an object lesson in the use of weasel words. Then serious conversation started, in one case between two officers who had not met for twenty years when the younger deserted from the elder, his company commander, to join the PL. I wondered how many of them remembered the Laotian proverb, 'three can keep a secret only when two of them are dead'.

Before I got any feedback from my party, Alan Davidson hosted a dinner party in honour of the Chinese ambassador and his senior staff. On one side of the menu were six 'lion and unicorn' crests and six three-headed Laotian elephant motifs. On the other were the dishes, listed as 'scotch broth, kippers, black pudding and chips, toad-in-the-hole, bubble and squeak, plum pudding and brandy sauce, cheddar cheese, english gooseberries and welsh rabbit'. To drink were 'somerset cider and guiness stout'. When she heard of the menu Mrs Davidson threatened to divorce her husband, so she told me, but she might have been joking.

The Chinese were unprepared for such bizarre food and merely played at eating it. I asked Chen Shu-lin if he wasn't hungry and he admitted that they had all had a 'decent' meal before they had left their embassy so there was no need to eat what was offered to them.

The feedback from my party, with who said what to whom, was reported, certainly for the royalists, to Sisouk, who was very pleased. This he told me himself when I took Ian Lawnder, the New Zealand attaché up from Bangkok (who had asked me to interpret for him when he paid a call on the Chinese DA), to visit him. During our talk Sisouk turned to me and asked me if he should take over as leader now that the Prime Minister, Prince Souvanna Phouma, had had a heart attack. My advice was an affirmative one with a warning and two provisos. The warning was that the morale of the RLA was so low that if he were not to take over, it might drop too low ever to rebound. The two provisos were to have a preparatory phase and to seek an opportunity to tell everyone when the LPF were discredited; I suggested that might be soon, when rice hoarding started, costs went up and the LPF minister in charge would have had his image tarnished. I sincerely hoped that the New Zealand DA would keep his mouth shut as to the part I played: it was innately sensitive but not to have answered would have been craven.

If that had been positive, I feared my next unexpected challenge was negative. I had flown down to Pakse and General Soutchai had lent me a helicopter ("be back before 10 o'clock") to go to an area of tension, Keng Nyao. The village had changed hands a number of times since the cease-fire and was on the border of the two zones. It so happened that there was a meeting of village headmen from the LPF zone in another village over the boundary river and the local commander, a Colonel, sent a runner to bring them all across.

At first they were afraid, thinking I was an American. But come they did and I was introduced as the British DA who had recently been to Sam Neua and would tell them everything that the British and LPF officials had spoken about. It was a tricky situation: say nothing and lose face, say too much and lose my reputation. So I started with some bland platitudes and gave them a harmless description of the countryside, fish farms, napalm damage and caves, to the growing agitation of the RLA Colonel, a shady-looking man who was half French and half Cambodian. After several minutes I had had enough and, in any case, I was already late in getting the helicopter back to Pakse.

To the Colonel's evident relief I wound up my short address and bade them goodbye. As I was leaving I heard the Colonel tell the audience that they had probably not understood what I had said as I spoke with a northern accent and what I meant to say was that all communists were bad, that none could be trusted and that it were better that all the headmen were to rally to the Vientiane side...

I crept away, worried how much of that would get back to the LPF and I be branded as two-faced. I was not my own master to the extent I should have liked but I felt I had avoided the trap of not showing diplomatic impartiality. I did not avoid the trap when, in a stupid effort to help General Soutchai plan interesting training for his men, I took down my personal copy of every Jungle Warfare School preçis for him to browse through. I thought I would get them back without any embarrassment – but I was wrong.

One Saturday morning I was invited around to Tao Ly's house and had a long conversation. He had given me a Top Secret document, an appreciation of the situation as seen from an intelligence angle, issued to ministers and generals. I congratulated him on it and said how much of it conformed with my ideas. "It should do," was his surprising reply. "It's based on what you have told me."

Communist successes in Indo-China were reflected in the more anti-western attitude of the two Indians suspected as having been 'bought' by the Russians. One was the man with ambassadorial status in charge of the ICSC, Gharekan, (denigrator of everything Britain stood for and who saw North Vietnam and East Germany as the 'book ends' necessary for the support of what was in the middle). The other was the First (and only) Secretary in the Indian embassy, both when they were in their cups. The latter had studied in USA where he had been 'trawled' for by the Soviets and in USSR – "in America all can talk but poor people cannot eat and in Russia all can eat but most people cannot talk" – told me that Nepal would be part of India by 2000 AD except in name, and much of what would happen has indeed come to pass.

I asked Chen Shu-lin what China's reaction would be if that were to happen. He said that China would punish India as it had done once already when it invaded the northeast of India. "We have no quarrel with the Indian people," he said, "only with the government if it violated Nepal." Was it coincidence that the 'Friendship Highway', linking Kathmandu with Lhasa, seemed to germinate from about that time?

In October I visited Phone Kheng for a talk with General Oudone Sananikone, the Director of Operations. He was worried as a crisis had arisen. Sisouk's wedding was to be commemorated by giving a medal to a hundred and one returned prisoners-of-war and the Director did not know which of two awards were to be given and, even if it was decided which was the more suitable, there were not enough of either sort to go round. Sisouk himself was already thirty minutes late in coming to present them. Oudone asked me if I'd like to go and talk with the POWs until the ceremony started. I jumped at the opportunity and accompanied him down to where they were lined up. The General turned to me and said, disarmingly and inaccurately, that I knew everything and understood everything better than they did.

By then I had become almost immune from the curiosities of Laotian life, almost but not quite. I thought of the staid British method of the award of decorations, the flamboyant American system and the nonchalant gong-grabbing French who boasted they never knew how many medals they had, but for sheer, unadulterated military inefficiency, this seemed to put all else in the shade.

The POWs may well have regarded me as an exotic appendage to the ceremony as I walked down the two ranks, shaking hands with and saying something to them all, and making some of them laugh. Sisouk arrived as I was finishing and the solution to the problem was apt: each row got a different medal, the front rank the lower grade but given out by the senior man and the rear rank the higher, given by the junior. Neat.

In October, at the annual Thad Luang festival, the PL were on parade with the RLA contingent. Later on the King, the Crown Prince and the Red Prince visited foreign stands. Davidson had briefed me to 'talk Lao loudly'. (I spoke in nine, including French and English that afternoon) I found myself escorting the Red Prince who was very haughty, so I spoke Lao loudly to two LPF ministers and their wives in his group. I made mention of the LPF cultural show of the night before, how I had enjoyed it but that the words of the songs were different from the Sam Neua ones. At that the Red Prince turned and said, in Lao, how well I spoke Lao. My riposte was that I feared to talk to him in Lao because he was royalty so had to be spoken to in French (to which he said, "Don't worry, carry on,") and I said that my reason for talking Lao was to act as a bridge between the two zones as befitted the Co-Chairman's representative. He was obviously pleased. As he smiled his eyes sparkled. What a game it was!

After dark films were shown outside some countries' booths. Scarcely anyone watched the Soviet or Chinese films but many clustered around the American screen, watching with great delight some vintage slapstick. The PL soldiers were there in profusion, laughing uproariously. After all, the Marx brothers could be related to Karl!

Over the months I paid visits to the MOD to have chats with the Minister of Defence, Sisouk, and the Commander-in-Chief, to brief them on any points I felt they ought to know about resulting from my visits. Both welcomed me and asked me to continue travelling around the country and helping the two sides bridge the gap of their differences. (I believe those who said that to me had an overblown estimation of what I could do.) The C-in-C was refreshingly frank. He himself found it hard to get around and "if you don't let us know what is happening then we don't know."

I called on the LPF's highest representative for defence in the Provisional Government, Kaysone Boupha, to try and glean any information possible. Kaysone was nobody's idea of a commander, being hesitant, unforthcoming and indecisive – wet enough to shoot snipe off was my uncharitable opinion of him. He had neither English nor French. The meeting in his office was studiously formal. The curtain over one of the two windows in the room was already drawn and the other was drawn before we started talking so we sat in semi-darkness. As he did not open his mouth and rather than sit in silence I started off: I told him that I reported to London about how I found both the RLA and the PL, how I had been to Sam Neua, how I had met both sides formally and informally in my house, that the Laotian quarrel was not mine and that I regarded myself as a bridge (the toadying in-phrase) in my ability to understand the two sides and, in a way, bring them together. This pleased him. I also told him that my successor would learn Lao, with reasons why, which also pleased him. (In the event I was not replaced.) A secretary wrote it all down. After twenty minutes I had run out of small talk so I asked about a visit to the PL battalions in Vientiane and in Luang Prabang, requested originally many months before. He spoke vague generalities for ten minutes and I left, no wiser than before.

Two weeks later I was back, asking about the visits but drew a blank so, nothing loth, went back a third time a couple of weeks after that, the week I had proposed. Having had no reply I went to get one. I guessed (correctly) that it would be a refusal but it was interesting to see their reaction. Forty minutes and much going off at tangents then "it is a problem." "It must be a big problem as it has lasted a year," I answered. I then, for the first time ever, got a direct answer. I could have a limited, less ambitious, meeting with some of the officials, sometime...

One result of my journeying around the countryside was that some RLA officers took advantage of me. On 28 November I was hijacked. Nothing bodily harmful, but hijacked. The background to it was dull and tedious so I suppose I had had my suspicions dulled. It had started in the previous July when I spent a night at a sub-area HQ at a place called Phone Hong, under a Colonel Somneuk Siharaj, my would-be matchmaker. He had arranged a *baçi*, a cultural show and a communal meal (in all I talked for eleven of the twenty-two hours I was there).

A month later, he suggested a drive round his area. We drove down a small feeder road leading to the dam that had been pointed out when I first flew to Long Cheng. A minor fishing industry had grown up and Somneuk suggested we visit it. On the way there we passed a dowdy-looking camp with a board that read 'MR 5 Resettlement and Development Unit'. Being interested in how we resettled our British Army Gurkhas due pension and wanting to compare notes, I asked him if we could call in on the way back. Grudgingly this was allowed.

It was pitifully bare of teaching aids, props, furniture and most facilities. There was no provision for livestock or handyman training. The Captain in charge gave me a drab and bland briefing that included statistics of square hectares of crops, of numbers of farm beasts and chickens – but where were they? – and had a soporific effect on me though I tried not to show it; it was not his fault that the subject matter was boring. He shot a glance at Somneuk who was lolling in a chair opposite. Somneuk suddenly straightened himself and turned to the Captain. In a voice charged with authority he interrupted him in mid-sentence.

"Tell him!"
"T-tell him?" the Captain faltered, patently distressed. "Tell him everything?"
"Don't worry. I will. You've done well. Thank you. This is my decision."

Somneuk turned to me and continued, "All you have been told so far is completely untrue." Thrown off balance I tried not to gawp. "The 'Resettlement and Rehabilitation' part of this is a cover for our real activities, the training of selected men to go over the line and make contact with the other side, either killing them or persuading them to surrender." Infiltration and reconnaissance were also taught. Not even the Americans (who paid for everything but had little to say beyond 'the point of audit departure') knew the school existed nor did the RLA officially know the school existed, so it had to be run on syphoned funds. I was told I was the very first foreigner to be let into the secret.

He paused for breath and I, riveted in fascination, merely nodded my head, not wanting to break the spell. How utterly unsuspected and totally divorced from the dull, lethargic briefing.

Somneuk turned to the Captain and said, "You've been here a long time. How many years?"
The Captain made a swift calculation. "Ten years, sir."
Again my head spun; ten years in one job and under such conditions. It hardly made sense even in Laotian terms.
"Care to look at our syllabus, our training programme?" Somneuk asked. "I'll give you a copy."
And how! This was meat and drink to me. I was told to keep it and that I would be invited back when there was a course running "so that you can really see what we're doing and talk to the students."

I had been back to see Somneuk twice since, once when he was ill and once when he told Khien to drive down a bumpy, dusty lane fringed with palm trees. Was this a back way to the training school? The lane petered out at a small *wat*. An elderly bonze came out and led us inside. Somneuk stopped and kicked off his shoes. I followed suit. Inside it was empty, dim and cool, and bare of the garish decorations so often found in larger *wats*. The two Lao went inside, knelt down and made obeisance to a large Buddha. I hung back. The others stood up stiffly, Somneuk with flushed face. Back in what had been an empty space I was surprised to see it filled with elderly people sitting cross-legged on straw mats. Facing them was a narrow wooden bench and two glasses of colourless liquid on the ground in front of it. I was gestured to sit down on the bench and have a drink of tepid well water.

Somneuk addressed the gathering, saying that he had called them together to listen to some wise words, to some teaching of an Englishman whose country, like theirs, was a monarchy threatened by communism. The *wat* was a place of teaching so it was right to have asked them to go there that morning to listen. He turned to me and said "It's all yours."

I am seldom lost for words but, even so, I was put in a most awkward position. Decline, and perhaps not get to the secret training camp; accept, and lay myself open to compromising misrepresentations. I racked my brains, cursing Somneuk and fretting inwardly. I stood up and taking the bull by the horns spoke about Britain respecting trusted and ancient traditions, that it was a most personal matter to each individual to make up his mind to back the system, not to buck it and, by example, to maintain it. More than that I would not say, as to comment on Laos was out of place. I finished off with some general remarks on the crops, the state of the weather, the sinking *kip* and the hope of a lasting peace.

The audience looked at me through old, calm, peasant eyes. They said nothing as there was nothing to say. This was ridiculous and I felt a sudden surge of anger and got up from the bench. I made the *wai* sign and left the *wat*, Somneuk trailing behind. Never had visit seemed less productive.

I fixed up yet another visit, on that fateful November day, this time definitely going to the school. I reported in to Somneuk with time to spare and was slightly disconcerted to see the Police Chief and the local District Administrator there. Our programme was to visit the school, me to address them, questions to me, a walk around and then finish.

Fine, I thought, but why the two civilians? My mind seethed. What the hell was this in aid of? I thought the two officials might just be cadging a lift. All of us got into my car and drove off towards the school, but passed it. Strange! We drove on and came to a large, American-built school that shrieked of 'aid', drove straight in, around the main block and stopped short of an open-sided building, packed full of students. A line of locals stretched from where the car stopped to the building. Who, I wondered, was the important person they were all lined up for? No, it couldn't be – but it was. Me, again. Misled, made of fool of. In short, hijacked.

The students were waiting for me to address them. This again was one of those situations that have a dream-like quality of unreality to them but have to be got on with. Twenty local dignitaries were lined up for introductions and I was ushered onto the stage where a chair waited me and those who came with me in my car. After several speeches it was my turn. I was escorted onto the little speaking platform and given a hand microphone. I was to be recorded.

I started by winning the audience over to my side. Just before I stood up I made funny faces behind the speaker's back as though I hated the idea of speaking, and I made a few more as I introduced myself. I said I was lucky to be made known to them before they met me outside and called me 'long-nosed foreigner', and I made my nose 'squeak'. I had a resounding cheer at that so, having thought out what I was going to say, manfully started. I spoke for ten minutes, long enough I thought. Colonel Somneuk stopped me from leaving and, using the mike, said I had been to Sam Neua and so I would describe it all. That took another fifteen minutes. Enough, I thought. But no – Somneuk yet again took the mike and said, "Has communism infiltrated into Britain? It has in Laos. Please comment."

I did my best and, rather lamely I fear, tailed off and made as to sit down. But no, Somneuk was persistent if nothing else. His next question was "Britain is a kingdom as is Laos. How can a country with royalty combat communism and what is the future of the royalty system in Laos vis-à-vis communism?" That seemed a favourite Laotian theme, made more apt by two narrow UK Labour party victories in 1974, the introduction of the 3-day working week in the previous March and Vassall's defection to the Soviet Union. I would have had difficulty in answering Somneuk's question 'cold' in English but I made a stab at it. As a gesture of defiance I pulled a rude face at the students, wobbled my eyebrows independently and smiled at them vacuously, with a terrible squint. Clown! Joker! Much laughter. Small comfort but enough for me to make an adaptation of 'the price of liberty is eternal vigilance', a few clichés about people's wishes and a final remark that enough was enough was enough...*phor di leew*.

In all I spoke for forty minutes and got a big ovation. All over. Finished. But no: the headmaster then got up and made a little speech and asked me to talk about the Co-Chairman's duties in the present situation in Laos. So I got up once again and tried my best. The student leader then came up to the rostrum and asked another question (fielded by Somneuk) and also asked my age, the population of UK and could I stay for four years in Laos? The students sang me a song and I was shown round, not really taking in much by that time.

I was driven back to the military HQ where I was pressed to stay for lunch, a meal of sticky rice, muddy lake fish and chickens' legs from the knees down. During it the tape was played back, my tinny voice jarring me. To Somneuk's chagrin I asked to be excused before the tape was finished. I thanked him for the meal and, trying not to show I was bitterly disappointed, said I presumed that that was not the last time we would be meeting. He said he hoped not.

I was not going to give up and made a call on a friend in HQ MR 5, a Colonel Douang Pi, wounded in the right wing *coup manqué* whom, when in hospital, I had visited, taking him 'goodies'. He was 'in my debt' and it was almost an anti-climax when I did finally get to the place where raids across the border were still trained for, despite the formation of the PGNU. We had a talk in the office, where I gave back the syllabus and suggested 'shadowing' techniques and memory training be added. (I got details from notes when I was Commandant of the Border Scouts in Borneo, which I sensibly did not take with me.) The students certainly looked tough and they regarded me with keen interest. I was invited to address them and was careful in what I said. We had a discussion and I left feeling that there was the future nucleus of men ready to fight for their King and country.

It was only long afterwards I remembered that they all had 'short back and sides' so were obviously military men. Were they really students at that place or a group especially brought in for me to meet?

'While still a boy in a man's league, I feel I'm now in the VIth form', I wrote home after I had given a lecture to RLA Staff College students. It was the practice for every attaché, once during his tenure, to tell them about the organisation of his own army. My turn was on 2 January 1975. I was sent a copy of the programme and saw I was to talk for two hours (far too long even with questions). The Deputy Minister of Defence, Kaysone Boupha, was due to follow me. I found some notes on the subject in the drawer of my desk, faithfully culled from the many préçis previous DAs had been given when students at the British Army's Staff College. I, never having been to that august establishment, did not feel its magisterial burden upon me, nor could I see the Lao being even faintly interested in anything that did not affect them directly. I decided to broaden my terms of reference. I asked the Commandant which language he wanted me to talk in, English, French or Lao. He said, with a grin, it was up to me but please not to speak in Chinese. In the event I risked speaking Lao (a 'first' I was told).

I began by saying that the students would only be interested to know that the promotion system of the British Army was designed to eliminate all but professional qualifications being considered and that officers were not allowed 'side jobs' to supplement their income. I then went into details of why and how the British had won in Malaya and Borneo, and gently reminded them of no non-communist victory in Indo-China. The audience was fascinated, especially as I traced the development of Chinese guerilla tactics, the Sino-Soviet quarrel and the Indo-China issue as and how they concerned Laos. I drew on my own experiences and my talks with the communists, especially the in-depth debriefing I had had with an NVA military adviser to the PL and many PL 'ralliers'.

After an hour I stopped and asked if there were any questions. There were, searching and penetrating, which I fully answered. So many were there that I stayed even longer than the prescribed two hours and the Deputy Minister, kept waiting, left in high dudgeon. I was invited back.

On the diplomatic front I had a permanent invitation to drop in on the South Vietnamese Ambassador and keep him up to date with what I had found out and, were I to go to Bangkok, to visit the West German Ambassador.

Meanwhile, as the communiqués had it, *la situation demure grave*. The country was effectively cut in two at Thakek at the top of the 'Panhandle'. There were strikes and student protests in most of the major towns, continued land grabs, rumours everywhere, false reports spread by the LPF who often disregarded their own terms of behaviour in the two 'neutralised' capitals (more men than officially allowed being one example) and a lowering of the already low morale among the royalist forces.

As if that was not bad enough, we had a visit from a high official in the FCO who told us that Britain was in a mess and faced only one problem, that of survival, with sixty left-wing members of parliament posing as grave a problem as any, and a referendum (which nobody really wanted) on the common market. Many were acutely worried about Soviet penetration in Britain after it was learnt what the Czech spy, Frolik, had said. It was hard for us to worry about the spread of communism in far-off Indo-China when now, by being in Laos we were aware as never before of its threat, we could easily see how it was penetrating and infiltrating the fabric of society at home.

My own views were especially influenced by four events. The first two were the recent removal of one hundred and five Soviet agents from Britain and the Prime Minister's friendship with Joseph Kagan (tainted by Richardas Vaygaskus [*The Storm Birds: Soviet Post-War*

Defectors, Gordon Brook-Shepherd, London, Chapter 13, pp 199-200]). The third was when the Chinese DA called in especially to say that he did so hope Wilson, the British Prime Minister, hadn't been taken in by the Soviets who, unlike the Chinese, wanted world domination. The fourth was that the person in charge of Overseas Development affairs in London, a Ms Judith Hart, did not allow us, the representatives of the right wing, to give them any material, only to the left wing. That we were only able to do without duly offending the royalists by giving medical stores to the refugees in the 'liberated zone'.

At the King's audience on New Year's Day, I greeted all the Generals by name as we circulated after His Majesty had retired. General Tao Ly said he hoped that 1975 would bring them political and military victory. I tried not to show my true feelings at this absurd remark and said that we had not had a chat for some time.

"Come to my house next Saturday, at about 5 in the evening. Plain clothes. I'll warn the guard. I want to talk to you." He seemed unusually serious. As he turned away he gulped down his half-full glass of champagne and grabbed another from a passing waiter.

I walked to the house and was shown inside. Tao Ly got up from his chair and, going to the windows, melodramatically drew the curtains. He called for some coffee for me. He had a brandy bottle and a glass in front of him. Even in the gloom it was obvious, from the outset, that he was worried, as well as verging on the broodingly maudlin.

He started off by telling me that he trusted me implicitly. We could talk openly, man to man. I inwardly stiffened, mentally alerting myself for something critical. His first point was about rumours of spies and agents becoming more active. He was forming killer squads to infiltrate their gangs once he had tracked them down and he wanted to be ready for his assassins to obliterate them. Could I provide him with miniature cameras, miniature tape recorders and silenced weapons? "Second, how can we beat communism?" He topped up his glass.

My mind reeled at the man's naïvety as he watched me intently, his normally happy face clouded and serious. I pursed my lips, looked for a long, long second directly into his eyes, and still holding his gaze, let silence hang in the air a little longer.

General Tao Ly was different from the other Lao generals. His promotion had been at American insistence, not on his superiors' recommendation. He therefore should have had a more balanced, impartial view of the true state of affairs. Almost without exception (Tao Ly was one of two generals with Soutchai in MR 4 the other) the senior officers of the RLA and many politicians had always shown more concern for their personal comfort than for their country's future in the way that they had nest-feathering business contacts (such as the monopoly in Pepsi Cola) and methods of manipulating the market. This was nothing new or unique in Asia but it had, unfortunately, the cumulative effect of making the communists' job that much the easier. Most Lao had a touching faith in their ability to get on with one another, family connections making a cat's cradle of inescapable contacts and very nearly unbreakable allegiances. With many of his friends dead or absorbed by constraint or conviction into the LPF, Tao Ly knew how absurdly stubborn the Vietnamese were, how easily they could bully their Lao neighbours and how soft many of the RLA General Staff and political leaders had become. He could read the signs of morale-sapping, fibre-loosening complacency and greed among his brother officers and political contacts. I knew that he had not amassed a fortune and he knew it would not be easy to start a new life in the States. He was faced with a decision: fight them, join them or escape from them. He would not opt out there and then as he believed he had a little time left before that option need be taken, hence his invitation to me. But he was frightened.

107

Tao Ly looked away and broke the slight tension that had started to build up. As his glass was empty again, he refilled it. I answered the first question. As regards the hardware he required in no way could I comply. I might be the UK 'unofficial spy' but my charter, I repeated, forbade me to help him. I presumed he had asked me, I continued with a flash of inspiration, because the Americans had already turned him down? Tao Ly nodded sadly. It was clever of me to have guessed or did I know already?

I assured him I had no foreknowledge but it was an obvious point. As regards the second question my answer would be in two phases, one now and one later. I drank up my coffee as I marshalled my thoughts. I thanked him for his confidence in me. He, too, knew that I, likewise, would respect mine in him. I spoke more softly than earlier when I had made it known that his outrageous request could not be met, hoping thereby to prevent him from asking me again

"I have been in Laos over three years and, brutally, I see you as being far too late in asking your questions. The French had no comprehensive answer nor have the Americans. Now, almost after the eleventh hour, you ask me. Had you asked me the question when I first came to Laos I might have given you, just might, a different answer, one that concerned tactics only. One basic mistake you and your allies have made is trying to find conventional solutions to unconventional problems. Another was to regard and plan your military responses out of context from political realities and cultural common sense, so you lacked balance and alienated much good will that you should never have lost. A serious blow. The North Vietnamese government also made similar mistakes if only because their pendulum swung too far the other way but they rectified theirs quicker than you realised your need to rectify yours. And by 'yours' I include South Vietnam. I can give you detailed examples later, if you want them. I tell you frankly you are too late and that now there is no way in which you can win militarily or politically. Any thoughts you may cherish are doomed to failure and are a waste of time."

The stark, chill words hung heavily between us. Tao Ly's expression did not change although it was a harsher response than he probably expected. None of them knew me when I first arrived and "we were prevented from getting to know you quicker by... until... much later." He hesitated as he tried to skirt round John Lloyd's left-wing leanings. He knew they had made mistakes, bad ones, in the past but why was I so sure in saying, in effect, defeat was inevitable?

I told him I was honoured at his thinking I could be of help at this juncture. He knew much more of what was happening in the PGNU than did I. I knew from the Accords and Protocols that provision had been made for elections after certain political stages had been reached. It would have been much better and infinitely more appropriate if the royalists could have achieved their aim by what the two sides in the Provisional Government worked out. I was sorry if what I had said was outspoken: that was about the past. I did not think I could be of any assistance in the future.

There was one last question: did I honestly think that the other side would abide by the Accords and the Protocols? I weighed the answer. Yes, I did, but only according to their advantage and the royalists' total eclipse. He had one request. Please, for his sake, try and work out a plan for long-term penetration of the LPF and ultimate success for the royalists.

I found out that Tao Ly had reciprocity of information with another person in the embassy and I was asked if I thought the request for assassination kit had any merit. I said that I thought he could prove an embarrassing security risk and that nothing of that nature should be given to him, if only because of his drinking habits.

It transpired that he was being funded to go to Paris and would be contacted there after which a final decision whether any hardware was to be given him or not would be made. My advice would be passed on. When in France Tao Ly also wanted to find out, if he could, the link in the chain of the PL's known supply of RLA officers although that seemed a touch late in the day.

However, the problem posed by the Director of Intelligence teased me in a number of ways: it was a subject dear to my heart, it was an intellectual exercise that intrigued me and it was a challenge. During my long walks over the next few weeks I tried hard to see if there could be an answer rather than what the answer should be. Eventually I struck on an idea, more of a mind-clearing exercise than anything, and that was to list the strong and weak points of both parties. That resulted in a paper for my London bosses titled 'Pathet Lao v Pathetic Lao'.

That done it further struck me that all I could really offer was a set of principles based on the right wing taking advantage of their own strong points and the left wing's shortcomings and, conversely, trying to eradicate their own shortcomings and their adversaries' advantages. It was not, as I had feared, an even balance sheet but one that could, possibly, be used as a basis for future planning. It would be the kiss of death to put anything in writing, unless it was unattributable; likewise it would be a waste of effort merely to pass it on by word of mouth. I wrote my answers in Lao and, substituting God and Satan for right and left wing, took my draft to the senior missionary in Vientiane, a brilliant linguist, a devoted Servant and a friend of mine, a Canadian by the name of Roffe.

"We're in for a bad time, Father," I explained, once I had convinced the devout men of my sincerity of purpose. I had wanted to put my thoughts down, in writing, of certain good and bad points that I believed could help the Lao people by having them pointed out so that they could try and enhance the good and eradicate the bad. I hoped he didn't think that a futile exercise, and I tried to smile engagingly. We were sitting in the missionary's book-lined study. He was in the final stages of translating the Old Testament into Lao. "Not at all, Colonel, but why come to me, delighted though I am to help in any way?"

I told the learned and dedicated scholar that, as he had been in Laos for fifty years, his Lao language ability was second to none and way, way above my meagre efforts, besides which I did not regard my aim as being incompatible with any message that he would want to propagate – indeed I would welcome it if he could add to my list. Regarding the final effort I wanted what I wrote to sound like how a Lao would have written it, not a European. "So much easier for them to follow what I'm driving at."

So we toiled away for a couple of hours, the missionary making sure of exactitudes of meaning from a filing cabinet full of notes, vocabulary and proverbs. I thanked him profusely and returned to my villa. There I took out some writing paper, ensuring that there was no watermark to compromise the source and, using locally bought carbon paper, switched God and Satan back to the unlovely present, not without a twinge of atavistic conscience. I only made two copies, both for Director of Intelligence, and took them to my office the next day, locking them up in my office safe, ready for his return from Paris.

While he was away, the stores for refugees that we had promised when in Sam Neua arrived. A ceremony was fixed up in the LPF HQ in Vientiane. A high-ranking member of the Politburo came, late, and was welcomed in French by Davidson and the Second Secretary. Without another thought I welcomed him in Lao, which pleased him immensely. We went inside and sat on opposite sides of a table. "You speak such good Lao you ought to be the ambassador," he said. I thanked him for his compliment.

Davidson turned to the Lao woman he had brought from the embassy as interpreter and asked her why, when he had told her to translate *everything*, she had not told him what had been said during this last exchange. She was understandably reluctant but, when pressed, blurted out what had been said. Davidson looked petulant.

All Socialist countries had been approached by the left-wing part of the PGNU for aid, as indeed had many right-wing countries (UK included) by the right-wing element. In North Vietnam's case its extensive road building was a good way to give aid as that merely authorised their army engineers who were in Laos already. Stores, cement I remember was one item, were brought down the roads they had built and, on arrival at the boundary between the two zones, the escorting tanks and anti-aircraft guns were put to one side, soldiers dumped their rifles, changed their uniforms for civil dress and drove the stores across the river at Paksane where they were loaded on boats and taken upstream to Vientiane for distribution.

In March I was invited over to Hong Kong to attend the Brigade of Gurkhas' annual conference. Before I went Tao Ly returned from Paris and called me to his office. I asked him how he had enjoyed his first-ever visit there.

He didn't like the French any more than he did before he went. The French who came out to Laos lorded it over them in a very superior way yet their own standards of behaviour in their homeland were, in many instances, inferior to the Lao's. He could see how some people had turned against them, was his succinct comment.

He asked me for my report on what we had discussed and I told him that I would only see him in his house. He pressed me to meet him on the Saturday morning, 15 March, but I said I'd be on my way to Hong Kong and would meet him on my return, on the evening of Friday, 21 March. He went to a wall safe and, fumbling badly as he inserted the key, took out a document. "I'll let you have this in return for what you've done for me."

As he gave it to me I noticed his hand trembled. It was a copy of the report on what he had found out in Paris (the document went only to the King and to the Commander-in-Chief), titled 'A Report on the Recruitment of Agents for the Lao Patriotic Front'. I was now in his debt.

In Hong Kong it was a marvellous time to renew old contacts, feel free and be back in a world I knew and had known for thirty years. Apart from giving lectures on the situation in Laos, I was invited to attend the Silver Jubilee cocktail party of the Gurkha Signals on the Friday and attend the summer ball of 48 Gurkha Infantry Brigade on the Saturday. The Brigadier, John Whitehead, a very old friend indeed, could not understand my refusal. "You always were jungly," he grumbled. "There's no war on in Laos, so why the hurry to get back? I expect it is a woman you've got hold of."

I let him think what he liked, unable to tell him the real reason. I managed to get back to my office in Vientiane before closing time on the Friday, as promised. I rang Tao Ly and was told to come round the next day. Having made that effort to come back as asked I said I'd be round in a few minutes. I collected my hand-written notes from my safe.

I walked to the house, making sure I was not being followed. The General's sentries did not acknowledge my greetings nearly so warmly as before. I went inside and saw Tao Ly's door open. He was sitting at the head of the table, slumped in his chair. "Good evening, General," I announced, loudly.

He turned to see who it was. "Go away," he said huskily. "I don't want you here now. Come back tomorrow morning." I told him that I was not coming back on the morrow and that it was then and there or never. He staggered to his feet, went and drew the curtains, called for hot, fresh black coffee and told me that he was still suffering from a hangover. Once we were alone I handed over one copy of the unattributable document, telling him it was what he had asked me to produce. He looked at it blankly. What was all that about he demanded crossly. He had never asked for it. He screwed his eyes up at it and announced that he didn't understand it. Why had I brought it to him?

I told him this was the answer to that second part of his question about how could they beat communism that I had said I would give him later. I tried to explain the format of the document, the principles I had thought necessary to base any future action on and the reasons for anonymity. But Tao Ly was having none of it and put his copy of the table in front of him and, holding his head in his hands, groaned that he was 'hung up'. How could I expect him to read all that nonsense?

Something snapped in me. I flung the second copy onto the table and, speaking roughly, told the General that I was leaving both copies with him. He would study them when he was sober, remember their contents, then burn them – the very next day. I would check whether he had destroyed them or not and if he said he hadn't, I would tell the C-in-C about the Paris report. Tao Ly looked at me imploringly.

Brashly and angrily I asked him to listen to me. I told him that I had noticed at various functions recently and in his office that he had been drinking heavily. It was doing him no good. He was afraid of being assassinated, he said. He had had reports that he was on a hit list. The only way he could combat this was to get drunk.

I had the bit between my teeth by then and told him, 'even if you're not interested, General,' that I had had a price on my head twice, once in Cochin China and once in Borneo. Both times, especially in Borneo, outnumbered and recognised wherever I went, I was razor sharp. At night even a mouse squeaking woke me up. The enemy hunted me but could never get me though they tried hard enough. "But you – your colleagues will mistrust you, your enemies – your future partners – will despise you and you've already lost self-confidence and self-respect." I had done more than I should have done and, as long as he was like this, I'd do no more. I bade him goodbye and left.

As I walked moodily back to my villa I wondered if I had said far too much. There was no going back even if I had.

News of the fighting in Vietnam was universally dreadful. It was the unexpected fall of Danang, four hundred odd miles to the north of Saigon, announced on Sunday, 30 March, that sent shivers down many a spine – chillingly for those fighting the communists and those who were feathering their nests like so many of the Laotian hierarchy were, despairingly for countless thousands who were fed up with the years of misery, joyfully for those communists who had been labouring so long for victory. Conventional wisdom on both sides of the political divide saw the battle for Saigon six months later, with the fall of Laos as 'Saigon plus two months'. It was this eight-month period that needed careful orchestrating in Laos by the LPF.

Both the South Vietnamese and Cambodian ambassadors were told by the LPF Foreign Minister to quit Laos within two weeks and reduce their embassy staffs. The USSR recognised Sihanouk. All the fighting superiority of the North Vietnamese would have been as nil if the Soviet Union and China had not flooded them with arms.

Meanwhile along the whole length of the two zones that divided Laos between the two contending factions more and more land was won back by the PL, eroding the morale of the RLA troops on the ground until, as I noted during my routine visits, the will to defend their homeland was almost extinguished. By the end of March only in the Sala Phou Khoun salient were PL forces not in possession of territory that they had held at the time of the 1962 cease-fire.

On 11 April Sisouk called me to the Defence Ministry. Outside his door was a PL sentry. I knocked and went in. I was beckoned to a sofa and the Minister sat beside me.

He was in sombre mood, glad that he had the chance to discuss a problem that was exercising him greatly. He had come to know that there were twenty-seven men, 'NVA advisers', in the PL camp at Ban Dong Nasok where the Neutralisation troops lived, not far from the Wattay complex. They had very recently arrived from Hanoi. He believed they were high-ranking political cadres, senior party members all. The advice he needed from me was should he try to have them exterminated or not?

Although by then I should have been immune from being astonished at anything I heard, I was momentarily taken aback. Before I could make any comment Sisouk continued, even more surprisingly, that he would do whatever I advised. If I advocated extermination it had to be complete, leaving none alive. "Whatever you advise will have an ineradicable effect on the future of the country."

Even allowing for exaggeration in the stress of the moment, it was obviously of great importance as Sisouk went on to explain that the country was lost if the twenty-seven remained, of that there was no doubt. The royalists might still have a chance to make future action easier if those men could be got rid of.

At that moment the telephone on his desk rang and he went over to answer it. My mind raced with possible answers: deny his request and miss out on a potential target; accept it and accept the moral obligations of failure and the perks of success; stick to my charter and miss out on a possible lead. A sudden thought made me reach out for the small table in front of me. As I felt under the flanges Sisouk put the telephone down and came back to the sofa. He looked at me. "What are you doing?" he asked with genuine curiosity.

I asked him if he had ever had his office debugged. Sounding peevish, he said he did not understand what I meant and asked me to explain. I fought back my impatience and told him what I meant. I was feeling to see if anybody unknown had installed a bug under this table. "But why should anyone want to do this to me?" came the astonishing reply. "This is the first time I've heard of such a thing." His surprise was genuine.

He was just the sort of person whom 'they' would do it to, I told him in a low voice as I gestured with my head to the sentry outside the door. The people in the other offices and in the passage did not know everything. They'd love to find out what he talked about. There might not be any such device there but we couldn't be sure and what he had asked me was far too delicate a matter to take any risks with. I suggested that we ought to talk in the open in a safe place and how about by the plunge pool in his garden? I had to consider his request. Today was Friday. Some time next week I would call and see him. Would he tell Princess Jasmine that John Cross would ring her up sometime before Tuesday afternoon and would merely ask 'when'? and she would tell me what he had decided. "I'll be there then. Do you agree?"

With a bit of reluctance, yes, he agreed. I saw he was still inclined to chat so I stayed where I was. It might be difficult, he said after a pause, as the Prime Minister wanted him to go to a monetary conference in Nairobi towards the end of the week.

Unthinkingly I did something I had never done before during my tour as an attaché, except to Tao Ly. I gave the Minister unasked-for advice. I told him that the morale of his army was so low it was hard to imagine it falling any lower yet if he were to leave the country at that juncture and the PL and the NVA decided to push their forces all the way to the Lao-Thai border, nothing would stop them. With him in Vientiane there was still a chance. As I travelled around the countryside visiting units, his name was on everybody's lips as the only person with any heart left to resist and fight back. Surely someone else could go to Nairobi?

A dejected Sisouk turned to face me and, with a sigh, said he believed I was right. He would not go. Staying in Laos was more important. Then, with ineffable sadness, he said, "You know even if I stay here it may be too late. I've got such bad generals."

I had never dreamt that I would be privy to such an admission and felt a surge of pity for this arrogant, ignorant, educated, lonely man. Without thinking I put my hand out and patted his knee, saying, "You are the Minister of Defence. What you say, goes, surely? Give them orders!" It showed the state of both of us that Sisouk never showed any reaction to having his knee patted and what I had done only dawned on me later when I was rehearsing the interview. I tried to imagine a Lao DA patting the British Defence Minister's knee in the latter's Whitehall office and I blushed at the thought of what I had done.

Sisouk glanced at me and scathingly said that I had been in Laos for two-and-a-half years, and I still thought that any general obeyed any of his orders if he didn't want to? I had the wit not to answer. It may have been a glimpse of the obvious to him but I saw I had gone far enough. I got up, made routine remarks about not wasting the Minister's valuable time, reminded him of our next meeting and took my leave. Alice through her looking glass never found such sound and sights as these, surely?

At a reception that evening the Australian and Filipino attachés came up to me. Almost in unison they asked me if I had noticed General Tao Ly? Only drinking squash! So different from before. I shook my head. "That's twice I've noticed it recently," said the Australian. "No, three times," corrected the Filipino.

"I hadn't noticed anything at all myself. Canberra and Manila *will* be pleased when you point out how observant you've been," I said in mock severity which the other two misinterpreted. They both turned away with a slightly superior expression on their faces, as though to show me I was losing out in the historic events that were sweeping that corner of Asia.

On 16 April I flew up to Luang Prabang with two Americans for the Laotian New Year in a Pilatus Porter, the only 'plane that could land on the pocket-handkerchief apology for a strip at Sala Phou Khoun where we stopped off. The other two, laden with whisky bottles and girlie magazines, moved up to the Command Post. Following them I noticed the expertly camouflaged 5.5-inch artillery piece, still as it was before. The Lao officers were sitting glumly around a makeshift table. The senior of the Americans called out to them that he had 'brought you some mo-rale boosters' and all the goodies were put on the table.

"Still not got yer gun fixed?" asked the other, knowing that to be the case. "Too bad, too bad. Never mind. This lot'll keep yer mind occupied for a while. Brother Gook might make himself impolite any day now so you might consider getting that gun fixed, not that it is anything to do with me."

There was not much point in staying for polite conversation after that as the Command Post staff had needed no second bidding to relax and were already clinking glasses and having a first lech at the magazines. "Never could get them to repair that piece," the pilot said, shaking his head as we strapped ourselves in. "Been like that for two years. It's so well camouflaged because they think the PL will be angry if they know it is there. Can you believe it?"

No sooner were we airborne when we picked up a message from the forward troops covering the gun position. The PL had started to attack: supporting fire was needed, supporting fire was being requested but no supporting fire ever came. I listened on my headset, hearing what the pilot was saying. He alerted the control tower in Luang Prabang and got the stand-by

T-28s airborne. They were over Sala Phou Khoun not long afterwards and strafed the PL positions. Nobody knew if it was that which stopped the PL attack or whether the forward troops were plain jittery and there had only been patrol movement.

The fall of Phnom Penh the next day, 17 April, following news of the NVA thrust south from Danang, made a deep impact on many people in Vientiane. Neither side had envisaged events moving so quickly but still no one forecast the fall of Saigon before the rains.

During the next ten days Sala Phou Khoun changed hands three times with doomsday rumours of the situation everywhere.

I learnt that one reason the Americans had to keep on flying in large quantities of artillery, arms and ammunition to Phnom Penh was that Lon Nol's army was selling significant amounts of all three commodities to the Khmer Rouges and getting US dollars in payment. I was unable to fathom what depths the level of corruption in the Khmer Republic had sunk as it was not 'my' country. I had my hands full, so to speak, in Laos, where it was hard enough to find out anything similarly specific as the British were not responsible for any military funding.

Before going to Luang Prabang I had rung Princess Jasmine and was bidden to be at their house on 18 April at 6 p.m. On the dot I reached it, an old colonial building on the bank of the Mekong, ineffectually guarded against natural and man-made disasters by an earth bund and bored soldiers, although the latter were drawn from the 'Scorpion' Division. They looked in the car, registered a trace of surprise as they saw a grinning Singha looking out of the window and let it drive in. As I got out, the front door opened and Jasmine, radiant with expectant motherhood, welcomed me. "He's round at the back," she said smiling. "Waiting for you."

I turned the corner of the house and there, sitting bolt upright on a hard wooden chair by the pool, with an empty chair drawn up beside him and a sentry in the bushes to the rear, was the Minister. I allowed myself a small thrill of satisfaction at what I saw, unthinkable two years before, improbable ever, yet now a fact. I walked up to Sisouk and was told to sit down. I was given a fresh lime, *citron pressé*, an anti-mosquito coil was moved slightly to one side and we started talking – or rather Sisouk did. I listened, absorbed.

It was hard for me to realise what it must have cost Sisouk in terms of pride and prestige to reach the state that now pertained. Years of wearing a public mask of dubious fit, months of pent-up frustrations and now looming defeat coupled with disillusion with the Americans rose up and spilt out in the garden that starlit evening. I sat, riveted, concentrating on remembering as much as I could of all that cascaded out during ninety minutes of nonstop, almost unbroken monologue, kept fluent by judicious prompting.

I learnt so much it was impossible to remember it all but the main strands of what he said stayed with me: how, since his heart attack, the Prime Minister, Souvanna Phouma, had been influenced to the point of erosion by his half-brother, the Red Prince, whose real aims had always been the dismantlement of the throne and a republic instead. I had always suspected that but our FCO-groomed stalwarts in the embassy would never accept it, especially as only very recently the LPF was discussing plans about the King's coronation. Before his illness Souvanna Phouma would never have countenanced that: "I know it all as I used to help him write his speeches," and now they were helpless; how Sisouk had three different intelligence networks – I knew two of them but the one run by the Provost Marshal, Colonel Loun Sisonol, was news to me – and which one was responsible for what; how, through various contacts, he had leads into the Politburo in Sam Neua and even farther back to Hanoi; who of his generals were crooked, who inefficient and who stupid – none was rated very highly; exactly what the LPF planned to do on the fall of Saigon – "I promise you I'll let you know when the PL start to move"; likely assassination targets in the Vientiane area; and, because the PL would only advance, initially, as far as Vang Vieng (where they were in 1962 and which marked the old Neutralist boundary) there would be no need for any evacuation plans for the foreign community (the Americans were needed, anyway, as they could be punished more easily by staying) unless, of course, the women and children would feel safer over the river for a couple of nights; who of the foreign community to be of and so much more that I felt my head would burst.

And then that question which I had been dreading more and more. "Now what about those twenty-seven North Vietnamese Army advisers?"

I had delayed saying 'no' to Sisouk initially just in case I found anyone who wanted to take action against such a target. Nobody did. As I sat in the dark garden, it was only in my mind that cocks crew – not once, nor twice but three times – as, inadequately, sorrowfully but officially, I heard myself say, "Your Excellency, I regret to inform you that my charter precludes me from acting on your request" and a silence, broken only by cicadas and stray background noises unnoticed till then, replaced the long lament of oral anguish that, litany-like in its completeness and sincerity, had poured forth for so long.

I, struggling with emotion, not he, broke that silence by lamely saying that I understood His Excellency's situation. "Thank you for telling me what you have and, within the limits of my charter and ability, I will do what I can for your country." *Cross, you pompous bastard*, I thought savagely, hating myself, as the Minister slowly got up and said, simply and forlornly, "I was afraid you would say that."

Prince Sisouk kept his word the very next night. We were in line receiving guests for the Queen's birthday party and, as he passed me, he leant over and softly said that the PL had started from Sala Phou Khoun at 1600 hours that afternoon but had not announced it yet. He had only got the news as he had left for the British party. "Vang Vieng first stop." I thanked him very sincerely and sent London a telegram as soon as I could.

In Vientiane the National Assembly was dissolved. The South Vietnamese ambassador fled to France the day after Saigon fell and the North Vietnamese moved into the embassy. I gather they had a field day in what they found. As Sisouk had foretold, a new development was humiliating the Americans. During my subsequent visits to the provinces I managed to avoid being involved in them, not that an angry crowd asks to look at passports before being nasty. The question about passports being valid or otherwise in this situation is recognised by a Geneva Convention to the extent that people are allowed one exit visa but that was cold comfort when the heady brew of victory and vengeance dictated minor functionaries' vindictive conduct and neither recognising the passport nor issuing an exit visa. A few senior Cambodians and South Vietnamese were given French passports but the others found themselves as stateless refugees. One young forlorn Cambodian who had run out of money said to me, "I'm dead."

I took the new First Secretary and his wife (Patrick and Maria Fairweather) around in the Beaver while there was still time. In every location RLA officers said to me, 'We are already dead'. Commanders were broken and unable to face the future. Up in Long Cheng I went to one battalion and found it consisted of three people, the CO, his wife and a driver. Everyone else had fled. How long that state of affairs had pertained I did not know but I came to the conclusion that the CO had been running a 'ghost battalion' for some time, using American-supplied jeeps as taxis – until there was only one left, hence the one driver! We saw the T-28 fighter-bombers take off laden with bombs for the spiteful little war over the hills. As we left General Vang Pao was getting reports of NVA reinforcements near by. He asked me about the situation, especially as I saw it. I think I helped him make up his mind about what he should do. I never saw him again.

Already MOD in Vientiane was virtually ineffective and a number of generals were away sick or on tour. There was a rift between Souvanna Phouma and all those under him. None of the royalists were happy and ministers were threatening to resign.

The communist victory consummated on 30 April by the capture of Saigon stunned the world by its speed, speed of advance and speed of demoralisation of the South Vietnamese. The appalling stories emanating from Phnom Penh had already struck terror into so many hearts that rational thought was hard to come by. Two evacuations in a little over two weeks; it had to be Vientiane's turn next, come what may and come it would. Laos as it was then known could never be the same again.

The news of the fall of Saigon reached Vientiane that evening. It was the one and only topic of conversation everywhere. Those who had emergency plans put them into action. Those without wondered what they had better do. In some quarters near panic was engendered as the full impact of the news sunk in. I recalled my garden conversation and knew there would be a long lull before the final course of events could take shape. I felt a thrill of the unexpected.

Sisouk and Jasmine threw a family party that same night to which I was invited. The Davidsons, Gharekan and his wife and some Lao, one of whom was their ambassador to the Court of St James, were there. Earlier in the day the Lao ambassador had had lunch with Davidson and had said that Sisouk was wanting to resign. A telegram was sent to London and the reply asked about any implications. It was, therefore, a fortuitous dinner party and Sisouk and Davidson. Next day, the Friday, the top four in the embassy pooled what our various contacts had told us, what assessments we had made and what were the implications. Two of our final opinions for a second telegram to London and their possible wording were 'we believe we can persuade the minister to resign' and 'give guidance if you wish us to dissuade the minister from resigning'. Looking back on it, I wonder how it came about that we were so heavily involved and I now believe that we were the only people the Lao could trust for impartial advice. At the meal there was no reference to our previous session in the garden. I never saw either Sisouk or Jasmine again.

In essence, the North Vietnamese victory in Indo-China came about because their political, not military, power base was stronger that than of the South Vietnamese. There were a number of reasons for this: a totalitarian regime, a censored press, fear as a weapon, overriding belief in their cause, dedication, discipline and inurement to unbelievable hardships being some examples. The South Vietnamese and the 'Free World' never had anything like such motivation as they never had any similar 'belief in a cause'. Inapposite democratic characteristics, the reverse of the communists' obverse ones, were grave impediments to success, the main military one being that a wrongly-slanted army was fighting a war it was never designed for. There were at least three other causes for American morale to falter to the point of no return: on the campuses hostile reaction, fomented very cleverly by adversaries of the war; a draft army that used a system that enrolled a larger proportion of those from the more unfortunate end of the social landscape than those more luckily placed; and the enervating abuse of drugs and prostitutes by so many servicemen – these last stark examples of Mao Tse-tung's 'sugar-coated bullets'.

There is also an historical aspect to the North Vietnamese victory that must never be discounted. For much of the past two thousand years Vietnam was regarded by the Chinese as a vassal state and this led to a burning desire to run their own affairs. Having got rid of the

Chinese, the Vietnamese bitterly resented the French arrival in the mid-nineteenth century and, by the late 1920s, were prepared to embrace communism the better to achieve their nationalistic desire for freedom. Once they had dealt with the French the American bogey had to be defeated. Nothing could eradicate this overwhelming desire, which had to be achieved at whatever the cost – and achieve it North Vietnam did.

It was easy to be wise after the event but my 'communist revolutionary warfare' antennae were very sharp, having had since early 1948 virtually nonstop involvement in such matters. I found that, but for specific details none of us could have foreseen, all that I had told London would happen, did.

Thursday, 1 May, dawned hot and sticky. May Day parades, already planned, were made more pertinent by the previous day's news. Participants and organisers had worked late into the night and their efforts added perceptibly to the shrillness of the occasion. Three sets of banners were in evidence: one listed the fifteen most hated and corrupt men in the Vientiane regime, starting with Sisouk na Champassak, working its way through ministers and generals and finishing up with the lowly Provost Marshal in charge of an intelligence network, Colonel Loun Sisonol. (He was spotted because the facts he was disseminating used a type of paper that was tracked to a source controlled by the Americans.) This set of banners also spat a vicious message: *Try these criminal traitors for crimes against the Lao people and then kill them.*

The second set blasted the CIA and feudalist lackeys while the third praised the two victories in the Khmer Republic, now confusingly named Kampuchea, and in Vietnam.

Attachés, communist-watchers and other interested people drove around town or stood watching at some nodal point while processions came and went, their LPF activists jockeying all and sundry to join in so vehemently that I was reminded of disoriented flying ants trying to find their new bearings on the ground after losing their wings.

The *kip*, that ephemeral and unstable currency that should have been at 1,200 to the US$ was 6,500 at 9 o'clock, 7,500 an hour later and 8,000 by noon. Tension mounted and panic spread as news of assassinations spread. Shops put up shutters and those that did stay open were those that had stock bought and sold with hard currency and were eager to sell their wares at bargain prices, so that their owners could escape over the border while the going was good.

We, in the safety of our diplomatic cocoon, had to consider what we would do if our situation became untenable; unpaid bills, rent of buildings, pets, insurance, bank balances and servants' wages were some of the items we had to think about. However, in Laos we were in a different position from the rest of Indo-China as the two sides considered themselves as being in the same provisional government and not, strictly speaking, as hostile adversaries. As for the man in the street, the widow in the hovel and the homeless everywhere, life was hard in any case. Thefts and violence were on the increase and, as I saw it in Vientiane, dogless American houses were the main targets.

I went for my usual Saturday morning walk on 3 May and, in the driest of paddies, I met two women hunting for fodder. One got on her knees and begged for help: husband died in March and eight children to care for. I had nothing on me. I looked at Singha, fit, well fed and contented, lying on the ground by my side, and wondered if the woman realised that my dog was eating a better diet, and probably more of it, than her entire family. To say, as nobody would, that to starve Singha would help the family or in any way solve the problem, but it did put her plight in a different perspective.

This year Constitution Day, 11 May, fell on a Sunday. Normally a full-scale march past down Avenue Lane Xang would take place, with the salute taken by the King. This year no details of whether there would be a parade were firm until late the day before, not that that, in itself, was anything new. Peter Shield asked me if I had heard the news. I shook my head.

Army cadets at Chinaimo Camp had gone on strike and set up a checkpoint, rather than a roadblock, outside the Lao-German Technical College, not far from Peter's quarter. They let him through, giving him a copy of their demands. He gave it to me. It appeared that, amongst other points that I now forget, they wanted to be under a neutralist agency not a right-wing one.

The day was already a scorcher. The seats were filling up as diplomats and their ladies arrived, the fatter ones sweating. Brows were mopped and fans fluttered. Pleasantries were exchanged and rumours about the cadets' strike kept everyone feeling in the centre of events. Then, as we sat waiting for the arrival of the King, the buzz started that the communist offensive had opened, that they were driving for the Thai border and a new situation would occur when they met Thai forces with no buffer between them.

I glanced over to where the generals were normally seated. There were not many there. They were never late. I glanced at my watch. The King was due to arrive at any moment. I noted that Etam and Tao Ly were the senior officers present after the Commander-in-Chief, now waiting on the road for His Majesty. I mentioned this poor showing to the others and the consensus of opinion was that those missing were over the Mekong by now and would never be seen again. Furtive but adequate precautions had been taken in time. As far as I could tell twelve out of the banner-listed fifteen had left. How long, I wondered, would the others remain?

His Majesty the King arrived and the parade started. He made a speech about unity and the future, as did the Prime Minister and General Bounphone. The march past was a tame affair, representatives of the Neutralisation troops followed by various social organisations, headed by the Boy Scouts. As the spectators began to drift off little groups formed, broke and reformed, hoping to squeeze enough rumours into a semblance of the truth to report back. Instant history was being written – but by what historians!

Later on that unusually hot day was a celebration soccer match, Customs v Police. I debated whether to attend and I felt I ought. Dressed in tropical service dress and sweltering, I was driven to the national stadium. In the VIP stand were the Prime Minister and his son, a UNO man, two American assistant attachés, Colonel Tsarkov – Gulag personified – the Soviet attaché who had taken over from Gretchanine's relief, Vasilli Soloviev and I. (I got to like Gretchanine. "I know why you jog every morning." "Why?" "So when you die, you die in good trim.")

Before the game started Tsarkov, sitting below me, turned and beckoned me down. I accepted. After ten minutes a goal was scored. Desultory applause rippled briefly before dying away in the heat. Calling me 'Comrade Colonel', he said that in our peace-loving socialist countries we had more spirit than that, hadn't we? He grinned malevolently. In a degenerate society like this – "but not for much longer" – what else could one expect? Quite soon we would see a change when socialist forces were unleashed all over the country, like in his and mine, eh?

I had seen enough of the Russian elite to believe, as a general rule, that they hated to be ignored. They never wanted to be loved – they often seemed to hate themselves too much to know what love meant and so they were content to be tolerated – but what they respected more than anything else was a person who refused to be bullied or denigrated. I did not rise to the jibe and concentrated on the football match.

Tsarkov made some remark about Britain and the USSR both being peace-loving nations of equal sincerity. This was too much for me. I rounded on him, telling him not to make the mistake of muddling my country with his. In Britain we linked 'peace' to 'good will', in the Soviet Union it was a case of 'peace and ill will', peace and malice. "Certainly we were allies during the war but since then what have you done?"

Scarcely pausing for breath and certainly not waiting for any riposte I read Tsarkov a lesson in post-war history, starting at the Berlin Blockade and working through until I reached current Soviet activities in the Horn of Africa. I compared the British giving up their old, colonial empire with the Soviet acquisition of a new, European one, including Cuban mercenaries. Tsarkov, in a lull, tried to steer me away from that topic by talking of 'Hitler, the fascist'.

"I hold no truck for him either," I growled, once again getting into top gear. The millions he had killed and the millions Stalin had killed were equally appalling. But at least Hitler had stood up as a leader and was counted whereas in the Soviet Union's case personal responsibilities and actions were shielded in a soviet. And what got me most of all 'your odious comparison between our two countries' was that when in his country a person said 'squeak' shrilly instead of gruffly, a knock came on the door in the small hours the next night and the person was put into a mental asylum and made mad. "I'd rather be dead than that, so would all true Englishmen. And I'd take you with me if I got half the chance."

I relapsed into silence. Damned tongue of mine, I told myself, but how immensely satisfying to get it off my chest, even if it was all in French. The final whistle for the end of the game shrilled out and the sweat-covered players dripped off the field. "But what about Scotland Yard?" demanded Tsarkov, vainly trying to counter-attack. I roared with laughter, recovering my good humour and stood up.

"You fool, Colonel Tsarkov! You absolute fool! That won't do. You"ll have to do better than that and we've had enough for one day." I told him that I wanted him to send me a nice, easily understandable book on his system so even a man like me could understand it. There must be something in it, I supposed. The two US officers grinned at me as we left. They did not hear what Tsarkov and I were talking about but they guessed I had 'won on points'.

The PL drive to the border was quickly executed. All major towns and military HQ were taken over. There was no fighting. LPF press releases gave us to understand that the PL came unopposed as victors, being welcomed by civilians and military alike. I had never got to grips with the PL as fighting men. My impression was that they were nothing more than second-class infantrymen at best, 'advised' by NVA cadres both politically and military, without any resources of their own. I was never able to get a view different from that, even when they were in Vientiane in force.

Americans in the provinces were given seventy-two hours to clear out. Military staffs were to be reduced. The French were to be the next target. The white man, whosoever he be, including the Soviets, is the lesser in stature following the American defeats.

I was sent for by General Bounpone and told I was the only person he knew who could give him a balanced opinion of how safe he was still working for the PL and whether I thought they would try and assassinate him when they had finished with him. My advice took the form of analysis of the situation to let him make up his own mind.

My continued touring of the country was considered by Davidson to be provocative so he forbade me to leave Vientiane. I wondered if the PL had found my Jungle Warfare School set of précis and what their reaction would be if they had. I fervently hoped they had not and I wondered how I would be able to get the wretched things back into my possession.

I crossed the Mekong to see Loun Sisonol, the ex-Provost Marshal, now hiding with the other Lao refugees in Nong Khai. None had much luggage and their main problem had been the time it took to get a forged passport. They asked me how I found them. I told them that I had seen a truck standing outside Loun's house as the PL were taking away his belongings. I had read what the bored driver had doodled in the dust on the cab and noticed his incorrect spelling of Nong Khai in the Lao script. The rest was easy.

It was even more difficult than usual to know what was happening for me properly to brief the ambassador and London. Trends were all a one-man band could look for. In most countries newspapers, bulletins and telephones would have made life simpler but not in Laos. I asked the Soviet Tsarkov what he had picked up and, to my surprise, he was as nice as pie to me, thereby giving me confidence that my contention of standing up to the Soviets pays dividends. Chen Shu-lin, gurgling with pleasure at seeing another revolution at first hand, was under the impression that all the manifestations were genuinely the masses' desire and the political awakening of the proletariat. He banged on for ninety minutes, which took quite some sitting through. I said I was one of the 'beastly rightists' and he grinned and said, no, I was the British DA – a diplomatic *non sequitur*!

The embassy needed to order the few volunteer British teachers and the fewer radio technicians lent by the BBC still in the provinces back to Vientiane but could not get the message to them. It had to be done by sending the Beaver and flying over their quarters to alert them, landing and waiting until they reached the aerodrome. Peter Shield was not able to contact General Soutchai on my behalf about my set of précis – served me right, I supposed.

Not for the first time did we find that the LPF were speaking with forked tongues, although the charitable would say that, such was the volatility of the situation, no right hand could know what its left was up to. They seemed determined to put pressure on those Lao officers who remained. Their only aircraft were a few borrowed Soviet AN-2 biplanes, flown by Cubans, so they had no expertise themselves. They forced the RLAF commander (General Souridh) to resign by accusing him of having ordered bombing raids on PL positions. This was incorrect as MR commanders or the Minister of Defence himself personally ordered all air raids.

There was enough rain to flood the swamps and paddies so many people went out catching snails and crabs, which not only may have helped fill their bellies but also did save their pockets. That was of real value as inflation was soaring. The LPF impounded every document needed to draw money from the banks so the Americans could not pay their many employees, such as hospital workers, drivers, storemen, clerks, house guards and domestic staff. But that was not all: the Americans, who had been supplying rice to some 50,000 army men since 1962, could do so no longer as they were not allowed to use aircraft and the PL had impounded all lorries. It also seemed that very soon what pittance of pay the RLA used to get would be no more with everybody on PL rates of pay; minuscule and all found, except that there was no one to find it.

Added even to that dreary catalogue were the Free World hard currency arrangements, which were about to run out and could not be renewed as the LPF had similarly impounded every necessary document and closed the banks. By early June Laos was worth US$6 million, equal to some twenty minutes' trading on the Tokyo money market. I was very sorry for the Americans. They had been pushed around almost to breaking point and something had to snap, if only Congress's temper. We, as an embassy, did what we could for them: the ambassadors of

Australia, India and the UK went to see the Foreign Minister to tell him about diplomatic immunity and related matters but at my level there was nothing I could do. After the Americans I thought the French would be harassed as they had too many soldiers in their Military Mission. It was all very dreary.

The LPF played their hands beautifully and the Western diplomats were taken for suckers almost without exception. We were in a communist state, for all intents and purposes. Every senior official went on intense indoctrination courses and those who 'failed' were punished. The Russians and the Chinese went around with grins the size of Cheshire Cats': for them the Revolution was as perfect as it could be. But there was still the problem of over a hundred thousand hungry people to feed. The loss of jobs, the loss of hard currency and the loss of confidence were not to be easily restored.

However, for the rest of us, everything was remarkably tranquil. Davidson's reaction to all these events was unbelieving if only because he still had only a very hazy idea of the mechanics of Communist Revolutionary Warfare. Rather like *Mien Kamf* and the Second World War along with Stalin's and Mao's works on communism, Giap and even the Lao Phoumi Vongvachit had written books explaining their plan to make Indo-China communist. I remember John Lloyd telling me he had been given a copy of one of Phoumi's books but I do not know whether the FCO was appraised, and if so, took cognisance or not. However, with the British Government's understandable desire not to become embroiled in Indo-China any more deeply than its Co-Chairmanship rôle, discontinuing the occasional payment into a blandly named Foreign Exchange Operating Fund and the need to concentrate on more urgent problems at home, I doubt it would have made the slightest difference even had they studied it.

9

Malice in Blunderland

'It ain't what you do, it's the way that you do it', is the refrain of an old song and it could well have been written for the LPF as it seemed to be their guiding principle. The slowness with which they filled the vacuum left by the hurried disappearance of so many senior people bespoke a rigid and carefully planned programme from which no deviation was allowed. That was how it struck us in Vientiane as we realised we were front-line spectators in a communist-inspired, political and cultural revolution.

The PL advance to Vang Vieng left the neutralist myth extant, but quite for what arcane purpose or for whose benefit was not clear. Those senior officials who had remained in their posts in the provinces had their movements restricted but were not harassed. Soldiers of the sad, dishevelled, bewildered RLA who had not melted into the landscape were given PL uniforms and were known as the Lao National Army, with its strength reduced by 20,000 to 30,000. It was announced that the countryside was liberated, with only the two 'neutralised' capitals left for similar treatment. Even so, in Vientiane, where 1,500 PL troops and three of their tanks only were authorised, there were 8,000 and eighteen respectively.

Overt political attention was applied in three spheres: humiliation of the Americans, launching a re-education programme of seminars and a purge of all military and civilian leaders. It was much milder than the horrendous reports coming out of Kampuchea and, to a lesser extent, Vietnam. A clamp on all road movement without a *laisser passer* was imposed and nobody could move more than three kilometres from their village without similar written permission. For foreigners it was five kilometers. Loudspeakers were installed everywhere people lived, towns and villages, and anti-imperialist propaganda blared forth raucously three times a day, at dawn, noon and dusk, each spell for two hours.

The atmosphere in Vientiane became less and less happy. There were many fewer cars on the roads and a number of houses and shops were shuttered. The main anti-US crusade was cleverly manipulated and, for the most part, the mass of the civilian population was unaffected. However, many more people started to feel the draught as breadwinners could win bread no more. A perceptible change in expression came over people's faces. Gone (for ever?) were the customary smiles. Folk were more pre-occupied than before. Nobody knew what the next move would be, nor when. I was particularly able to observe the difference as I exposed myself far more than did my colleagues in that I walked, most days, to the embassy as well as out into the countryside at weekends. Out in the paddy one Saturday a man spoke to me roughly, accusing me first of being an American and secondly a Frenchman. When I told him I was an Englishman he smiled, shook my hand and wished me good luck. Yes, it was strange to live through an orchestrated revolution and I would be quite happy not to have to experience another, although in no way had this affected me physically. The lawlessness engendered by the looting recently had extended to the left-wing socialist countries' houses with complaints that they were not being properly looked after.

It seemed that LPF policy was to by-pass what authorised organs of government there were and to force the pace by manipulating the students with their pre-placed agents, civilian and military. They infiltrated their own soldiers, in uniform only when tactical, into the crowds and these directed their energies as and where already planned. Gangs of students roamed the place with banners demanding such matters as the immediate removal of US aid workers, implementation of protocols and the forcing of right-wing sympathisers into the open. Chen Shu-lin told me he was thrilled to see 'people's power' at work. Tsarkov, on the other hand, having sent me a well-produced book about the Soviet Union (which I gave to my illiterate driver because the pictures would amuse his many children) was not thrilled. He became so abusive to the Lao, saying that they were so useless they were bound to make a nonsense of their victory 'which you never won by yourselves', that pressure was applied to have him removed.

This was mob rule called, by the communists, Social Democracy – 'the will of the populace'. The strike of cadets, similarly orchestrated by the LPF – nothing was spontaneous – spread, slowly at first, to every military unit in Vientiane still tainted by the old persuasion. The method was always the same; to hang banners up near the unit concerned demanding that all those who had participated in crimes against the Lao people be tried and punished. Loudspeakers blared out the charges and the background to them. If passers-by did not take enough interest, they were hauled in to listen to the proceedings. It was difficult for people to get done what they had to because not to show sufficient interest was tantamount to showing that the revolution did not emanate from the people.

In one RLA engineer unit a corporal vehemently addressed a group of his few remaining comrades and forced a vote on who should be the commanding officer, the major who was in command or he, the speaker. The major, a good and popular commander, won 85 per cent of the vote. A plain-clothes member of the LPF then emerged from the shadows and said the voting had been carried out unconstitutionally, that it was therefore null and void, that they would all go into recess for an hour then vote again. During that period considerable pressure was brought to bear and an hour later the result of the new vote was 85 per cent in favour of the corporal. The major managed to escape over the Mekong with his family that same night.

It did not seem to matter whether a Military Region commander was the man under discussion or the man in charge of the Military Police at Phone Kheng; the same rigmarole had to be adhered to. I came across one of the last units to have its revolution, a signals detachment that had somehow been overlooked when the programme was made out. There was only one man demonstrating among the by-then tattered banners. He was on a chair, fast asleep, while the words, now meaningless so dulled were they by repetition, cackled out their eroded message on a cheap tape recorder. It showed vividly that format was all-important for the communists.

Every government department was subjected to this 'spontaneous' demonstration of popular will, while the rest of the population was subjected to a programme of seminars, twice a week, with no excuses accepted for non-attendance. Then unintelligible topics of imperialism, feudalism, reactionaries, neo-colonialism, socialism, were introduced to audiences that did not understand such esoteric ideas, felt they were nothing to do with them, had to be taught so many new difficult words, were bored stiff and who wanted to be left in peace but were too frightened to disobey.

I kept tabs on the MOD, which was like a morgue. A few people were in evidence, either lowly residents doing nothing or the newly-elected, groping about in a strange place where they'd never been before, trying to find a PL liaison officer. Those senior officers not in exile were on a re-education course elsewhere, confined to barracks and, so I believed, undergoing self-criticism – no one was spared. Cards and gossip were the order of the day for those underlings yet to be re-educated. "Your turn for brain washing next?" I asked a Captain in the Survey and Map branch. He grinned wryly but said nothing.

Luckily I had kept my contacts with the PL troops and they were friendly to me, calling to me over the wall of their buildings ("How does your dog understand English? How do you wobble your eyebrows?"), crossing the street to talk to me and letting me visit them in their offices. On one occasion I told the LPF official, a mid-ranking man, that the LPF were 'jealous' of the Americans. I had a 20-minute diatribe as the man, Thong Damdouane, worked himself into a fury. In his wish to convince me that the LPF had their finger on the public pulse he told me how they went into the streets to monitor what people were saying, doing 2-hour stints and reporting back to a co-ordinating cell where they collated their material for further use – and a whole lot more I now forget. I do remember he was remonstrating with his arms to such a degree that he did not see a woman orderly bringing in two glasses of soft drinks on a tray and knocked both of them out of her hands onto the floor. Even that did not stop his tirade.

I felt I needed to cool him down and told him I was a fool, thinking that I knew how to speak Lao when I made elementary mistakes. "I do apologise: I realise I said 'jealous of' the Americans when I meant to say 'angry with' them." I was forgiven, smiles and handshakes, and given an invitation to come back. It was a ploy I would be wise to use sparingly but it made a useful contribution to our knowledge of their methods.

All this time the wretched Americans were being harassed and even when some agreement had been reached (with the students as representatives of the people) about how many would be allowed to leave and when, that was not the end of their discomfiture. The strident, virulent and odious things the re-named elements of the Royal Lao Army had been putting out about the Americans, by radio, loud-hailer from their camps, and broadsheets would, in any other circumstances, have been pathetically naïve. One interesting factor was that their written expositions were all in some quaint, new spelling the LPF had devised for themselves, thus giving the game away that it was not the non-PL that had composed them. However, in this case, it portrayed the absolute victory of communist propaganda, subversion and inspiration of fear – to me it was sinister and frightening.

The Lao people are not, broadly speaking, vicious. For centuries the peasants living on, or just above, the breadline have had to accommodate to their masters' will. The locals were in no way anti-anybody, nor did they feel that the many manifestations that had been such a feature of life in Vientiane were anything to do with them. They wanted to be left alone to live their simple lives, make love, bring up their families, earn their living in peace. But when hunger, the PL, or both had everyone out in the paddy fields adding to the 'plough power' all day and the PL had them on re-education lectures in the evenings, a quiet life was a thing of the past.

The American embassy only just managed to close its doors before a rent-a-crowd student mob reached it and the Marine guard inside took the necessary remaining security precautions. Shredding of classified material had already been carried out. The crowd attacked the commissariat and looted most of the hooch and the tinned goodies. Power to the deep freeze was turned off and the stench of rancid meat later overpowered the besieging mob.

The ambassadors of Australia, India and the UK again went to the Foreign Affairs Ministry to complain on behalf of the Americans about their diplomatic immunity not being respected, but it made no difference. Some agreement was reached about numbers being allowed to leave – the amount of household stores that had to be left behind must have run into tens if not thousands of dollars' worth.

We had evidence that the hard-liners among the LPF were gaining strength: these were the dedicated communists, tied to Hanoi and Moscow's apron strings as opposed to the more nationalist-minded lot who did not want so much foreign control. Souvanna Phouma was a 'busted flush': a sad old figurehead and his half-brother, the Red Prince, had lost considerable influence. Both they, and the King and Queen, would be kept for only as long as they could be used.

One of the stranger aspects of that period, tame and bloodless though it was in comparison with the Red Guards in China and the Khmer Rouges in Kampuchea, was that diplomatic relations with the Americans were never severed; they were needed to be tormented and humiliated. The hapless Yanks' only crime was to have backed the wrong side; their stupidities were to have surrounded themselves with expensive trash and to make no provision for a quick getaway. It was unedifying to see the inanities of one cumbrous system pitting itself against another similarly ponderous one.

Unemployment became rampant and the supply of rice grew shorter. With money either valueless or nonexistent, black market dollars became even more sought-after and normal commodities became scarce. Heavy penalties were exacted from anyone caught with dollars and when an LPF functionary was found to have some in his possession, his answer was that that was the only way he could manage.

Despite rumours to the contrary neither water nor electricity was ever turned off so those few families that had refrigerators and had stocked up did not go short of commons. Not so the ordinary people: on my walks I saw groups digging for insect grubs, stalking lizards with makeshift catapults, hunting for toads and mudfish in the swamps and trapping small birds with net and lime. Later on there were no birds to be seen and when that happens people are hungry. I toured the town and bought a carton of steak and kidney puddings, thirty-six in all, as a reserve, and hoped that a full sack of dog biscuits would last Singha for some time.

Most people were bewildered, many afraid and all were powerless to do anything except tick over with a sense of doom never far away. The shrill anti-American orchestra continued its frenetic chant, not believed by the great majority of normal folk yet having to be heeded for self-protection. Eventually, humiliated and humbled, provoked and persecuted, the Americans were allowed to go, mostly without their belongings.

Meanwhile the various student leaders who had dictated terms to the American Chargé d'Affaires, Mr Christian Chapman (a fluent French speaker and a highly decorated pilot) also went. When the LPF first descended on Vientiane they hotly denied that they were communists. Nationalists and patriots, yes: socialists and democrats, yes: communists, no. When the top brass of the old regime fled, one set of social pressures was released. With the fear of communists out of their minds – after all, who objects to helping nationalists? – the natural leaders were invited to come forward and come forward they did, cleverly and firmly guided from behind. Once the American-bating phase was over, the Central Committee issued a decree saying that, although fervent patriots and revolutionaries had a part of play, there was more in the struggle than what they had been doing in the recent past and now it was a time of consolidation and re-education.

It was as though the LPF had changed political course, if only by a few degrees. They were clever for, at one stroke, a small and insignificant country had humbled a mighty nation, gained considerable international sympathy and prestige, and had managed to find out who the natural leaders were. Now these leaders had been identified they had to be purged for, if they could rise up, without a knowledge of Marxism-Leninism, against one government, why not against another? Those who did not flee across the Mekong were taken into communist-held territory for further political education for an unspecified, protracted and unpleasant spell.

Towards the end of May I learnt that a special seminar, lasting for two weeks, was taking place in Chinaimo Camp for the remaining senior RLA officers and that General Soutchai was among those attending. My problem was how to contact him about the recovery of my set of précis without letting any intermediary know the true reason for my wanting to meet him. One answer was to drive to Chinaimo and meet the General yet I knew that the camp was fully guarded by zealous PL soldiers. It would not be easy.

I sat down at my desk and composed a letter. It was very simple. It read:

Dear General Soutchai. I hear you are in Vientiane. You have given me so much hospitality when I visited your headquarters over the months I want now, in some small measure, to return it. Can you contact me between now and 7 June and let me know when you can come to my house in Thad Luang?

I signed it and put it in an envelope which I left unsealed, called Khien, whistled up Singha and drove back to my villa to put on some smart uniform.

At Chinaimo, the dog's head stuck out of the back window, the PL sentry flagged us down. "Why do you want to enter the camp?" he asked in a surly manner, keeping the barrier in the down position. Khien mumbled something about the *Tan Thud* [attaché] in the back of the car needed to go inside the camp. "I have had no warning about any foreign cars coming here. Can't let you in."

I looked out of the window and said that I knew he was only trying to do his duty but he should recognise the flag on my car and see that I was the British Defence Attaché. "Now you know my credentials there is no need to tell you more."

The sentry scowled back at me but made no effort to lift the barrier to let us through. I felt anger rising in my gorge. I fought it back. I told him I had a letter for General Soutchai who was attending a seminar. I had no intention of disturbing him but would go to HQ MR 5, contact one of the staff and tell him to give the letter to the General. I showed it to the sentry. "Would you like to vet it first?"

The sentry moved slightly forward and ordered the driver to open the boot of the car. This was against protocol, but I was powerless to prevent it. He came round to the window and I opened the envelope and showed the letter to him. I saw from the way he looked at it that he was illiterate but too proud to say so. With great reluctance, he lifted the barrier and let us in.

I found Colonel Douang Pi in one of the offices, gave him the letter and asked him to deliver it. We did not talk much but the look on his face told me all. I got a telephone call a couple of days later telling me when to expect General Soutchai.

Over a cup of coffee in my villa he told me that my preçis were still at his HQ, locked up. "No, I did not bring them up with me. Maybe I should have done but I have had other things on my mind." After some small talk he leaned forward in his chair and thanked me for the very understanding way I had conducted my affairs and dealings with him. Initially he had been inclined not to believe my answers and comments to his questions as they were so different from what the Americans had said. He particularly remembered one comment I had made, about the Meo General Vang Pao, to the effect that when the Americans left he would be like a man up a ladder with the ladder taken away. As a result of the collapse in the Sala Phou Khoun area, which Vang Pao should have held, he saw what I had said was absolutely true. He now trusted my judgement and wished he had taken advantage of it earlier. It was too late except in one respect: he wanted me to go to Pakse, any time before mid-June.

"Meet me in my office. I'll give you a briefing but we may have a PL audience so it won't be a very truthful one. What I want you to do is judge the situation in Vientiane, come and judge it in Pakse, then advise me whether to stay on or leave. Please, you're the only man I can trust."

I found myself saying, yes, of course I would, unless it was physically impossible. He stayed for ninety minutes and, after he had gone, I told myself never to be so stupid again.

Surprisingly, some of the Generals were allowed out of their seminar to attend the farewell lunch for Tsarkov, hosted by Chen Shu-lin, when he was posted to Hanoi. One of the Generals came over to poke me in the ribs after lunch and told me that he thought our politics in Britain were the cleverest in the world. I pressed him for more and his answer was that between the two world wars we had been No. 1 imperialists but not only had we changed but we had handed over our territories in a far better state than anyone else had and we had changed with the times. When we left places there were senior military officers, judges and doctors; an administration, hospitals and schools; roads and railways. When the French handed over there was nothing. I said that that was what I had been saying to anyone who cared to listen ever since I had been in Laos.

I told Davidson that I thought my presence in Pakse would help get the one remaining English schoolteacher out and he relented, allowing me to go. At Pakse we saw how very different it was now, no RLAF aircraft, sentries in PL uniforms and anti-aircraft artillery pieces all round the perimeter. As I turned to go to HQ MR 4, Peter Shield said, "Go and exercise your charm on these PL, Colonel, we might be able to take off more easily." Two scowling PL sentries had sidled up to investigate what we were about.

I greeted them with a smile and asked them if they had come to guard us against the imperialists' attacks? No answer but a spark of interest showed on their faces. I told them to stay around and that I was going to see Brigadier General Soutchai.

The two soldiers, unsure how to react to a Lao-speaking foreigner, watched me as I turned away. They had been told that any 'plane that wanted to land would be allowed to but, if permission for takeoff was not granted anti-aircraft artillery would shoot it down if it did try to fly away.

Inside the HQ building the General happened to be by himself. He looked tired but brightened up when he saw me. To my intense relief he gave me back my set of preçis, still in their envelope, so rashly given in the best of faith. I did not dare to ask him if he had ever looked at them.

He told me about the current situation. It was not so much that the PL had taken over everything but rather that the NVA had been pouring reinforcements into the area in such strength that a thrust into Thailand as far as Bangkok could be made with no logistical trouble and Kampuchea could be reinforced by NVA troops at the drop of a hat. All the NVA had been issued with PL-type uniforms and most of their weapons, ammunition, vehicles and fuel were American. Did I know that? I said I had heard some rumours to that effect but had no idea in what quantities.

It grieved him to have to tell me this but so much American equipment had been sold by the officers of his army that all the NVA had had to do was to supply instructors to teach the men how to use it. In fact, all the requirements, less air, for any offensive in that part of Laos could be got from ex-US stock. How corrupt could one get? And the currency paid for it all, by the North Vietnamese or their agents, had been American greenbacks. Most of the RLA never had been interested in winning the war – only in making as much money as possible.

But I already knew it was not only with arms and ammunition where the black market thrived. I had already discovered for myself that many administrative and medical needs were lacking at 'soldier level' because entitled stores were never sent to the front line. 'Not available': no, not for the soldiers, that is, but 'yes' for those unentitled people who paid a good price for them and could flog them elsewhere. When, at one unit I visited 'in the sticks', I was told that the soldiers looked tired because were sleepless. Oh, Why? Not because of the PL or the NVA but because of mosquitoes and sandflies. These latter are tiny little creatures that get into ears and eyes, can drive a person to distraction and infect liver and spleen. I told the soldiers I had managed, when in Borneo, to combat both types of insects, if only to a certain extent. We each made a chain of pungent chillies by splitting them lengthways and tying them at the tops with cotton every six or so inches. Depending on how many chillies could be got hold of and the length of cotton, the 'chain' could be either be worn round the neck, placed on the head as a halo or even tied to poles where a bed net would normally be tied. Many a good sleep has been had using this method. The young RLA soldiers were delighted at the idea and a hunt for chillies started there and then. It worked and the news spread to other units.

I thanked Soutchai for the précis and the information. I told him it was time he left. I was sure he was of the same opinion. A man like him had to leave, if only temporarily – that was to say for a few years – until the present madness had burnt itself out. He nodded, tears in his eyes. I would fly him out if he wanted me to.

He thanked me for the offer and said that that would mean we would both be prevented from leaving. We said goodbye, as friends, and went together to the airport. He told me to have a word with the sentries, he would go round to the tower. "Goodbye and good luck."

The sentries told me we could not take off otherwise we would be shot down. I told them not to worry themselves. This British 'plane had been to Sam Neua and had permission to travel to Pakse and back to Vientiane. Comrade Soupraseut [the PL overall commander] had given me his personal word, I lied. I looked at them closely. "You two are Rhadé men from around Kong My, aren't you?" They were and said we could go safely. That, and what went on in the tower, was enough to ensure an unscathed takeoff.

I never met Soutchai again.

On the way back I recalled the very first briefings I had had on my very first tour of all Military Regions. It had taken me some time to learn one reason why the war had gone on so long so inconclusively: before one side attacked the other, the defenders would be warned so that they could slip away quietly. Why should Lao kill Lao? Even then it had never occurred to me that another reason why the dreary little Laotian war had gone on for so long was due, in great part, to unscrupulous commanders flogging, to their enemies, the kit given by their friends, the Americans, to fight them. How many of the current higher and middle level officers would live the rest of their lives on riches gained this way? The thought sickened me but it was the only answer that made sense in the context of what I had been reporting on for so long. Only at the very end of it all had I stumbled on the truth which I would not have done had it not been for those wretched précis. Such were the people for whom I had been getting more and more involved. Why? I knew my answer, because it was what I was paid for. Back in London that thought would be seen as neither a cross nor a crown, but an irrelevance.

Nevertheless, London sparked. Simon wrote:

You have achieved an almost legendary reputation here and even if you were never to send us another line of intelligence it would not be impaired…if anyone can contrive to build something from the ruins you are the man and we all know you will do your level best.

The man two up from him wrote:

I thought I should drop you a line to let you know how much all of us here value your frequent reports with their wealth of insight and judgement on people and events.
As with Vietnam, things have acquired considerable momentum in recent weeks. Thanks to the fund of knowledge that your previous reporting has built up for us and to your most conscientious and timely

current reporting we have been able to cope with all requirements for briefings and assessments without difficulty. I am extremely grateful to you for this.

I imagine you must be feeling pretty sad at seeing things crumble in this way. The events themselves were not unexpected, but I for one thought they lay a little further in the future. However that may be, Laos continues to attract the attention and interest here both politically and militarily. In this latter connection we would very much appreciate whatever reportage and assessment you can send us, although I know that you could well find increasing difficulties placed in your way, in spite of your careful building up of contacts on both sides. With every good wish...

It was very nice of them to have bothered to write.

Thieving became very bad. Armed vigilante groups were organised to patrol the streets. They were efficient for a few nights then the standard dropped off. One night the head of Shell was returning late from a party and was stopped by a vigilante. A bribe was sought but, having no money on him, he was forced to wait until the man procured a pipe and syphoned enough petrol out of the car to fill his own motor bicycle tank. Shell supplied fuel to both sides in Laos: it was always embarrassing for those flying in the AN-2 to be refuelled by a 'free-world' set-up.

The Soviets were interesting during this time. On three separate occasions I was told by them 'people did not matter, only the leaders did'. I met General Tao Ly once more, after the Constitution Day parade, when he thanked me for 'opening his brain'. He had recovered his former aplomb and seemed intent on what he could do 'from the inside'. He asked me my views on whether he should escape or stay. I said that if he felt strongly about his country he would stay. So he did, along with a number of others.

It may have been the wrong advice. I heard what had happened to them when I was invited to the Staff College graduation ceremony. (I was surprised that the course was allowed to run its time.) At dawn one morning soon after our conversation, four generals, 37 colonels and 103 lieutenant colonels and majors were told to report at a certain place at 5 p.m. that day, with necessities and eight days' rations. About a dozen of the more junior managed to escape over the Mekong.

When the officers reported in they were stripped of all their insignia, told to call one another 'comrade' and on the morrow were taken to an area to the north of Vientiane plain and allotted plots of land that they had to clear with their own hands. They had to build their own camp, otherwise there was no shelter. It was then the rainy season. If they collected materials for making their camp there was insufficient time to collect food to eat, and *vice versa*. If they asked any villager for food, it had to be paid for by work. It was an appalling position to be in. I can remember how I ended the report I sent to London: '...*sans badge, sans brooch, sans braid, sans everything.*

At one dinner party I attended I met the Principal Secretaries to the Ministry of Foreign Affairs and of Propaganda and Tourism, the former having orchestrated the anti-American activities. He asked my views on the situation and did I think they had achieved their political aims? My answer was a Laotian proverb, a 'Yes and No' type that intrigued them. I was pressed to expand my answer, indeed I was to be given an invitation to continue the conversation in their HQ. I never did have one for that but, on learning that I was due away in February 1976, I was asked to stay another couple of years. I told them that I would be out of the army in five years, at which they suggested I be an English language teacher with them.

It so happened that the LPF were not the only people who offered me a job. It had been suggested that I work for the FCO after I left the army but before I took any decision a telegram arrived, 'out of the blue', asking if I would go to Nepal as one of the two recruiting officers. I sent back an immediate affirmative. When I told the First Secretary, Barry Denny, he sent a telegram to London that started off 'We have lost John Cross to his first love'. Later I was asked by a visiting FCO person why I had chosen that job, tucked away by myself in the west of Nepal, rather than with them in London. I quoted a Chinese saying, that I would rather be the head of a chicken than the tail of an elephant.

By the end of June the cultural side of the revolution was still continuing unabated. By then it was the turn of such people as taxi drivers, bar girls, prostitutes, Peter Shield's gardener and the cook's aged mother-in-law. Rumour was rife: a PL victory parade was in the offing; the NVA would force the Lao to do in Vientiane what the Khmer Rouges did in Phnom Penh, all foreigners were doomed and more. I continued my walking, meeting the PL based in the villages helping the farmers in the fields. I was always treated politely. In fact, I was cast in revolutionary mould: short back and sides, a total abstainer and I walked to work. LPF staff often stopped me to ask why I walked to work and my answer was that I could not afford the petrol and, anyway, if I were to go by car ('like the others') I would not meet such interesting people as them. This answer they accepted at face value.

I still kept up my visits in and around town. I would drop in on the MOD, the River Flotilla or the air force and, being known, I was always made welcome. I seldom learnt much but it stopped me from becoming bored.

Also, at the end of June, two British technicians on loan from the BBC, and just about to go home, went flying in the Vientiane flying club Cessna aircraft and did not return. The next morning Peter and I set out in the Beaver, my last-ever flight, and searched the area. We found the 'plane at Vang Vieng but my instinct warned me not to go below a thousand feet, let alone to land, so we flew back. We made enquiries and were told that their paperwork was not in order and that, until Sam Neua gave orders to release them, there they had to stay. In fact it was thought they were spies. However, it was the army's responsibility to get them out and I was told to write a letter to the MOD, addressed personally to Kaysone Boupha, asking him for help. Davidson wanted me to go by road to Vang Vieng and visit the two men. I paid the ministry two visits to try and arrange this and the upshot was that I had to go to the Joint Mixed Commission in town for a *laisser passer*, not for me, as a diplomat I had my own card, but for the driver and the car. These I eventually got.

Dressed in smart uniform, with an overnight bag, I was driven north. We passed a large notice board with 'Liberated Zone' painted in large letters and, over a small hill, was a PL-manned barrier. We crawled to a stop, behind a few lorries and a couple of taxis. When our turn came the sentry stood in front of the car and another armed man came and beckoned the driver to follow him up to an office. I sat still, waiting. A third man came and opened the back door. He saw my overnight bag and searched it thoroughly. I kept quiet and the man ordered me, in halting French, to follow him. We went up the slope together and, seeing Khien's forlorn glance at the *laisser passer* on a table, I realised that the document I had so sedulously striven to acquire had not worked. The unexpected comment about it was that, as it had been issued in Vientiane which was not yet in the liberated zone, it had no currency outside it. I remonstrated and quietly pointed out that one of those who had signed had actually written LPF under his name, but that carried no weight either. Vientiane was not in the liberated zone, therefore nothing produced there was valid.

I had begun to give up hope of getting any farther that day when I changed my tack. I congratulated them on their soldierly appearance and said that, despite my having diplomatic immunity, I understood their caution. I continued by saying that I presumed they realised I was the attaché for all Laos, not for one side or the other. I added that I had been to Sam Neua and met members of the Politburo, which was perfectly true but had no bearing on the actual problem of being allowed through the barrier into the liberated zone. I told them I had fought against the Japanese in Burma (but forbore to mention what I had been doing since) and, at that they perked up, full of interest. The Japanese were either 'feudalists' or 'reactionaries' in their lexicon (I forget which) and so I had taken part in the same struggle as they were now participating in. At that the *laisser passer* was countersigned and I was allowed to continue my journey – an hour later.

It was a strange feeling to have the barrier behind me. These people had yet another thought process I did not understand. It was not so much a question of accepting or rejecting normal authority but rather there was a whole range of invisible buttons that had to be pressed before the right combination clicked into gear. It had been rather like that during the Queen's birthday party and the 'PL in the residence garden' conundrum. I wondered if it was not something to do with a distortion of oriental face or if they were waiting to see how much homework had been done or humble pie had to be eaten. It is still an unsolved puzzle.

When we stopped in a village for a bite to eat no more notice of us was taken than ever had been the case before the arrival of the new regime. Some folk talked to us, some ignored us. Before we left on the next part of our journey a local military commander strolled up and asked to see our documents. He was a Lao, not being bullied by the Vietnamese, so was his normal polite self and even had a chat before wishing us a safe journey and letting us go on.

I now felt more hopeful of reaching the two Britons but was quite prepared to be foiled. We reached the junction where the recently-built road from Long Cheng joined Route 13 and in the very middle of the highway I saw a rough booth that had not been there before and a crowd of some fifty locals milling round a couple of LPF officials. One of them turned to us as he heard the car. He held out his hand in a gesture that meant halt. I told Khien to stop short of the booth. I got out and went to see what the hold-up was.

There was an air of disquiet among the small crowd. They looked at me as I came up and some of them averted their gaze. I gave the official the *laisser passer* to examine and asked if we could drive on.

"No."

The man looked at me unsmilingly and turned away. I went into the booth and showed my other documents to the other man, the elder of the two. He glanced at them. Didn't mean a thing to him, he said. "None of you can move north from here. You can't, they can't," and he indicated the crowd around him.

I explained how I had followed all the rules till then and what my mission was. How long was he going to keep me waiting? The man paused before giving me his crushing reply. As far as he was concerned I would not be going up this road for a long time, ten, twenty or a hundred years, nor would any Westerners. "I'm not even allowing these people here to go where they think they want to until they learn to take note of our new socialist democratic republic."

To me here was a prime example of the world's most dangerous man, the over-educated idiot whose education outruns his common sense the day he learns how to sign his name. I wondered if the refusal was due to a rumour about NVA troop movements in the vicinity that were directed against ex-Irregular Meo, now rebels. There was nothing to do but to return to Vientiane, which I did, giving a lift to a PL soldier caught in a rainstorm on the way back. The two BBC men were released a few days later. For the first eight days they were treated as spies and the last eight they were used politically. They were delighted to be out, had lost some weight and ponged a bit as they had no laundering facilities. They were very, very apologetic for the bother they had caused. They confirmed that, had we landed, we would not have been allowed to take off again and had we flown within range of small arms' fire, we would have been a target. Not a word of any of this came out in the world press and the LPF let us know, had it, the release of the men would not have been so quick.

Before the end of the month, all French (remnants of the MMF and schoolteachers) and Japanese (voluntary aid workers) in the provinces were told they had a few days to get out. The next morning they were told to leave that day. The ten Japanese in Savannakhet, teaching judo, were about to give a show but the day before an LPF broadcast denounced judo as a non-Laotian activity, forbade the show and ordered them out there and then. Only half got away that day, with a crowd of Lao asking them for their banned kit before they left.

An interesting sign of the times was that, as never before, the reply to the French toast on Bastille Day was given in Lao. In fact, apart from the assistant Chinese attaché and myself, none of the foreign community spoke Lao and, in the various LPF offices, the only language allowed was Lao. Interpreters were provided for important people – if they were important enough.

The Beaver had to fly back to England, a most challenging task for Peter. Before it took off on the first leg of its journey to England on 1 August, a *baçi* was given for it and Peter Shield in the hangar at Wattay. The two PL guards were invited over and enjoyed being part of the farewell ceremony. We sent a report about it to London and, in due course, we got an answer from the Head of the South-East Asia desk at the FCO:

> ... *The removal of the aircraft marks virtually the end of a period of unique British involvement in Laos. The character of the involvement had always been regarded as exceptional but the departure of the Beaver had a special and rather sad piquancy for all that...*
> ... *The departure of Col Cross will be almost as big a milestone in our relations with Laos as was that of the Beaver. Please convey our warm thanks to him from all the Department.*

It was indeed the end of an era. Apart from the Americans, who were in a different league, having an aircraft had enabled us British to visit places few other nationalities were able to get to and it had allowed me an undreamt freedom of action. My relations with the Lao and my coverage of events would have been miniscule without it.

As for the others, I knew that the Thais had an intelligence network as a major incident developed when their spies were caught. It was even on the BBC news for a day or so. The French also ran an extensive network: one of the characteristics of the job was never to know how much the other man knew. I often wondered what the other attachés did with their time and how they got any knowledge of what was really happening. Despite the Beaver, in the early days I managed precious little of substance, yet all the time I was working to the day when contacts, language, Beaver and luck kept me abreast of the situation.

By the middle of the month there were scarcely any cars on the roads but bicycles (many of them presents from Russia) and horses instead, no doctors in the hospitals, no drugs, no dentists and the surplus population in the fields. Every Saturday and Sunday gangs of youths would be seen working on such jobs as filling in potholes and cleaning out drains.

"You come from Britain, another socialist country. Join in," they would call as I walked past them. "I've done my share already," I lied cheerfully as I declined.

Youths whose hair was considered too long were the targets of mobile barbers. Some who did not like their hair forcibly cut and remonstrated had a swathe cut from front to rear and across the top.

Simon Hutchinson visited me again and I managed to get him to a Chinese Army Day party at which all the personages who had been names on paper till then were met in the flesh. His visit did my morale an immense amount of good.

Meanwhile Britain presented ambassadorial credentials to the Government of Vietnam, having previously only been accredited to the Mayor of Hanoi. John Stewart was the ambassador and the possibility of my being doubly accredited was finally turned down. I gather I was the only runner considered for the post and, apart from the time 'not yet ripe' for a Vietnamese attaché being accredited to Britain from France, my relief would not have my particular span of oriental languages and his speaking French only would be considered by Hanoi as London not taking the post as seriously as when I had been in it.

Villages in the close neighbourhood of Vientiane were 'liberated'. This entailed new leaders being chosen and a new vigilante corps being set up. I sensed a feeling of tension between the 'liberators' and those whom they hoped to 'liberate', the honest, decent, solid citizen who now saw the whole tenor of his life put in jeopardy with irrevocable changes. It was a very strange and not uninteresting process to be in the middle of. I saw one liberation seminar (from which only the unborn, dying and demented were excused) being held in the grounds of a *wat*, with armed PL sentries guarding it. After the LPF's '18 political points' had been rehearsed it was announced that from then on any person caught without the necessary permission was to be apprehended and measures would be taken against any person not turning such an offender over. No foreigners were to be allowed there.

At one village one of the participants asked about the English colonel and his dog. Was he to be allowed? The questioner was reminded what had been said and the answer was no. Another villager said that I made the people laugh, I gave the children things to eat and that I was welcome. "Is this a people's revolution or not?" the political cadre in charge was asked.

It was indeed and a vote was taken as to whether or not I should be allowed to continue walking around. A show of hands confirmed that I was and a delegation went to other villages, told them of their decision and I was approached in the embassy. The questioner, who was on the village committee, was a British embassy office cleaner. "You can go anywhere you like," he said. "You and the 'little soldier'." I knew that the new Australian ambassador liked walking and so I asked if I could ever take a friend with me. "No, this is for you only," I was told.

I used to walk the dog once around the area before going to bed. One night, on my way from the house, I noticed a man tinkering with a jeep. I said nothing to him and, on the way back, he was still there. I stopped to talk to him, asking what the trouble was.

He was waiting for his wife who worked as a cook in the house opposite and, to avoid suspicion of loitering, he had to make it seem as though he was having trouble with his motor. At first he could not place me (he offered American, French, Italian, Russian and Canadian) and when I said what I did he immediately remembered me. He asked me if I recognised him. I did not and he told me that he had been Colonel Somneuk's staff officer up at Phone Hong and had helped organise the occasion when I was hijacked. At the outbreak of the revolution he had denounced the colonel, the police chief and the local administrative chief – the three men who had travelled in my car that time – and had been put in charge of the area.

"So you can travel quite easily?" I asked.

No, it was not that. He had surreptitiously left Phone Hong, come down to Vientiane to take his wife across the river, as he had planned all along. I asked him why, therefore, he had denounced these three if he had no intention of staying. His only way to escape was to make them think he was one of them. He had to do something drastic otherwise he would never have been trusted.

It was remarkable to have found him and he to talk so freely and truthfully. I wondered how many others like him there were. Countless, probably.

In late August Vientiane and Luang Prabang were 'liberated'. Only the Lao could have a situation where a neutral zone could be liberated and the zone stay neutral!

Ambassador Davidson voluntarily retired and told the staff that his replacement was 'a long way from Laos'. "Who isn't?" was my rejoinder. He was in Brasilia.

Somehow or other the Commander-in-Chief had not been sent for re-education as had the others. I met him and his wife at a large dinner party given by the Brigadier General in charge of the MMF to say goodbye to Jean Laboucheix. (The last time I had been asked I had to translate French into five Asian languages, for the ladies, and after ten minutes I was suffering from mental constipation and came to a complete halt.) At table I sat next to Jubilation who very quietly spoke to me in Lao. He had been waiting to ask me again, should he escape now or wait a month or so? He had been warned that he would have to go to Hanoi some time in the future. It was impolite to keep up a conversation in Lao when we all spoke French so we had a two-tier talk. During the non-French part of it I told him he were better out as soon as possible. It was to his evident relief; he sighed and said that his wife would not agree. Would I, after dinner, try and persuade her to go? "She takes no notice of me but will do of you."

I knew he thought well of me as he had, not long before, asked me if he could write to London for me to be extended in post. Not that London would have been swayed as, even before my second extension, I was too old for further promotion and to be an attaché.

The French looked on me as gallant, a *loup blanc*, and popular, with the story of how, in the middle of a proposal of marriage, I had forgotten the girl's name and, in my confusion, used her mother's, tickling their sense of humour. So when, after dinner I manoeuvred Madame Bounpone, a large lady well past her prime, into a corner, it was accepted with knowing smiles. We had a long chat. I knew that she was the business brains of the two and that the casino in Savannakhet was their property so she was understandably unhappy to leave it. I told her that she would never see any gain from staying where she was and, eventually, she nodded her acceptance.

Two mornings after that the Chinese DA went round to their house and said that would be both on an aeroplane, initially bound for Hanoi and thence to Peking, that afternoon. A notice in the press said that the General had gone for medical treatment. I never saw them again.

It could have been the intention of the authorities to get rid of the Bounphones before the end of the week when we had a 'liberation' festival. The group of young leaders, emerging after the first lot of firebrands had been fully used and then disposed of, arranged this. It started at 8 o'clock in the morning and was scheduled to last for forty-eight hours, then twelve, but it only lasted three and a half with some of the crowd leaving after two. We were advised to keep away in case of trouble. I went for a walk and heard the speeches being broadcast as I passed houses. People did not seem particularly happy about being liberated but, being powerless to do anything about it, accepted it philosophically.

During this period I found myself being sustained by my own convictions and my religious faith. I had been treasurer of the church for over two years and, by the end of evensong, the two back pews would be full of children waiting for me. We would walk to the Evening Market (that and the church were near my villa) where I would sit them down in an eating booth, order them a large meal, pay for it and go back to my own. I also helped pay for their hospital and school bills.

I was sustained by having sight of a letter that the Assistant Under Secretary of State at the FCO wrote to his opposite number at the MOD about my last annual report:

> *...It seems probable that this will be the last Annual Report from Colonel Cross and I should like to take this opportunity to pay tribute to his work over the last two and a half years in Laos. Thanks to his personal qualities and his ability in the language, we have enjoyed the benefit of a unique insight into one of the key areas of Lao society on both sides of the political divide.*
>
> *I should like, on behalf of the Foreign and Commonwealth Office, to endorse these words. HMG has been remarkably well served in Laos by the Army officers appointed to the embassy. The qualities and linguist and other qualifications Colonel Cross brought to his duties were of a very high order. I was lucky enough to be about to observe what a tower of strength he is when I visited Vientiane earlier in the year.*

Acorn to oak trees, I mused when I read it, but I had never thought of what I had done in those terms.

For those who offended against the new order there were various penalties. Some were benign: a 'spontaneous' mass demonstration against a local official, 'chosen' by the public three weeks before, was organised overnight. People were told to be outside the local *wat* at 5 o'clock in the morning to 'demonstrate' against him, demanding that he resign. Others would not be kindly dealt with.

Others not: revulsion therapy was applied to dissuade venial activities as card playing, visiting brothels (a popular if not national pastime), asking stupid questions at seminars and petty thefts. A zealous PL patrol came across half a dozen elderly women playing cards; they were taken to a police post and made to play cards from 6 o'clock in the morning, nonstop, until midnight, their faces heavily made up with rouge and lipstick to shame them. Eating and sleeping were allowed from midnight to 6 a.m. This went on for seventy-two hours.

For a man who had answered a question at a seminar incorrectly the punishment was being forced to listen to a tape recording of the question and its correct answer for a similar 72-hour span. It nearly sent him mad, he said. However, he was luckier than a person who had just finished a 6-month re-education course who unthinkingly said the forbidden Americanism 'OK'. He had to undergo the whole course again.

Any man caught in a brothel had to wait there until it was established whether he was married or not. If so, his wife was sent for to take him away; if not, he was forced to marry the whore. In both cases man and woman were made to walk around the town together for the rest of the day, he with an explanatory label hung around his neck. One lad of five or six stole an onion and also had to walk around all day with a notice, detailing his crime, round his neck.

No one from the losing side was spared re-education. The knock on the door in the small hours became a commonplace. One ex-royalist police captain was called for at 3 o'clock in the morning as his wife lay dying in childbirth. He requested the authorities to send him another time, so that he could do what he could for his wife and his ten children. He was told that his country was more important than his family. He then asked if he could be given until 3 o'clock in the afternoon instead of the 10 o'clock morning deadline. No. I had recently read an article in which this caught my eye: *the puritanical Marxists who, however Utopian their curious religion may be in theory, invariably increase the amount of human misery...* So it seemed.

I met the children, still in a state of shock, outside their house. I tried to comfort them but to no avail. My dog was better fed than they, despite food shortages, as I had that sack of dog biscuit. I wondered if I should put the dog down and, having soaked the dog biscuit in water, give it to the children. I did not but I thought of them each time I saw a television advertisement for dog food.

And yet...? One Saturday morning, as I walked out of the town with the dog, I should have counted the number of folk who greeted me before I greeted them, how many taxis blew their horns in greeting and how many people waved at me from car or taxi windows. Even a stern-faced PL driving past waved at me. I never knew why but was I all things to all people? And yet...?

The LPF were not having it all their own way. That same day a heavy-handed PL arrested a well-known Lao who had public backing to an unusual degree. He was anti-US and anti-communist. On the Monday evening I heard firing and learnt that the PL were trying to disperse a crowd of students who had gathered outside the man's house to demonstrate on his behalf. Next day his daughter emerged from the house and told the PL to shoot her if they wanted to. The man was released.

It coincided with an unusually long article in the LPF daily paper which, most surprisingly, went into details of how, in fact, they had been following a communist line the whole time. As Davidson had never accepted my word that the LPF were communists (so the FCO presumably were of the same opinion), I felt that I was fully vindicated.

As if to show the world its communist credentials, more was to come. Preparations were being made for big celebrations to take place on Sunday, 12 October. All the emphasis was on Laos becoming cleansed from the nastinesses of the modern western world. Local cultural groups practised their dancing and their new revolutionary songs. The sound of drumbeats was heard where before transistor radios would have blared out. Great efforts were made to fill in the potholes and clean the place up generally with local voluntary labour – 'voluntary' not being synonymous with 'willing' – but brave indeed is the spirit that dares oppose the people's wishes!

In that same month I wrote an article about the communist takeover in Laos for the regimental journal:

> ...and the saddest part of it all, as I see it, is that what has taken over from the old regime had, initially, to be better than that which it replaced. That which could not sensibly evolve by its own peaceful methods was ripe for change to be brought upon it by violent means... Decent men and women had ceased to have faith in their own institutions yet were powerless to root out the enemy in their own midst...all because the leaders gave them no sign that they had understood either the problems or any of the dangers that were besetting them, nor that there was enough willpower to change what a few good men and true had already needed changing. Is Laos the only country in that unenviable position?

10

From Hanoi with XXX

The Lao Patriotic Front, as a political force, even backed up as it was by the Pathet Lao as its military arm, would never have won the civil war by itself. It was the Vietnamese from the north, 'lacquered bamboo', with their age-old dreams of an Indo-China dominated from Hanoi, that was the propelling force, the guiding light and the overwhelming impetus behind the LPF that allowed its victory.

The cold war of the superpowers, the communist quarrel between USSR and China, the US policy of trying to contain communism on the mainland of Asia were powerful ingredients that prevented the civil war in Laos from being settled years before. The backdrop against which the drama of Laos was played out, with Vietnam using communism for nationalistic reasons, has never been in doubt. The way they had put their people, as Lao, in the east of Laos over the past decade and more – deny it though they always did – proved their policy. Had the Vietnamese leaders been true communist 'internationalists', they would have aimed their strength strategically towards the borders of India and Burma: this they did not. All their thinking was tactical and national, moving down the Indo-China peninsula to realise the hegemony that they had desired for so long. They had been stalled by the French colonialists but, once the French had solidified the concept of Indo-China and had been driven away, the rest was a matter of time, opportunity and very clever tactics. However, in the context of the cold war, to say that the Russians fought almost to the last drop of Vietnamese blood would only be an exaggeration.

By 1 May 1975, the northerners had captured the south: Kampuchea – called Cambodia again in 1989 – where lived their hereditary enemies (who also hated the Vietnamese and would offer their American advisers the liver of any Vietnamese they killed), could wait. For Laos, the programme for completing their colonising task seemed to be before 1976 was out.

On 12 October 1945 the Japanese decreed that Laos was thenceforth to be a sovereign state, with King Sisavangvong as King of all Laos. Over the centuries the geographical area of modern Laos had been split up into smaller kingdoms and had been invaded by Thais, Red-Flag and Yellow-Flag Hos from south China, Tonkinese, Khmers, French and Japanese, but it had never been a single sovereign country until the Japanese decree. This state of affairs did not last for long; the French came back again, still regarding Laos as a Protectorate within the French Union.

The date, 12 October 1975, had a strong attraction to the Lao communists and their whole take-over programme could well have been anchored to it. It was ironic that Laos, never having been able to attain independence on its own, only managed it by relying on the 'Elder Brothers', as the North Vietnamese were known, to achieve it thirty years later. Common though that knowledge was, it was taboo to the extent that the whole of the LPF lived their myth with a devotion that meant not only was the Secretary General without clothes but that the whole of the Politburo also went naked. Skilful propaganda deflected the public's view from this fact of life, but in any case, as most Lao only wanted to be left alone to make love and play their *khene* violins, the propaganda did not have to be unduly subtle.

Celebrations were to take place in the Thad Luang area, which was increased in size. Earth-moving plant sent up clouds of red dust as the heavy vehicles took off the topsoil, knocking down shanties, booths and shrubs as they strove to complete the task on time.

The first event was on the previous afternoon. A large pictorial exhibition had been put on display in a new wooden building by the side of the grandstand. Some of the pictures were anti-French but mostly they were of what the Americans had done; bombing was a favourite subject, ruins of Sam Neua and other towns, followed by views of napalm scars, refugees and harassment of US aid officials.

It was not my business to defend the Americans and much of what they had done was anathema to me but I always took the opportunity to put the record straight in pointing out the good things the Americans had done, the British stood for and the dangers of getting into the grasp of the USSR. By this time I was positively glad that successive British governments had declined to send armed forces into Indo-China, although that had not always been my view. Fundamentally I firmly believed that having American allies was better than having Soviet ones.

The Russians were in festive mood. Ahead of me was the Soviet ambassador who laughingly congratulated, in French, a pretty young hostess on the part she was playing in the exhibition. I could not help it: as I drew near her I asked her, in Lao, if she knew who had spoken to her? No, she didn't so I told her, adding that if the Soviets really were friends of the Lao, they would bother to speak the language. She took my point.

The LPF representatives were brimful with an 'I-told-you-so' look on their faces and the North Vietnamese were as ebullient as I had ever seen them. It was seldom that I saw happy communists, they nearly always wore grim expressions. However, among the Asians, I never saw a hard-core communist who was fat. If nothing else they shared the misery of the people under them. Since then I have never really believed any man who asserts that his political faith is communism or socialism if he carries too much weight.

At the exhibition the head West German television man in southeast Asia, up from Singapore for the celebrations, approached me. He had been to the Jungle Warfare School in my day to make a film and now he wanted me to take him into the surrounding countryside and, while I was talking to the villagers, his team would record it.

That evening at a reception in Phone Kheng hard liquor, stolen from the raids on the American commissariat earlier in the year, was offered. Wives of husbands being re-educated made the small eats. Wanting to escape to go to another party I tried to slip away but was prevented so I could watch a firework display. This was the finest I had ever seen, with salvos of bombs that were full of star clusters being fired from Chinese 81-mm mortars. Chok Di, in my villa, thought the noise was war breaking out again.

Unseasonably, it rained heavily in the night and the red desert was changed into a red quagmire. Dressed in full ceremonial fig, we were seated in the grandstand by half past 6 next morning. On the far side of the ground was a tiered stand full of men with coloured squares on poles which, when raised, produced giant 'wall posters'. There were policy slogans, a map of Laos and the LPF emblem. It was cleverly and spectacularly done, all squares being changed in unison. It must have needed much practice.

A long speech was made, vituperatively anti-American in particular and anti-western in general. The fraternal community was lauded, as was the USSR. For the third time in recent weeks they were given credit for winning the Second World War single-handed. Later Davidson and I bitterly complained to both Soviets and Lao about the wilful disregard for historical facts and, in both cases, got a rueful grin in return.

International media merchants were there in strength. The march past, all troops dressed in new green uniforms (no badges of rank) and white gloves, was marred by their slithering in the glutinous red mud. As we were leaving, I went to talk to a group of PL women military police, muddy and tired, standing to one side. I commiserated with them on their dirty shoes and stockings, saying what a shame it was that all their practice was ruined. They talked happily until they realised several microphones were being pushed our way. The television fraternity must have had some film they wanted to finish off. I wondered how many people, there and viewers, saw the irony of the now-admitted communists talking to a western military man on such friendly terms.

I changed and went for a walk. It was very hot by then. I spoke to a number of those who had been parading and they were very glad it was over. They had been practising for a long time and some of them had to get up at half-past midnight to be in time, others at 2 a.m. The PL were worried that there might have been trouble and had billeted one man in every tenth house all over the town.

The German television team hired a car and picked me and Singha up. I briefed the driver to tell any local revolutionary committee that the Germans had government permission, which was not true. I got out of the car on the near side of the village I had chosen and the German team drove through it to the far end. The idea was that curiosity in what they were doing would have cooled enough for me to be the attraction as I moved towards the cameras.

I did not know that the PL had reinforced the village against any disturbances and as I walked along four of them came towards me so I stopped and had a brief chat. I asked them if they knew me and, as they did, there was no trouble. Another uniformed man came hurrying out of a house, saluted me as an old friend and asked, most nervously, who the strangers were. I told him not to bother as I had cleared it in Vientiane and was responsible for them. He saluted again and, relieved, went back into the house. All that was filmed, as was my one-man cabaret act with the children. Twice, as the crew asked me to wait while they took up another position. Their efforts won them an award for the best news coverage of the year.

The last remnants of a French military presence, the MMF, folded up, abandoning their dog and cat pets: within a week the PL who had taken the camp over had eaten every one.

The Americans were very interested in finding out my views on the solution of the communist revolutionary problem in those parts. With my experience, I was told by one of their staff from Bangkok, I ought to be in an unrivalled position to provide the answer. By then, the more I had seen of the problem, the harder I found it to give a definitive answer, which may have been the start of true knowledge. I said I would have to give the problem much thought: the West might be in a pendulum swing of history that made it impossible to find a permanent solution so, while the present wave of killings and misery burnt itself out, all we could do was try to hasten it on its way as best we could. A council of despair, maybe, but an interesting topic to write on, making it my final gift to the Ministry from the last of 'their men' in Indo-China.

I had a chance to see more of a communist country when I visited Hanoi as courier at the end of the month. The Vietnamese authorities in Vientiane had said that there would be no difficulty about a visa but, at the last minute, there was. It was alleged that I was an American spy. A hurried signal was sent to the ambassador, John Stewart (through Darwin to Peking then by land line to Hanoi), who managed to convince the Hanoi authorities I was a genuine British citizen.

I flew up by Aeroflot full of unsmiling and grey-faced mid-Europeans in baggy clothes. At Hanoi our passports were taken off us and the functionary at the airport would only give them back if the owners could recite the number. Most of the passengers could not so were made to wait. I refused to answer in French and the official seemed so surprised when I spoke in Vietnamese that he gave me mine back at once.

I was there four days and had time to wander around on foot and on a bicycle. The city is well laid out and I was fascinated to see that there was no bomb damage in the residential area. All the talk about Hanoi itself being bombed was fabricated, although one bomb did fall in the

Indian ambassador's garden. The ugly student riots in France were shamelessly orchestrated showing the age-old dangers of the gullible being swayed by the plausible.

So few vehicles were there that, at each of the many crossroads, they had to stop and hoot a warning of their presence. Most people used bicycles and, so many and so silent were they, I likened going around the place to being in a room with too many cats and always in danger of treading on one. There were, in fact, only cats in Hanoi, no dogs being allowed by government edict.

Crocodiles of school children passed me, the leader giving them the order 'eyes right', with the word of command being the Vietnamese for 'Soviet'. I replied in English but not a blind bit of notice was ever taken. I was stopped by a sentry and roughly told I could go no farther. Who was I? I told him and he demanded to see my passport. "It's in the ministry," was my answer as I was turned back.

I stopped and talked to people in the streets. One and all seemed delighted to be talking to an Englishman. In the International Club, built by the Soviets (no locals allowed except staff), I made the Vietnamese bar girls laugh. I talked to Vietnamese when at a cocktail party, the only European to do so. The Khmer Rouge representative, who had been there many years, surprised me by calling the women men, so poor was his command of Vietnamese grammar.

I went into a small shop. The proprietor, a man in his fifties, thinking I was an eastern European, asked me in French what I wanted. I told him who, what and where I was. The reaction was immediate and impressive. He told me to sit down at a small table at the back of the shop, the other side of a screen. I faced the far wall on which hung a large picture behind plate glass that reflected the entrance to the shop. "Watch that," the man said as he sat down with his back to the wall, "and if anyone looks in here for more than five seconds, tell me."

He told his wife to bring coffee and to play an old-fashioned wind-up gramophone. For the next hour, in a mixture of Vietnamese and French, he poured out his heart. Although the communists had been in power for over a score of years, many similarly aged men (he claimed 80 per cent) had never come to terms with them but were too scared to remonstrate or say that life was very difficult under them. He spoke of territorial friction between the Vietnamese and the Chinese, not only in the context of the Paracel and Spratly Islands but on the common border. As I did not recognise the border names, I asked him to draw me a map: within fifteen seconds it was drawn, shown me and destroyed. I found it sad that anybody had to live under the strains that he and his wife, among many others, evidently did.

Despite the communists having been in power since 1954, the Catholic church was filled by all ages every Sunday (and not there to make a nuisance), but the one Protestant church I came across was used as a library.

John Stewart and I went for a walk in one of the public parks and met groups of soldiers. I talked to them, making them laugh, asking what the signs on their uniforms meant. They asked us to take their photographs, which John did, suitably posed.

I met the Indian ambassador to Vietnam, Gharekan, late of the ICSC, who was at pains to create a good impression and be pleasant, a nice contrast from his behaviour in Vientiane. As for Tsarkov, he was more than pleasant. He claimed that the victory in Indo-China could not have happened without Soviet help – 'our socialist victory' – but then he would do. His table groaned with delicacies, as did those of the Hungarian and Romanian attachés. These both admitted to having been taken in by Vietnamese propaganda about the bombing of Hanoi and were bored stiff. I was invited to their houses where taped music was played loudly to drown any eavesdropping devices and the freemasonry of soldiers allowed frank discussion.

My visit to the Chinese DA was of great interest. Back in Vientiane I had told Chen Shu-lin about my visit and he said I should go and see his counterpart, and that he would write and tell him I was coming. We had a long and earnest conversation. The message I was given was to tell the Americans that, despite public pronouncements to the contrary, the Chinese wanted an American presence retained in Thailand as they feared what they saw as a greater, Soviet, evil would fill the vacuum.

A remark such as that can only be evaluated as being wholly true, wholly false or somewhere in between if its originator and the person to whom it is given have also been graded for reliability. I reported the matter and, as is normal practice, never heard any more about it.

In November I paid a fleeting visit to Burma where I met a one-time foreign minister and several Shan opposition leaders who had been let out of jail within the past few days after many years. The view of Laos from both neighbouring countries made me realise that there was less in it than met the eye.

Back in Laos the weather was cold and the locals were looking for kindling. By that time I was a familiar figure on my long walks (I calculated that I walked and jogged 12,500 miles during my stay there; I think I'd have gone mad if I had not had the countryside and my dog). The Saturday after I returned from Hanoi, when some distance from Vientiane, a lone man came up to me in the paddy fields and asked me if I liked the new situation. I said no I didn't and he started giving me his views – most uncomplimentary to the new Lords and Masters. It was so strange to come across the roughest of roughs in the middle of nowhere and hear him parroting the advantages of socialism and the disadvantages of imperialism. I said to him that three years ago, when I came to Laos, nobody had ever heard of those words and did he really know what they meant? He said, no, of course not, but added that 'the elder and younger brothers' taught them to talk like that. That week the seminars were busy with a 'hate America week', with the most stupid and far-fetched things said about them. If the people cavilled at what was said, they were brandied as traitors, but both teacher and taught knew that most of what was said was a tissue of lies.

By then some of the harvest had been gathered, making me happy to think that people would be having a square meal once again. In one village I saw all the villagers in the temple precincts being lectured, with Pathet Lao soldiers standing guard outside, rifles at the ready. In any war, especially the civil kind, the vanquished lose their dignity. It again struck me how very lucky we were in England despite strikes fomented by a hard core of stubborn union men and how lucky I was not to have watch much more of such nonsense, *and* soon to be leaving it behind. If there was one thing above all else that I had learnt in Laos was that my eyes had been opened, much more than in any 'normal' job, about Russian-Marxist-Imperialism, as I now thought of the communist system as actually practised, and the dangers it posed for my own countrymen, who had not seen it at first hand, so could not believe what it was about nor that it could happen to them.

An embassy driver who had gone on retirement down in the south only a matter of a month before returned. The state of affairs was so bad that he could not stomach it as normal family life was no more.

The week after I came back for Hanoi I wrote home:

We have the annual festival of Thad Luang on our hands...the ageing and useless Prime Minister came and opened it, thereby making one of his rare public appearances. All the socialist countries tripped over themselves in their efforts to out-comrade one another, which makes me laugh. I must say that this revolution in the name of socialism is not much more that a despicable charade. The way in which the Authorities poison the minds of the credulous populace with the most unlikely of tales, as well as keeping them very much afraid, makes me wish that all the weird, bearded creatures that prattle about left-wing nonsenses in our great halls of learning in Britain could go to Laos, not only to see for themselves what it is like 'on the ground' but also to undergo the humiliating treatment that the revolution has brought. I know that there are no rules in politics nor even in victory but that does not make the victors' behaviour any more easy to swallow. Meanwhile the 'seminar' remains a daily feature which everybody has to attend. As far as the embassy local staff is concerned this has resulted in there being no drivers, for instance, or no one being on duty for passport renewals or telephone switchboard work. The telephone in my villa has been out of order since mid-August...but despite many requests for it to be repaired, every time the answer is the same, namely that all the repair staff is on seminar. In Hanoi, despite their victory over the French so many years ago, such seminars are still a permanent feature of everyday life. Thank the Lord I don't have to live permanently in one of those countries. I find it hard to imagine such splendidly loyal people as the Scottish coal miners happily or willingly submitting themselves to such aspects of party discipline – how blind they all are!...

...in the old-isms there was any amount of nastiness, sure, but nobody tried to disguise the fact that there was privilege at the top. Nowadays there are still any amount of privileges, but those at the top try and pretend that there are none. No, there is too much cant and hypocrisy at the top for any decent person's liking. Only dupes and fools lap it up.

Now that the revolution had been achieved in Indo-China (or had it?) the Soviet Union declined to pay its share of the cost of the ICSC. There being no money it was wound up, not that there had been anything active for it to do all the time I was there. I was sorry to see their Indian Army representative go. The present man, Brigadier Pathania and his half-Nepali wife, were delightful people. He had commanded a battalion of the 8th Gorkhas and I had twice managed that we three went to Radio Laos and made a recording for the British Army Gurkhas' radio service in Hong Kong. Before Pathania was Brigadier Tony Michigan, another delightful man, a staunch Christian, a lay reader and a wonderful speaker of English. (I recall his telling me about something 'tantamounting to hullaballoos'.) All three senior Indian officers, Brigadier Bakhshi to start with, were of high calibre, good friends and a pleasure to work with.

Around that time I had a long chat with Princess Golden Fairy's parents. They were most unhappy at the way the situation was developing and 'the King hated it'. I was told that they would be sorry to lose me as I had been of use to them. I was always suspicious of such 'end-of-term-candy floss' remarks, from both sides.

There were shortages of fuel and food and I was very glad of all those steak and kidney puddings I had bought. Roadblocks were maintained around the town. An Australian and a Lao drove through one of the barriers and the PL opened fire on them, forcing them to stop. Both were put in jail. Wanting to see what reaction I would get, I went to that same village and was warmly welcomed. I still jogged in the early mornings, slipping under the barriers while the vigilantes, weapons loaded, stayed inside their temporary booths trying to keep warm.

With the longer nights dawn would break after I had been out an hour or more on my Saturday and Sunday walks. I was never scared, having complete confidence in my 'license to walk'. I often met PL dawn patrols in patches of jungle, in the fields or as I walked through villages and I would be asked where I was going. I knew the countryside like the back of my hand and would explain in detail, not that they were any the wiser. Wasn't I afraid? I would be asked. "No, the *phee* [thirty-two personal souls that inhabit the thirty-two parts of a person's body and can be mischievous] will not let me down, they know me well enough," was my standard answer. The younger men would look abashed as they were no longer allowed to believe in *phee*, although all true Lao knew they existed.

142

At times I would meet a PL soldier by himself. Materialising out of a ditch or from behind a tree he would accost me, asking which direction was northeast. Home lay that way and he was unhappy down in Vientiane. On several occasions I was asked if I understood all these strange words such as 'imperialist', 'lackey', 'feudalist', the man first looking around furtively to see if there was anyone within earshot. "No, not really," I would answer, conspiratorially. "Nor do I," was the standard answer.

On Friday, 28 November, shortly after some local elections for low-level representatives, we heard about a sudden and secretly conceived plot to overthrow what semblance of the façade there was of the PGNU (that had only concerned Luang Prabang and Vientiane since 'liberation'). Orders were received during the night and by 10 o'clock the next morning the political cadres were collecting their cell members and making placards that demanded the overthrow of all the trappings of government that had been so painfully worked out after the cease-fire.

Conventional wisdom had been that every vestige of the Kingdom of Laos – monarchy, flag, stamps, currency, national anthem –would be dispensed with in April 1976 after elections, so this move took the diplomatic community by surprise. On my walk the next day the PL were as nice and charming as ever they were to me and, some way off my normal radius, I was called over to what had been the local cell, invited to sit down on a bench and asked my views.

I countered that I had not heard exactly what had transpired from the previous day's demonstrations and the answer was indeed that every vestige of the old regime, including the prime minister, had been done away with. My answer was that if that what the Lao people wanted, fine and dandy, but I was a foreigner and that any criticism I might make was barred on the grounds that I was an impartial observer. I did not want Lao interfering with affairs in England and the Lao did not want me interfering with their affairs – an answer that brought many a nod of fervent approval. I quoted a number of Laotian proverbs (including "Silkworms are not fed when they are asleep' and 'To judge an elephant you must look at its tail; in the case of a girl you must look at her mother') and said that we in Britain had socialism but, unlike in Laos, we had liberty, freedom and a tolerance of individualism. To rob that remark of any snub I quoted the political slogan of the LPF. I added that my one worry was that the imperialist Russians would infiltrate them as they had infiltrated so many state organs and caused such havoc in UK that we had had to expel one hundred and five of them. Surprised at my use of 'imperialist' for the Russians, I was asked to explain what I meant. They then asked me if I liked the Russians and I said that it was their system and intolerance of individual dignity that I hated.

A few days after that I was walking back to my villa after work in the office and I heard a voice from behind, calling me softly. I did not turn round and a Lao on a bicycle passed me. "I'll be round after dark," I heard as he overtook me. He had been a soldier then worked as a barber. We became friendly. One day I noticed his absence and I asked where he had got to. Nobody knew, or if they did, nobody said.

He told me a little about himself when he visited me after dark. He had reported to the Americans and, suspected, had been taken to a re-education camp. He had escaped six weeks later and made his way down to Vientiane, hoping to cross the Mekong that night.

On his way south he had passed through and been hidden in a number of villages. The pattern of the revolution was the same: everyone up at 4 a.m. and, all together, in the fields by dawn for communal work until the morning meal, communally cooked and brought to them by the women, then more work for the rest of the day. After their day's labour, they returned, in a group, at dusk. A wash and a meal were allowed before an hour and a half's political indoctrination. Only then were they permitted to go home to sleep – day in day out, the same.

He had not gone home to his family in Vientiane as he knew his house was under surveillance. After leaving me he was going to Thailand, hoping to join the 'Black Horse' programme. This was continuing and clandestine support for the Meo Irregulars-turned-guerillas, when unmarked helicopters ferried men and stores back into Laos to help them continue the struggle. He gave me many details of its organisation.

Up till that time many of the LPF men in Vientiane were personable, nice people who could smile and were easy to get on with (within limits) to the extent that, to a casual observer, enforced socialism had not blunted their natural Laotian graces. People believed them, partly because they wanted to and partly because they were plausible. They disappeared overnight, so all the contacts I had so sedulously cultivated over the years were no more. This allowed the real leaders, the hard men, to emerge from the shadows, confident that there were no more contenders to obliterate.

At the end of November two of the King's sons and thirty-seven others, disguised as peasants, fled over the Mekong. On the following Tuesday, 2 December, I was jogging at dawn and came across a group of men hastily painting slogans on placards. I stopped but was shooed away. During the morning we were warned to stand by for an important announcement and, in the early afternoon, it came. His Majesty, the King of Laos, had abdicated. No longer was there a Kingdom of Laos but the People's Democratic Republic of Laos. The banners I had seen being painted earlier that day were paraded around the town, one group of demonstrators being school children. From the look on their faces it was clear that they were there because they had to be. Many walls had slogans daubed over them. I only heard one man complain about the way that that good, kind, friendly man, who read Voltaire before he went to sleep at night, was ousted so shoddily. It was only earlier in the year that the LPF invited him to Sam Neua to discuss arrangements about his coronation. I felt sick inside.

(He was forced to work as a peasant on his one-time estate and only in December 1987 was it reported that he had died of starvation.)

For a day or so loud speakers toured the town, bawling out revolutionary communiqués and slogans, with the sound of stylised hand clapping. The whole charade was most carefully planned and manipulated.

The situation became tenser than normal and prices rocketed. In the Morning Market edibles were cockroaches and skinned toads with little else. Onions were 82 new pence each (all three of them). The soft drink and beer factory closed down, such drinks becoming almost impossible to obtain. There was a dribble of black market goods from over the border and some PL started flogging petrol.

By then many of the vendors could count up to ten in Russian and knew the Russian names for common commodities. Russian behaviour, however, did not endear them to the restaurateurs. They would take their own drink with them, sit at a table, order the staff to buy them food from the cheap vendors by the side of the road and eat it inside. In the shops their haggling made them brasher by far than the Americans ever were.

Britain's recognition of the new regime came through on the following Friday afternoon, just in time for the embassy staff to respond to an invitation to the Presidential Palace (the erstwhile royal palace) to meet the new rulers. There was an air of expectancy: Cubans – all of whom had immediately received decorations from the new regime – winked and sniggered, while the Soviet ambassador threw himself on one Lao and embraced him as though he were his prodigal son. In contrast the Asian diplomats there behaved normally and with restraint.

At last I was to meet the Lao communist hard men who had never so revealed themselves to either the western world or in Vientiane since the end of the Second World War. It was a dramatic moment when they came outside into the spotlights of the many television cameras. The new President, no longer the Red Prince but now Mr Souvannouvong, led his Politburo out of the palace with great panache. They stood, in line, immobile. The shadows cast were unkind and the 'faceless' ones seemed to be wearing death masks, so gaunt, tired and uninspiring did they look.

The President read a speech, starting the applause himself at appropriate moments, after which the doyen of the diplomatic corps, the Vietnamese Ambassador (no North or South now), read out a pæan of praise. The audience, in the dim lights on the lawn, listened intently, each wrapped, no doubt, in private thoughts.

The presidential party left the steps and wended its way round the line of diplomats. First the President, then his Prime Minister and the rest of the bunch and, at the very end, looking so fragile and unhappy about it all, came Souvanna Phouma. I was standing behind the Chargé and his wife, and the group took no notice of me. Souvanna saw me and came through the front rank to shake me by the hand. I was touched and the thought did flit through my mind that he regarded me, in some strange manner, as a link with the past.

For me it was all over, probably including the shouting. I was due to leave in early February but I might have got away earlier if I had wanted to unless I was branded as a 'useless mouth' beforehand. I did not go for two reasons. I wanted to help the new ambassador, Mr Donald Cape, in his first month and I wanted to inoculate myself from ever wanting to live in a People's Democratic Republic.

I noted to London that the Russians, not the Chinese, had the upper hand in Laos but I doubted that would be so a decade later. I believed that Chinese influence would eventually dominate. I finished writing my thoughts on combating communist revolutionary warfare in an Indo-Chinese context and sent it to London. In it I listed a number of points that I felt were essential for a successful counter, so preventing communism prevailing over similar 'Free World' governments:

1   The stability of their own political base, coupled with a national faith strong enough to resist Communism.

2   Having an over-riding national aim for survival, based on an awareness of Communist tactics, and embracing all aspects of policy, i.e. political, economic, cultural and military as one combined 'rope' rather than utilising individual 'strands' haphazardly. The corollary to this requirement is to have strong, effective and 'clean' Security Forces.

3   The willingness and ability to foretell areas of pressure and to act positively before a negative 'knee-jerk' reaction results in divisive and counter-productive measures.

4   Having a strong and reliable intelligence system that can recognise and evaluate the threat.

5   Balancing the intelligence requirement with a counter-intelligence organisation. Apart from conventional requirements, prevention of such facets as refugees and unilateral aid donors from setting up subversive infrastructure should never be forgotten.

6   Having an effect 'white' propaganda machine.

7   Having requisite specialists to train for and counter various areas of subversion, insurgency and terrorism by guerillas in urban, jungle and mountainous areas.

I saw that conversion to communism depended on:

8   *Already committed Communists using people who have an ability to appease their personal scruples by setting themselves a principle so demanding that they are forced to overcome them; or a purpose that makes every sacrifice worthwhile (and then probably jettisoning them) while*

9   *Getting others to abuse their positions in society by rating social contacts higher than their oath of loyalty or normal disciplinary caveats.*

I was to learn that it was, most unusually, given the status of an FCO despatch that was sent to all embassies. As there were no sources in it I also took a copy of it round to my Thai counterpart, Colonel Mana Varamit, to see if he was interested.

On Christmas Day I listened to the Queen's speech. It gave me a lump in the throat as she seemed to be speaking to me personally, so aptly did she describe the dead weight of officialdom. I particularly recalled one phrase Her Majesty used, 'grains of sand versus lumps of lead', very eastern and parable-like.

A small boy came up and shyly gave me a Christmas card he had drawn himself. "I have no money to do anything better for you," he said. Another brought me two strips of embroidered yellow ribbon made into book markers, one stitched, in Lao, with *Laos* and the other with *love*. I have them yet.

On the morning of 31 December Patrick Fairweather called me into his office and gave me a signal to read. It had come in on 17 December and had been burning a hole in his pocket ever since, and it simply said that Her Majesty the Queen had graciously approved I be made OBE. In a letter home started on 1 January 1976 I wrote:

About three years ago I wrote to you and asked if an acorn in the ground felt idle as it stayed there, apparently doing nothing. May I say that it looks as though that little acorn has not only grown into a tree but also had a little acorn of its own.

Peter Shield was made MBE in the same list, a rare occurrence in the attaché world. None of the staff said anything about a 'lucky dip'.

I was so overjoyed when I got the news that, instead of walking on New Year's Day, I jogged twenty miles. Singha hardly made it. That evening I was entertained in the house of one of the few remaining Americans to a movie depicting the golden age of comedy. I laughed more than I had done since I had been an attaché.

I continued my walks and met a couple of peasants whom I had helped out by buying some land for them. The husband was peddling a bicycle and the wife was perched on the back. It was the first time he had seen me since I gave the money to his wife. They got off, doffed their headgear and, taking me by the hand, prayed to their Christian God in the middle of the road in thanks for what I had managed to do for them.

Mr Cape was allowed to present his credentials, this time in Vientiane, within days of his arrival and took me with him as part of his team. After the brief ceremony I was presented to the President and got a warm smile. He murmured *le polyglot* and made some nice remarks, as did the Minister of Foreign Affairs.

Every morning, everywhere, the ritual of political indoctrination would take place. One Saturday morning, early, miles out 'in the sticks' and still a bit chilly, I saw a group of PL soldiers sitting cross-legged in a circle in a harvested rice field away some way from the nearest village, weapons resting against their knees, being lectured by a hard-faced 'cadre'. They were directly in the line I was taking. I did not deviate but kept on towards them. I did not want Singha to disgrace himself so I talked to him, in Nepali, telling him not to chase the goats or the

146

pigs. He was an obedient dog and stayed to heel. They saw me coming, then heard a strange language from a few paces away. The cadre stopped talking and stared at me.

I walked into the centre of the group and, still in Nepali, told the dog to sit, give me one paw and then the other. He obliged me. I said to the group, "That's discipline. That's how you won the war. Without it that's how you'll lose the peace." A pause while I indicated the dog. "You can call him the 'little soldier' but don't call me the 'big dog'."

Blank amazement greeted this eccentricity. Nothing existed in the book of rules for such behaviour that was not hostile, rude or unseemly. I wobbled my knees and eyebrows, asking the young soldiers if they could. They burst out laughing, all semblance of severity gone. I went up to the cadre, a hard-faced man, probably a Thai Dam from the Dien Bien Phu area of Vietnam. I put my arm round his shoulders, one hand on his head and made a squeaking noise with my mouth. He gave a start. Such an occurrence was evidently not yet a common experience.

"You've got a mouse in your head," I said sympathetically and inanely. "I hope it doesn't hurt. And you still teach politics?" By then I had gone as far as I dared so, telling the dog to stand up and follow me, turned and left without looking behind. For a brief moment I felt it mighty cold on the back of my neck. I often wondered what was said about that trivial, unnecessary and entirely unexpected incident.

At the villa the packers moved in and Singha mooned around, knowing that I was going. In the office my clerk and I were busy closing down. Socially I was asked out to farewell parties. In one I had to get up and make a speech and I said that, despite all the traumas of the past three and a quarter years, part of me hurt at the thought of leaving. "That is as it should be: the more one gave, the more it hurt and the less one gave, the less it hurt. If it did not hurt at the end of a job, the person should never have been sent and had been a failure. Only by giving can one receive."

I had a wonderful letter from Simon Hutchinson who said that my citation was for a CBE:

> *...I don't know whether to rejoice or curse! Rejoicing and congratulations are certainly in order both for your own more than well deserved reward and your success in getting Peter Shield his MBE. But a plague on the hidebound, unimaginative, obscure, muddled, parasitic, dull, orthodox, anachronistic, wrong-headed ineffable* functionary *who decided that all your effort was worth no more than the sort of reward that can confidently be expected by a competent Town Clerk!*
>
> *However long I remain in Crown service I shall never begin to comprehend the 'Official Mind' with its ludicrous belief in pedantic precedent and the reduction of all human activity for a cumbersome and almost entirely meaningless ritual dance...*
>
> *But this is* not *the sort of letter that I intended to write. So let me return to my original theme of heartfelt congratulation and say how glad we all feel that you now have a visible token of your success in Laos. And success it was. I am sure that one of the reasons for not appointing a relief was the sheer impossibility of finding anyone who could begin to approach the standards that you had set. Of all the SE Asian countries Laos was the only one where we always felt quite confident that our intelligence was streets ahead of anyone else's...*

There was an upsurge of fighting near Vang Vieng and forty wounded PL were flown into Vientiane. In Vientiane itself, all mail written in Lao, Thai, French and English was opened. Most of the letters were thrown away, so one of the censorship board said at a party with many of the Party Faithful there. However, he announced in a loud voice, for a small sum he would 'pass' all mail given to him. I wondered how long he would remain in the Land of the Privileged.

I had one more duty to perform as acting doyen of the attaché corps, as I had by then become. Some time before, I had asked the new Minister of Defence if all attachés could meet

147

him, in a bunch to save him bother. I was rung up to say that such a meeting was impossible. Later on in the day I was told that, as it was the army's 27th anniversary, it was possible and we were to meet on the morrow. I was given the time and place; would I arrange for the rest to be there? Sure. I contacted them all and, at 5 o'clock that evening, received a message to say that the time and place were altered. As the Soviet and Chinese embassies did not man their telephones after 5 in the evening, that set me a problem that was not easily solved.

The acting Chinese attaché, Lin To-nan – a Lao speaker – had earlier rung me to ask if I knew how to address a group of senior army officers of the new regime in correct Lao? Such had not even occurred to me and he dictated the long and complicated mouthful for me, including the new and cumbersome name. I was most grateful to him.

At the Ministry (both time and venue had again been changed since the previous evening) I, as senior man, was taken into the presence first. There were three deputy ministers there and I was supposed to know them all when I only knew one. I was offered a chair next to the minister and made small talk for two minutes when the next senior attaché was ushered in. At two-minute intervals the others came in, the Russian, Vasilli Soloviov (back again), being late.

Champagne was placed in front of everybody and, nobody knowing what to do, we all stayed quiet. Was it up to me to propose a toast? I glanced at one of the LPF whom I knew quite well and he nodded. Nothing loth, I rose and, turning to the senior man, addressed him as taught by Lin To-nan: "Mr Minister of Defence of the People's Democratic Republic of Laos and Commander-in-Chief of the Lao People's Liberation Army," then paused for breath.

Emboldened, I went on to say that I was the spokesman for the attaché corps who, one by one, I introduced to the Lao. After that I introduced the Lao to the attachés. I did not know the names of two of them but I covered my ignorance with a neat bit of improvisation. I went on to say that we were honoured and happy to be allowed to pay our respects on this day, the 27th Anniversary of the LPLA, and we hoped that the army would be successful in the future in guaranteeing the country from all dangers, and a little bit more. I then gave an English version, having first ascertained if the new French attaché needed a French rendering also.

A toast was drunk and the minister answered, I interpreting. I broke the ensuing heavy and sustained silence by saying that I hoped my Lao was up to all that the minister had said. Another silence followed. Bored to tears, I made an outrageous remark, "I can speak eleven languages but I cannot speak the language of love. I am still a bachelor but I not a queer."

That galvanised the minister to make an answer to the effect that my Lao language efforts were appreciated. He then asked how many people there were in the French embassy who spoke Lao? I interpreted. None. I turned to the Russian and asked him how many Lao speakers were there in his embassy, knowing the answer to be nil.

None, as there was no Lao language school in Moscow. I translated this to the minister to the embarrassment of the Russian and the joy of the American. "I expect the government of the USSR will soon establish such a school," observed the minister. Vasilli stayed quiet.

I went one further. I called across to the American DA, Colonel Len Wood, and asked him how many Americans had there been in his embassy who spoke Lao. He could not say how many but quite a number. When I interpreted that to the minister I added that the Americans learnt to speak Lao because they liked and respected the Lao people.

Whether it was time to go or not, that remark ensured we stayed no longer. Twenty minutes after we started we were outside. It had been hard work. Len said "you were just great" and what would they do without me? I replied that such occurrences were few and far between so any opportunity had to be taken. I had been plugging the Americans' good points to as many people as I could over the past few months. The Pentagon sent me a present for my efforts.

The Capes wanted to give me a farewell party, despite my asking them not to. Most of my old attaché contacts had gone and none of my Lao contacts were in town. He prevailed and I stuck my neck out. I suggested that he invite the senior men in town to a sit-down dinner. I think Mr Cape was just a little apprehensive that I was aiming too high, but he gave me my head.

The Lao guests were the Deputy Prime Minister/Foreign Minister, the Minister of Education (Phoumi Vongvachit), the Secretary of State for War (Kaysone Boupha), the Director of Political Affairs, the senior woman in the Politburo, the wife of the Air Force Commander, the Ambassador designate to Britain, the Head of the Protocol Department, and the ex-ADC to the King and now the President's whom I particularly wanted. I rang the Protocol Department to see if the ADC would accept the invitation.

Nobody seemed to be able to contact him, so, with the help of the girl on the embassy telephone exchange, I rang the next man up who, along with the ADC, had come to escort the new ambassador on the morning he presented his credentials. I asked where So-&-So was. He who answered had never heard of him. So I explained who he was and his one up told me to wait while he found out his name! I was told he worked in another part of Protocol, which we duly rang up, only to be told that they had no idea who we meant. So I had the invitation card made ready and took it down to the office myself. On the gate the sentry had no idea who I wanted, and I was directed into an area which transpired to be the girls' wash place. A PL girl came out, in 'bathroom attire', as I got there, all very embarrassing. I was passed from one person to another to a third, to a fourth, eventually giving the card to some fellow who seemed to have just that veneer of authority to let me take the chance. I sent my driver down there the following morning, but he wasn't there, although I'd learnt that that was where his 'office' was. Luckily I'd given Khien (who had the most terrible trouble remembering the chap's name) another place to try and he managed to run the fellow to earth. In the event he could not come. But what a way to go about organising a dinner party remembering that most of the other Lao guests posed similar problems. It was certainly an eye-opener for Mrs Cape.

The turn-out for the formal dinner was impressive. Apart from the Lao guests, some with their ladies, (the only man invited who did not come was the President's ADC) were the Indian Ambassador and wife, and the American Chargé d'Affaires. It so happened that I knew them all. Cape gave a most gracious speech in which he said how honoured we were that such a distinguished gathering had come...that the Queen had made me OBE but he was sure that I was equally proud of those who had come tonight to the farewell party...and then he gave a toast. I took over and made a speech, which Cape had vetted beforehand as it was to be given in Lao. In the event I strayed from the original and that got the Lao guests laughing. I proposed a toast.

The most influential guest, Phoumi Vongvachit, stood up and made a speech, in French. He thanked Britain for what she had done over the years and said that the LPF was entirely satisfied with what I had done, except for one thing, and that was I had not married one of the many beautiful Lao girls there were. There would always be a corner of my heart in Laos and that I was always welcome to come back whenever I wanted to.

After the meal I told Kaysone Boupha that I was sure that Phoumi had not really meant all that and was rounded on severely. Of course it was meant. We were also told that, except for a national day, no such senior group of officials had ever gathered under the roof of any foreigner's house. The Capes were able to use me as a shoehorn, becoming more informally friendly with these powerful men than they would have been able to in months. In fact I was very proud to think that there could be such a turn-out for a mere DA. I know that the new ambassador was delighted. The guests stayed until much later than normal, taking the opportunity to talk with the American and Cape himself. I went and talked to the ladies with nothing but bonhomie. In fact nobody could have told that they were all dedicated communists. A far cry from November 1972!

I went to bid all the attachés farewell. Chen Shu-lin was away so I spoke with his Lao-speaking assistant, Lin To-nan. To start off with we talked unofficially, so we spoke in Lao.

He gave me a painting on silk and two lacquered vases. "One for you and one for your future wife." He also said that he had learnt much from me in the way to comport oneself; not only in the way I spoke to high and humble but also in the way I had such strict self-discipline. Even taking Oriental flattery into consideration, he repeated himself several times. (So did some other attachés: maybe they did not have unconventional soldiers in their armies.) He said that I was a *good* friend of the Chinese people and that although we had many points in disagreement we had many in common, which were the ones to concentrate on and the others would eventually cause no friction. When we started talking officially we had to use the French interpreter. By then my Lao was better than my French and I had to smile to myself when, stuck for a word in French, I had to ask Lin, in Lao, what it was and then he said the word in Chinese to the interpreter who then told me what it was in French which I then used back to the interpreter who then translated it into Chinese for the non-French-speaking Lin, who knew what I was going to say all along! That lent an air of frivolity, if not unreality, to the proceedings.

I said that my time in Laos had let me understand the Chinese point of view much better than before, and that I saw no threat to my country by the Chinese, so could feel that I was a friend of the Chinese, despite not liking communism. I further said that I saw the greatest danger to world peace as Russian expansionism, with my own country as a target, to which he heartily agreed. "What can one man do?" I asked.

He quoted one of Mao Tsu-tung's aphorisms, about the one spark that could start a prairie fire. I countered by saying only a few men over the ages were ever in a position to act as that spark and I was not one of them.

He asked me what my answer was and, after some thought, I answered that 'never falling from the standards I set myself and being true to myself' was my creed.

I had expected so say farewell to the Russian in the embassy where I was fully intending to be pointed about Angola but, in the event, I was asked to his house where a table had been spread with biscuits, sweets, chocolates, grapes, brandy and tea. His wife, who only spoke Russian, was present. We had to toast each other in brandy and make polite conversation. I toasted to the mutual understanding and sincerity of the Russian and English, Soviet and British people, and was then embarrassed when I was given a present of two classical music gramophone records, a calendar and a desk diary. So all I managed was pleasantries, which maybe was just as well.

My time came to an end. I had Singha put down, in the knowledge that he would pine mercilessly or be eaten. It took five of us to hold him down and the look in his eyes still haunts me. I had broken trust. I wept bitterly and folk in the fields asked me where he was. When they knew I was going, some of the people came to me, knelt down and clasped my knees. I had fixed Chok Di to be the Cape's major domo. If he had not been married, he told me, he would go with me wherever I went. I learnt later that he escaped over the border with his family.

My 'journey of a thousand miles' had come to an end.

Postscript

I felt desperately tired and emotionally drained. I was debriefed in Bangkok before going to Hong Kong en route for a 4-month trek in Nepal. Only after that would I return to Britain.

In Hong Kong I saw a boy put his arm round a girl while waiting for a ferry and I instinctively looked round to see who was watching him, ready to take him away, but of course no one was. Had I been under the communists for less that a year? I saw another youth choose which cassette he wanted to play in his recorder. I again looked round to see who would stop him from choosing his own tune, but of course no one did. I *had* been under the communists for less than one year. If their system could do that to me in such a short time, what did it do to those who could not escape and to those who knew no better?

My trek in Nepal let me unwind. Laos was never far away from my thoughts as I saw another landlocked country with China to the north and a good friend of Russia's to a flank, this time India. I saw some of the same mistakes that the Royal Lao Government had made and my heart wept within me. The one overriding impression I still carry of the Lao is that they are one of the nicest people I know and it still grieves me bitterly to see how that godless religion called communism can so change charming men, women and children to act so spitefully and irrationally.

I got home, mentally whacked, and learnt that a coup had taken place in Thailand. I read in the paper that the new prime minister, an army general, had said that he had a 5-point plan to beat the communists. They were five of the six points in the paper I had prepared for the counter to communist revolutionary warfare. So Mana Varamit had forwarded his copy to Bangkok, or was it coincidence?

I was debriefed by senior officials and I was disappointed that they were unwilling to extrapolate my experience in Laos from the 'Indo-China case book' to the 'Northwest European case book', as it must be almost unique to have watched a communist takeover from the grandstand, so to speak, been accepted by and kept faith with both sides. "But we have read your reports with great interest."

I spoke to a senior official in the FCO, whose answer was that the MOD and the FCO could only advise government, not dictate policy. "You had better write a book to get it off your chest."

I felt that to write the truth was too raw and that it were better in a work of 'faction'. I started on it in mid-1972, while it was still fresh in my mind. I called it *A Stranger Truth*. People who read the draft believed only some of it and said that I over-exaggerated. In fact it was the fiction that they believed, not the facts. No publisher wasted his time on it, but writing it was cathartic and therapeutic. That, and all the weekly letters home provided the vivid details, when I started on this in 1987. I kept none of the official stuff, nor had I sight of it again and that has made some otherwise interesting details sketchy and tame.

At Buckingham Palace Her Majesty noted that I had been an attaché somewhere and what was it like?

If I could not tell the Queen, who could I? I told Her Majesty where it was and that it was all right till the end when there was an acute food shortage for a long time. The only food that people could buy in the market was cockroaches and skinned toads.

"Good gracious. What did you do?"

A happy thought struck me. "Luckily I had thirty-six steak and kidney puddings, Ma'am, and so I ate steak and kidley puddlies for thirty-six days."

Index

1 Place names are given in italics.
2 Place names are also used for seats and departments of governments; e.g. British Government will be found under *United Kingdom* and *London* can mean the Foreign and Commonwealth Officer or the Ministry of Defence. The context will determine which.
3 A country's national is indicated by that country's name.

154

FIRST IN, LAST OUT
An Unconventional British Officer in Indo-China
J P Cross, Brassey's (UK) 1992, £27.50 ISBN 0-08-041787-6

In the autumn of 1945 Colonel John P Cross, served with the Gurkhas who then successfully suppressed the revolution in Southern Vietnam (Cochinchina), with the assistance of two Japanese battalions, and gave back to [sic] the country to France. This is how Cross came 'First In'. Then he was out for 26 years, serving British interests elsewhere. From 1972 to 1976 he was Defence Attaché at the British Embassy in Laos, thus experiencing the final phase of the Second Indochina War in a country where the gradual transition from one regime to another reflected the more dramatic events in Cambodia and South Vietnam. After four years he was 'Last Out', leaving the Lao (the nicest people Cross knows) 'to the godless religion called Communism'.

The unconventional officer's reminiscences from these two episodes in the history of British involvement in Indochina (and in his life of jungle war) have for some reason become a book. Part I adds nothing to our understanding of what happened in Indochina in 1945-1946. It serves mainly to expose the author's francophobia (his love for his Gurkhas is expressed in an 'antescript').

The second and by far the longest part does provide an (at times fascinating) account of the atmosphere within the strangely insulated international community of Vientiane, where a few Russian, Chinese, French and British diplomats could conspire against each other and with some outmanoeuvred Laotians while the Americans and the Vietnamese were staging the war at a distance. The closer we get to the Spring of 1975 the less dull does Cross' account become. He gets to know some of the leading personae on the Laotian political scene, first the less-and-less US-sponsored generals, then the doomed figureheads of the traditional regime, and finally but not really the communist 'baddies' who turn up only in 1976. Cross has some arresting episodes and conversations to recount, but they are drowned in the author's unrelenting attempts to satisfy his own vanity. The story has one hero, Cross himself. Virtually everyone else is either wicked, stupid or, at best, mistaken. Cross writes over and over again about his great linguistic abilities, how much better informed he was than anyone else, how he understood the communist danger before and more profoundly than others, and how his work was praised by his superiors (long quotes) earning him in the end an OBE. He even takes pride in telling in minute detail how he resisted the attempts of a named female language teacher to seduce him (this proving that he could not be compromised by foreign agents). The Colonel remained a bachelor through his stay, but kept a dog.

Cross most probably did a good job. The normal reader is likely to be so disgusted by the author's frenetic self-praise that he may jump to the conclusion that Cross had simply been put away in Vientiane in order not to do harm to other places. It would be a pity if too many reached such a conclusion. By staying as long as he did and using his ability to speak Lao, Cross must have assembled a good deal of useful information. The better passages of the book give reason to believe that the Defence Attaché's reports will be valuable sources for historians of Laos 1972-76, once these documents are made available at the Public Records Office. But if you do not have to read the book, don't.

Stein Tonnesson
Nordic Institute of Asian Studies, Copenhagen

BUFFETED BUFFER STATE
HUGH TOYE
FIRST IN, LAST OUT

J P Cross, bachelor, teetotal, eccentric, a man of outstanding gifts, has spent a military career of thirty-seven years in the Far East. Early convinced by personal tragedy of the importance of languages, he learnt those of the people with whom he had to deal: nine of them. In First In, last Out, Colonel Cross recounts two episodes: South Vietnam (Cochin China) in 1945, when a British Force took the Japanese surrender (First In), and this three-and-a-half years as Military Attaché in Laos, 1972-76 (Last Out, as he was not replaced)> In 1945, as a young officer in the Gurkha Rifles, actually commanding for a time two Japanese battalions, used to keep order against Vietnamese guerrillas until the French returned, he found much to admire in the Japanese and disliked the French. That dislike came to be unfortunate - since his years in ex-French-colonial Laos occupy all but thirty pages of this book.

Little Laos, the mountainous, thinly populated hinterland of Vietnam, traditional buffer between Vietnam and Thailand, had become in the 1960s a subsidiary theatre of the American Indo-China War. When Cross arrived in 1972, it was divided between Laotian Communists backed by the Vietnamese in the uplands and, in the lowlands, Laotian non-Communists backed by the United States. The Vietnam cease-fire of 1973 brought a scaling down of American activity, which allowed the North Vietnamese to triumph in 1975 and Pol Pot to overrun Cambodia with hideous consequences. In Laos, because the Communists, to begin with, simply took their places in a hitherto nominal Government of National Union, penetration was more gradual, but no less ruthless. The former civil and military leaders who did not escape were killed or "re-educated", the King, Queen and Crown Prince driven and starved to death. Before the author left in 1976, Laos had endured a year of bleak, poverty-stricken Communist rule by loudspeaker, complete with secret police and the whole dreary apparatus.

The impact on this developing situation of a British Military Attaché who could speak all the languages involved was of unique value to his masters. Cross mingled in Lao society at every level: the urchins in the villages who loved him and his dog, the soldiers, the generals, the politicians. He was allowed where no foreign attaché had been, and he addressed assemblies of villagers or military students at length in their own language. In the last painful phase, he managed to establish reasonable relations even with the Communists.

He has a story to tell and, to an extent, he has been allowed to tell it. There are good accounts of the dedicated and cultured King and his court, as well as of the Communists' hide-outs in the mountains, and the charm of the country and its people emerges. He also tells of a determined (unsuccessful) attempt to seduce him. But there are obvious gaps which mar the narrative, and perhaps too much point-scoring between attachés. There are also mistakes concerning Laotian personalities and history. It remains a remarkable story.

The conclusion is sad. Colonel Cross arrived in 1972 fresh from the Jungle Warfare School in Malaya, thinking that some of the techniques he had taught there might be of use to the Laotian Army. But it was not that kind of war:

> Before one side attacked the other, the defenders would be warned so that they could slip away quietly....Another reason why the...war had gone on so long was...in the great part...unscrupulous commanders flogging to their enemies the kit given by their friends, the Americans....Only at the very end...had I stumbled on the truth.

Noise and silver bullets - Lin Yutang said it all in My country and My People.

Times Literary Supplement 6 August 1993

For thirty years after the Second World War, the major focus for much professional soldiering was South East Asia. In the aftermath of the Japanese surrender, the old Colonial powers of Britain, France and Holland struggled to reassert authority in their former possessions, in Indonesia, down through the Malayan Peninsula and across Indo-China, nationalist and communist ideology rose from the jungles and padi fields. Power sprang from the barrel of a gun, and the theory of the dominoes gripped Western strategic planners. Danger seemed greatest in Indo-China where French and American defeat contrasted with British success in Malaya and Borneo. The Vietcong, Pathet Lao and Khmer Rouge entered the military lexicon as formidable adversaries for conventional Western Armies.

For those of us soldiering at that time with the British Army in the Far East, John Cross was a legendary, if somewhat eccentric figure. His exploits in the jungle during the Malayan Emergency, leadership of the Border Scouts in Borneo, parachuting with the Gurkhas, an extraordinary facility with languages, a profound knowledge of Counter-Revolutionary Warfare doctrine, all combined with a shrewd intelligence and a deep affinity with Asian people, made him a formidable Commandant of the Kota Tinggi Jungle Warfare School. If, for many, his Spartan life style and disdain for the more conventional approach brought him into conflict with some of his peers and seniors, I and many others recognised and admired the deep insight that he brought to the political and military changed that was all around us.

In First In, Last Out John Cross describes two distinct periods in his Asian soldiering life. In the first, at the end of the war, he is with his Gurkha Battalion in Indo-China attempting to disarm the Japanese, yet with their help, fighting the Vietminh. Twenty-seven years later he is back as Defence Attaché in Laos during Britain's Co-Chairmanship with the Soviet Union of the Geneva Accords for Indo-China. The ambiguities he witnesses in his first experience and indeed, all that followed in his subsequent career, serve him well in his last involvement in Indo-China. For four years as the tragedies of Vietnam and Cambodia gathered momentum around him, Cross operated in the hotbed of intrigue, national rivalry and corruption that was Laos. His account provides a deep insight into the complexities of events unfolding in Vientiane as communist supremacy is asserted over the whole region. But what makes this book unique and highly readable, aside from its contribution to the history of this most unhappy part of the world, is the pace, style, compassion and wit with which it is written. The idiosyncrasies of Cross himself come over in much that he writes, yet the often acerbic and highly uncomplimentary comments that pepper his account ring all too true and give the book a liveliness and originality that similar volumes seldom achieve. It deserves to be widely read and enjoyed.

Journal of the United Service Institute
last issue 1992
Lt Gen Sir Peter Duffell KCB, CBE MC
Inspector General Doctrine and Training MOD

Stiff Upper Lip

Subtitled An Unconventional British Officer in Indo-China, J P Cross' military memoir describes his two stints in this troubled region. First, as a Gurkha regiment office during Britain's brief occupation of southern Vietnam after the Japanese surrender in 1945, provocatively codenamed "Operation Masterdom"; and later as defence attaché to Laos, in 1972-76, where he witnessed the "quiet victory" of the communist Pathet Lao over royalist forces.

Trained - and fully psyched - to fight Japanese forces in Burma, Cross arrived too late to see combat in World War II, but instead found himself working with Japanese troops in repelling Viet Minh guerrilla attacks in southern Vietnam. Initially welcomed by many Vietnamese, British troops faced tough resistance when it became clear that French colonial rule would be restored. Still green, Cross (rightly) bowed to the greater combat experience of a Japanese officer during one skirmish, and found himself taking orders from the former enemy, who were now his ward. In the heat of battle, a Japanese soldier yelled to Cross: "Respected sir, Captain Yamagishi... Not 'yelled', 'hissed' (page 14)respectfully asks your respected permission to fire his mortars." Cross gave his respected permission.

The most intriguing incident during the author's spell in Vietnam in 1945-46 involved identifying the body of America's first MIA in Vietnam, Lieut-Col Peter Dewey, who had been ambushed and killed outside Saigon, and his body unaccounted for. Following a tip-off, Cross and a couple of US army officers spent a macabre day digging up coffins in a graveyard, in a bid to locate and identify Dewey's body. Their grizzly efforts proved inconclusive.

The author comes from the "old school" of British military and diplomatic training. The British, he declares, "seem to be able to hit it off to a remarkable degree with various ethnic groups". "Americans are naive and the French arrogant and cruel," while "Asians can be worse than either, and then to their own sort." Cross' blatant dislike of all things French and/or communist made his presence in Vietnam and Laos a little surprising. Ending a heated debate with a Soviet diplomat, Cross yelled that he would rather be Not 'yelled', 'growled' (page 169)dead than Red, and "so would all true Englishmen. And I'd take you when I went if I got half the chance."

Americans, on the other hand, appear as fools. For instance, the Pathet Lao decision not to sever diplomatic relations with Washington in 1975 - in stark contrast to events in Vietnam and Cambodia - is explained thus: Americans "were needed to be tormented and humiliated. The hapless Yanks' only crime was to have backed the wrong side; their stupidities were to have surrounded themselves with expensive trash and to make no provisions for a quick getaway."

The author revelled in his defence attaché posting to Laos in the closing years of the civil war, and enjoyed remarkable access to the myriad sides. The key to Cross' apparent success in Lao circles (though we only have the author's word) was his knowledge of the Lao language. Indeed, Cross boasts knowledge of nine Asian languages, fired by the needless death of his elder brother in 1944 as a result of poorly communicated orders.

The author's only handicap - a major one in diplomatic circles - was in being a tee-totaller. The German attaché would eat "a pound of butter, drink the oil from several tins of sardines and a pint or so of milk" in preparation for vodka-sodden meetings with his Soviet counterpart. A Lao-speaking, non-drinking and non-womanising diplomat was initially regarded with much distrust in Vientiane.

Despite Cross' deep aversion to communists, he recognised the inadequacy and corruption of the royalist forces in Laos. A report on events, bound for London, was tersely edited "Pathet Lao v. Pathetic Lao". Given the corruption of Indo-China's pro-West military leaders, perhaps developments in Laos and throughout Indo-China were inevitable. Cross witnessed the entire liberation struggle and his highly opinionated biographical account provides an intriguing warts-and-all report of events on the ground.

Far Eastern Economic Review
25 March 1993
Nick Freeman

'Unconventional' Colonel Cross certainly appears from the two periods of his career covered by this fascinating book. The first - and all too short - phase describes his time as a comparatively inexperienced young officer serving with the force sent in 1945 to French Indo-China, as it then was, to take the surrender of the Japanese troops there and maintain order in the country until the French administration could take over once again. The second phase, and the greater part of the book, describes the author's experience as Defence Attaché between 1972 and 1976.

Aged 20, Cross had been posted to 1 Battalion First Gurkha Rifles in Burma, shortly after which the battalion was ordered to Saigon as part of Operation MASTERDOM. Once in Indo-China the British found a state of chaos, with the Vietnamese determined to gain their independence from the French, the Japanese having been disposed of: Cross's frank comments on the oppressive pre-war French colonial rule and the behaviour of individuals on their return, make the Vietnamese desire to rule themselves only too clear. But the Japanese had not been got rid of: in fact they were the only disciplined body of troops in the region, apart from the small British force sent to accept their surrender. So the author finds himself in the strange position of commanding a battalion of his erstwhile enemies in an effort to subdue the Vietminh, whom he had ostensibly come to liberate, so that the French could once again take over.

The political complexities in South East Asia were making themselves felt even at this early stage and, though the author makes every effort to clarify the situation, it is no fault of his that it is sometimes difficult to follow. Nevertheless, Indo-China soon exerted its own fascination on our author and Cross, unlike so many of his compatriots in similar situations, learnt several languages of the region and came to understand the people and their customs better than most.

One would like to have read much more of that little written-about period immediately after the end of World War Two, but it is the author's time in Laos, occupying most of the book, which really captures our attention. Because of his knowledge of the people, his ability to speak their language (almost alone amongst the diplomatic corps in Laos at that time) and his willingness to walk about amongst them, invariably accompanied by his dog, Cross gained the confidence of the Laotians, from the highest in the land to the lowest peasant: he was evidently widely known and trusted, uniquely by both the Lao Patriotic Front, doing their best to overthrow the Government, and by the Government and Royal Family themselves. As a result he was allowed to visit the military and other closed areas of both sides, forbidden to almost all other foreigners; surely an extraordinary situation.

The author is very critical, not only of the appalling corruption within Laos, but also of the various diplomats and others with whom he came in contact, not excepting the first British Ambassador under whom he served; there was evidently a clash of personalities with this avowedly left-wing representative of Her Britannic Majesty's Government, plainly anti-American and apparently unwilling to believe that the Patriotic Front and their military arm, the Pathet Lao, were either Communist or planning to take over the country. Fortunately he was in due course replaced by a more discerning diplomat, who gave the author greater freedom of action.

The oppression and regimentation which followed as the Communists gained power is made abundantly clear as the author watches the take-over in Laos from his privileged position. As various people he knew in the Government and armed forces disclosed their plans to escape the inevitable, the phrase 'I never met ------ again' occurs with depressing frequency. While American policy in South East Asia does not escape the author's criticism, his loathing of Communism and all its manifestations is evident. Talking of his imminent departure at the end of his tour, Cross comments that he could have left earlier but one reason why he stayed on right to the end was that he 'wanted to inoculate [himself] from ever wanting to live in a People's Democratic Republic', which is what Laos had become.

Cross left with sadness, having clearly formed a great attachment for the Laotian people. From the Foreign and Commonwealth Office came enthusiastic appreciation of his efforts - 'of all the SE Asian countries Laos was the only one where we always felt quite confident that our intelligence was streets ahead of anyone else's'. That must have been some balm to his soul.

This is a very readable book, though the author lapses from time to time into somewhat schoolboyish slang. It is sadly marred by a surprising number of misprints and by the abbreviations and acronyms which splatter every page; the titles of parties and organisations etc are difficult enough to follow when spelt out; understanding is not helped by having to think about the meaning of incomprehensible jumbles of letters. The reader is only partly helped by the glossary provided which, strangely, lists the title first and then the acronym, the reverse of how one would wish to consult it: also it includes, unnecessarily, a number of titles which are not abbreviated in the text. The idea of providing a list of 'Dramatis Personae' is good, especially with the difficult Loatian names, but serves little purpose since most of those shown omit any description of their position in the scheme of things.

However, these circumstances aside, the book provides a fascinating insight in to the intricacies of the South East Asian scene and a picture of a truly extraordinary man who has served his country well. It demonstrates all too clearly the dangers facing a Western country if it becomes closely involved in that region: when the author comments on the wisdom of the British Government in declining to involve British troops in the Vietnam War, on the evidence of this book one can only agree fervently with him: how the Americans must now wish they had not been involved themselves.

Tank Journal
Bill Woodhouse
[date not known]